Comparative Politics

The Quest for Theory and Explanation

Comparative Politics

The Quest for Theory and Explanation

Lawrence C. Mayer
Texas Tech University

2007
Sloan Publishing
Cornwall-on-Hudson, NY 12520

Library-of-Congress Control Number: 2006927113

Mayer, Lawrence C.
  Comparative Politics: The Quest for Theory and Explanation / Lawrence C. Mayer.
    p.   cm.
  Includes bibliographical references and index.
  ISBN 1-59738-002-4

Cover design by Amy Rosen

Printed in the United States of America

10 9 8 7 6 5 4 3 2 1

ISBN 1-59738-002-4

To Etta and the kids:
Gabi, Arthur, Nathan, and Josh

Table of Contents

Preface

In the first decade of the twenty-first century, our world has become engulfed in waves of fundamental transformations, making humanity's eternal struggle to comprehend the natural and social forces that define that world exponentially more difficult and complex. The well-understood principles that governed the relations among nations that characterized the centuries of classic diplomacy were challenged by the events of the World Wars of the 20th century and virtually abandoned by the theologically-driven assaults on the civilization called "the West." The struggles of the early twenty-first century were not between nation states pursuing their national interests, but were driven by the attempt to impose a theologically-defined lifestyle. The legitimate interests of nation states and the essence of warfare itself were being redefined.

Meanwhile, the nation states themselves and the patterns of social and political behavior were similarly transformed in their adaptations to this transformed world. Socioeconomic cleavages, deep-seated cultural attributes, and the party systems that represented them that had characterized the Western world for much of late modern history were changed in essential ways. Widely-accepted conventional wisdoms (that had not been empirically tested yet formed the bedrock of our former understanding of social and political behavior) are being challenged by this transformed world, and the world has lost faith in them.

The discipline of comparative politics has responded to this need for new explanations with a burgeoning body of explanatory literature. The postwar redefinition of the field from a largely descriptive enterprise to an explanatory and predictive one has been a settled issue for decades. However, this volume will reveal that there is considerable lack of consensus on the essential principles of an explanatory enterprise as it relates to the study of various aspects of human behavior, and this lack of consensus is a major theme of this book.

With some notable and admirable exceptions, most of our textbooks and the organization of the courses we teach do not reflect this now-established explanatory purpose of the field. Countries are described as idiosyncratic entities without answering the question that must occur to many students, "Why do I need to know this material?" This risks discouraging and alientating them from the study of politics, which should be an exciting pursuit in this rapidly and fundamentally changing world.

This book is intended as a critical survey of the major literature of the field of comparative politics in light of this explanatory purpose. The intent is to show how the facts presented contribute to one's understanding of not only major trends in the field, but why they have occurred and what impact they are likely to have. For example, facts about how the British Parliament operates with its unique set of procedures are addressed from the perspective of how they may contribute to structuring accountability of political leaders. In addition to describing the attributes of a nation's culture, these attributes are shown to be part of a broader theory on the nature of cultural change. By its focus on the explanatory literature in the field, this book hopes to contribute not only to students' knowledge, but to their understanding as well.

Rather than confining myself to one theoretic framework, this book addresses several of the alternative approaches and paradigms showing students the conceptual richness of the field. By taking a critical approach, it encourages its readers to think critically about the literature being discussed. The theoretic and explanatory focus of the book provides a useful criterion for the selection of descriptive data to present, and thereby provides a means of avoiding overloading students with facts about politics for their own sake, without any sense of relevance or usefulness.

The ability to think critically about explanatory literature requires a greater understanding of the nature of a scientifically adequate explanation than is possessed by most students. Therefore, the book begins with an extended treatment of how the norms of the scientific method can be applied to the "soft" sciences whose subject of human behavior forces serious modifications of that method. Comparative political analysis offers a unique opportunity to adapt social science methodology to the study of politics. It is therefore important for students to *understand* the comparative method and to *see it applied to a range of research questions* in order for them to think critically about the attempts to build explanatory theory in political science.

The excellent treatments of this topic in the philosophy of social science literature tend to be very challenging to typical political science students; hence, this book attempts to offer a full but readable treatment of that method and its applications aimed at upper-level undergraduates.[1] The intent is to provide students with what they need to know about this inherently difficult subject so they can analyze the comparative literature without becoming full-fledged philosophers of science. The topics for the application of the comparative method are those typically found in comparative textbooks; hence, the book can serve as a theory-oriented supplement to many large descriptive texts or to collections of readings.

A project of this nature always incurs debts to people whose generous encouragement and assistance makes a work like this possible. First, I must single out my editor, Bill Webber of Sloan Publishing, whose support of and faith in the original idea provided tremendous motivation to bring the task to completion. Two reviewers, Gunther Hega of Western Michigan University and Maria Fornella-Oehninger of Old Dominion University, provided both encouragement and constructively thorough critiques of parts of the book, most of which were incorporated in the final product. Three of my comparative colleagues, Dennis Patterson, Glen Biglaiser, and Frank Thames, generously gave of their valuable time to read and comment on other portions of the manuscript. I profited from their suggestions. However, I must state the usual boiler-plate declaration that the responsibility for any remaining flaws in the book are mine.

Lawrence Mayer
Lubbock, Texas
April 2006

1

Comparative Politics as a Field of Study

In the first decade after World War II, the field of comparative politics was redefined by some of its scholars. The redefinition was eventually accepted in principle by most, but not all, of its practitioners.[1] This redefinition was at the heart of an effort to bring political science in general and comparative politics in particular into the universe of academic respectability. This transformation of the field was to attempt to do with *our* subject matter, the institutions and procedures of government and politics, what several of our sister "social sciences" such as sociology, psychology, and economics, and the natural sciences, such as physics and biology, were already doing with theirs: to explain and predict occurrences.

Before this, the study of "comparative government" was essentially a *descriptive* enterprise. Scholars in the field were engaged in producing increasingly detailed descriptions of constitutionally designated structures and the processes by which they operate. The field was defined geographically as the study of foreign governments, a conceptualization of the field that excluded serious consideration of data from the United States; American Politics was defined as a distinct subfield from comparative government. Moreover, these foreign governments were examined one at a time. Generalization across nations or cultures was considered epistemologically invalid because the phenomena we study—institutions and events—were regarded as so unique as to render such generalizations meaningless.

Of course these phenomena were and are unique; there will never be an event exactly like the French Revolution of 1789, which occurred in a context and state of technology that can never be repeated. The French Socialist Party, the British Labour Party, and the German Social Democratic Party are each distinct from one another in important respects because they are each products of a distinct history, culture, and a myriad of other factors. Every human being that participated in these complex events was himself or herself the product of every person or experience he or she encountered. Had Maximilian Robespierre been a well-adjusted, mild-mannered human being, the French Revolution would have taken a very different course. This perspective argues that the political institutions and events on which we should focus are the product of a unique configuration of historical, cultural, geographic, and demographic factors. It is therefore meaningless to attempt to generalize from one such context to another. As the saying goes, "you cannot compare apples to oranges." Hence, our misnamed field was strictly noncomparative. We strictly constructed our descriptions on a country-by-country basis.

Yet, we know that comparisons of social and political phenomena are regularly undertaken in modern political analysis. The obvious uniqueness of these phenomena is not a barrier to such comparison. You *can* compare apples to oranges. They are both citrus fruit containing vitamin C for starters. The essence of comparison is to identify aspects that phenomena have in common even when most other aspects are different. It makes no sense to compare phenomena that are identical. Thus, to say all revolutions are X is merely saying that revolutions that are otherwise unique have at least X in common.

Over half a century ago, historian Crane Brinton studied four great (and unique) revolutions—the American Revolution of 1776, the French Revolution of 1789, the British Revolution of 1688, and the Russian Revolution of 1917—and found a number of patterns in the way they all unfolded.[2] They each occurred in a time of socioeconomic change when conditions for the strata leading the revolution were improving while the incumbent regimes became bankrupt. They all went through an initial moderate phase that degenerated into a chaotic radical phase that was in turn ended by an authoritarian retrenchment. The point is that comparison and generalization are possible even among the idiosyncratic phenomena that social scientists study.

This is an important point because the essence of the scientific method, that is, the basis of our modern goal of explanation, is generalization. The debate that divided our field for several decades in the postwar era is now over. The question of whether it is possible or appropriate to apply the epistemological principles of science to the study of political phenomena has been largely resolved in the affirmative.

Thus, there is an answer to the question, why compare? The answer is that comparison contributes to the discipline goal of building explanatory theory. The scholarship discussed in this volume will be evaluated by its contribution to that goal. It is therefore important to understand the logic of comparative analysis and how it forms the basis of the application of the principles of the scientific method to the study of politics in order to appreciate the contributions of the scholarship discussed in this volume.

THE APPLICABILITY OF THE SCIENTIFIC METHOD TO THE STUDY OF POLITICS

Despite pockets of resistance, there is a widespread consensus that there is a scientific method that can apply with appropriate modifications to all fields of inquiry and the adherence to which is the criterion for whether a set of conclusions can legitimately be called knowledge.[3] The structure of explanation in the natural and social sciences is the same in this view. The difference between the natural and social sciences (or, otherwise put, the hard and soft sciences) lies in the completeness of their explanations and the accuracy of the predictions derived from them.[4]

The structure of any scientific explanation consists of a principle or general statement of a relationship among two or more concepts from which the phenomenon or events to be explained can be logically deduced.[5] Thus, if the principle were true, the phenomenon to be explained (called by philosophers of science *the explicandum*) should occur or be present given certain stipulated conditions. However, while natural scientists can deduce the necessary occurrence of their *explicanda,* students of society and politics can at best deduce their probable occurrence.

The reason that the predictions of natural scientists are deterministic while those of social scientists are probabilistic is that the explicanda of social science are *overdetermined*—the product of such a numerous array of potential causes that one can only analyze a few of the most prominent ones. Meanwhile, in natural science, investigators are often able to isolate possible causes and their presumed effects from the context in which these outcomes occur. This analysis of the most prominent causes of the explicanda in social science while ignoring other factors that may have a causal impact is what Brodbeck means by the concept of incomplete explanation. These unanalyzed factors—factors outside the causal model being presented—are called *exogenous* in the philosophy of science literature. The inevitability of exogenous factors is the major difference between social and natural sciences.

Thus, when natural scientists can say X causes Y, they mean that whenever you have X in a particular set of circumstances, Y will invariably follow. However, when social and behavioral scientists make that assertion, they can only mean that the presence of X makes the appearance of Y more likely or that the presence of X will tend to bring about Y, other things being equal. This other-things-being-equal qualifier (often referred to in its Latin form *ceteris paribus*) attached to all social science assertions of relationships means that that X will bring about Y if all other factors that may impact on the occurrence of Y cancel themselves out.

Since the explicandum, Y, is not expected to follow every instance of A, tendency statements create a danger of imprecision in what exactly is being claimed.

How many instances of A without Y can be rationalized before one abandons the assertion that A causes B *ceteris paribus*?

THE EMPIRICAL BASE OF SCIENCE

This concern with the precision of the predictions entailed by explanatory principles in the social sciences is driven by the second criterion for the scientific status of one's truth claims or conclusions: they must be falsifiable in terms of sensory data. This means that the predicted phenomena entailed by the principle should in fact be observed in the appropriate situation. In other words, there must be a precise category of observable data which, if encountered, would force the investigator to revise or reject the truth claim as stated.

Note that nothing was said about proving a proposition to be true. Logically, such proof could never be offered. Truth implies the proposition in question is consistent with all relevant data. However, since scientific explanations should enable us to extrapolate from what we can directly observe to what can expect to see, scientific propositions refer to an infinite category of data. Hence, one can never exclude the possibility that the next relevant data point one encounters will disconfirm the proposition. For example, you could never conclusively assert all swans are white, even if all the swans you have ever seen are white because the next swan you meet may be black. However, precise truth claims could be disconfirmed in a single test.

It is for this reason that noted philosopher of science Karl Popper argues that "the criterion of demarcation" (distinguishing a scientific from a nonscientific proposition) is falsifiability.[6] A proposition has scientific status if it logically implies a precise class of observations which, if encountered, require the rejection or revision of the proposition. Thus, when Seymour Lipset, in his oft-cited work on "some social requisites of democracy" says that unique circumstances in individual cases could cause democracy to exist in any number of cases without those "social requisites" or could result in democracy not existing in any number of cases in which the requisites are present, he is claiming the truth of his proposition no matter what is found.[7] This is a classic case of the "saving the hypothesis" fallacy in which the proposition, by purporting to explain all findings, explains none.

This criterion of falsification is critiqued as crude positivism by the oft-cited works of Thomas Kuhn and Imre Lakatos. Kuhn has attained the status of a scientific guru in his characterization of science as dominated by a single "paradigm" or theoretic perspective by theory-hungry political scientists. However, properly understood, Kuhn denies the very essence of the history of science, the progressive building of a body of cumulative knowledge.[8] Kuhn claims that the meaning of data or observations is determined by the theory; hence, data cannot be an objective test of that theory. Yet, once the concepts are defined and indicators specified, the compatibility of the data with theory is intersubjective. After all, scientific progress is undeniable. Diseases are cured, the vehicle runs, computers process their data, and the bomb explodes. In their zeal to worship a guru of real science, Kuhn's followers failed to notice that his description of the history of natural science is wildly inaccurate. Natural sciences have not been dominated by a single paradigm or theory; Newtonian mechanics and Einstein's relativity coexist in physics, for example. Theories are not merely fashionable; new theories gain acceptance when they account for phenomena not explained by existing theory.

Lakatos' critique of "naïve falsificationism" is more sophisticated. He claims that the mere capacity of predicting disconfirming data does not make a proposition scientific. Rather, a scientific theory must be "superior" in the sense of progressively accounting for as yet unexplained phenomena.[9] This may be a matter of semantics. Scientific propositions in the sense of Popper's positivism may be more or less useful and Lakatos wants to deny scientific status to propositions that do not advance the cause of incrementally building a body of explanatory theory.

We call inquiry whose propositions can be falsified in terms of observable evidence *empirical*. First, we frame our discourse in terms of ideas or concepts. For example, we may claim that discriminated individuals are liberal. Here we have two concepts: individuals who belong to discriminated groups and those who are liberal. We render inquiry empirical by either defining our terms or concepts by a set of observations (an operational definition) or be specifying observable data from which we can infer the presence and strength of the concept. The latter use of indirect indicators for a concept raises a question of whether those indicators measure the concept as essentially defined. For example, one's score on any one of a number of IQ tests supposedly measures one's innate intelligence but is not considered to be intelligence as essentially defined. We may define a liberal as someone who expresses certain attitudes on a particular questionnaire or as one who votes for a particular class of political parties.

There are two types of nonfalsifiable propositions. The first type is characterized by vagueness with respect to tolerance of deviant cases such as we encounter in tendency statements such as Xs tend to be Y. This implies that not all Xs will be Y but we are not told how many non-Y Xs we can tolerate before giving up on the proposition and admitting the X has no causal impact on Y. Lipset's proposition, by accepting any number of exceptions to his proposition, is of this character. The second type of nonfalsifiable proposition is comprised of terms or concepts that do not refer to the world of experience. Thus when St. Thomas Aquinas claims that natural law is higher than civil law, or when Plato claims that the world of experience is an imperfect representation of a reality that exists in the realm of ideas, there are no conceivable data or observations that are logically inconsistent with those claims. Such statements are known as metaphysical statements. Such statements are derided by positivist philosophers such as A. J. Ayer, not as untrue, but as "meaningless" because they tell us nothing about the world of experience.[10]

The truth claims in these two types of nonfalsifiable propositions cannot be demonstrated so that anyone, regardless of their dispositions and confronted with the same information, would have to agree on whether they are true. Hence, such conclusions are subjective; they vary with the internal dispositions of each subject. The questions raised by such propositions cannot be resolved. We do not know any more about the nature of justice than did Plato, despite innumerable treatises on the subject throughout the ages.

Of course, we have already shown that no statements, even those that logically entail precise predictions about the world of experience, can be proven true. However, such falsifiable statements can be shown to be consistent with the relevant evidence insofar as that evidence is known. When the consistency of a proposition or a truth claim with the relevant evidence is demonstrated, we tentatively assume the statement is true and we can proceed to build on that knowledge. Science is interested in the ability to explain phenomena more completely and thereby to predict them more accurately. It is not interested in final, essential truth in the sense of a theological truth.

The answer to the question of whether a properly constructed empirical proposition is consistent with the known and relevant evidence will not vary from one individual to another, given the way concepts are defined. In that sense, scientific inquiry is objective although we will see numerous subjective aspects of such inquiry remain.

The ability to tentatively resolve certain puzzles, to reach tentative acceptance of certain truth claims, enables scholars in the field to build on what is accepted and resolved and to address new, more complex questions. Knowledge in any scientific field is built cumulatively; the work of each succeeding generation of scholars build on what is already known.[11] Thus, work in modern nuclear physics could not have begun without the work of previous generations of physicists on the nature of atoms or even on Newtonian mechanics. Otherwise, each generation of scholars begins from square one and asks the same questions as did all previous generations, as in the case of political philosophers who have pursued the essence of justice ever since Plato.

THE COMPARATIVE METHOD

The foregoing discussion of the application of the scientific method to the study of social and political phenomena makes the point that the inevitably incomplete nature of the explanation of such social and political phenomena derives from the inexorable presence of exogenous variables, factors that may affect the outcome we wish to explain but are omitted from our model. The comparative method is one of three methods that may be used to deal with the ubiquity of exogenous variables.

The experimental method, most appropriate for the natural sciences, involves the physical isolation of endogenous variables under analysis from exogenous variables that may affect the outcome. This is normally accomplished by the selective administration of the putatively causal factor to one group (the experimental subjects) and not to another (the control group) when both groups are alike in other respects. If no other stimuli affected the experimental group, one could then assess the impact of the explicans. Obviously, it is usually impractical to selectively and deliberately apply such a causal factor, which may include a very harmful state of affairs or a very destructive set of attitudes, to actual human beings. Such causal factors, moreover, are complex phenomena such as war, poverty, oppression that cannot be administered or withheld at will. Since behavior must occur somewhere, it is normally impossible to isolate behavior from a setting or context.

A second method for addressing the pervasive presence of exogenous variables is the statistical method, a mathematical system for estimating the probability of error in inferring causation from an observed relationship. Causation is always inferred in social research; it is never directly observed. (Inferred findings involve a certain amount of interpretation in moving from one's observations to a conclusion.) That is because we only see a sample of the universe of phenomena to which refer. We observe a number of people with a given characteristic from which we draw conclusions about the infinite number of people past, present, and future with that characteristic. This is not an issue in the natural sciences because all cases of say, a given quantity of a certain chemical, are identical: hence, to observe one unit is to observe them all. In social research, we may observe a pattern in which individuals with attribute or attitude A engage in behavior B. However, we cannot say for sure if B is due to A or to some other exogenous factor. We may have drawn an unrepresentative sample such that individuals with A just happen by chance to engage in behavior B. If we infer that A causes B, what are the chances for a given number of observations (sample size) that we are wrong and that the observed pattern is due to sampling error? Statistics can precisely estimate the probability of error in making causal inferences from a sample to a universe. This in effect tells us what an observed relationship would be if all other factors that might influence the explicandum were to cancel one another out.

The third method for dealing with the pervasiveness of exogenous variables in social research is the comparative method. Among the most pervasive of these exogenous variables is the context or setting in which such social and political phenomena occur. These phenomena—which consist of patterns of behavior and interaction—occur in a cultural, historical, geographic, and demographic setting from which they cannot be separated for purposes of the study. Therefore, a relationship between one set of attitudes—say a degree of anger and frustration—and a particular behavior—engaging in a particular kind of violence—may hold true in a setting in which the resort to violence has become an accepted way of resolving political grievances. This held true in France where a "theatre of revolution" had romanticized and legitimized the resort to violence, but it did not in another setting like Great Britain, in which established institutions and processes had acquired great acceptance.

Since we cannot isolate our explanatory propositions from the settings in which they occur, we must strive to ascertain the impact of those settings. As in all matters of scientific inquiry, we ascertain the impact of a class of phenomena by generalizing about them. These settings about which we strive to generalize are the attributes of entire political and social systems: their history or pattern of nation building, their culture, their social structure, the geographic setting, their demographics, or the nature of their political regime. One can identify these contextual or whole system factors by asking whether the proper noun name of a political system can be an adjective for that variable. Thus we know that culture is a contextual variable because we can reasonably speak of the French culture, the Swedish culture, etc. A political system identified with such a proper name is a repository of a number of contextual variables.

When a principle relating two empirically grounded concepts referring to the attitudes, attributes such as social class, or behavior holds true in some political systems but not in others, we can reasonably conclude that something in that repository of contextual factors is causing this distinction. This author found, for example, that women voted more conservatively than men in a number of European states (Italy, Germany, France) but not in others (Britain, Sweden, and Norway).[12] To say that our generalization holds true in these three countries but not in the other three ends the inquiry there because we have no logical basis for projecting our findings beyond the named states. Proper nouns refer to idiosyncratic entities while scientific inquiry seeks to extrapolate from direct observation, which is purely descriptive, to an infinite category of cases yet unseen. The obvious next question is, how is the one group of states different from the other in such a way as to affect the outcome in question? The answer will lie in the patterns in the repository of contextual variables for which the proper noun names of these countries are but a label. In this case, this author found that in the first group of countries, religiosity was still an important factor—a significant portion of the population still attended church more or less regularly—while in the latter group religion did not play a significant role in the lives of most of the population. We now had an amended theory, that women are more religious than men and people who are more religious tend to be conservative. In countries where religion played a significant role in such a small segment of the population, significant differences in religiosity between men and women disappeared; hence, the foregoing proposition did not hold true. We can now infer the expectation that the religious difference between men and women will also disappear in the infinite category of states that also has a low level of religiosity.

Such determinations can only be made by generalizing about the attributes of whole systems or countries. When you have a proposition that holds true in some systems but not in others, or holds true in a different way or to a different extent in some systems compared to others, you have a research question that requires comparative analysis. Of course you can only tell if you have such a research question if you apply your proposition to a variety of countries and hence a variety of contexts.

Comparative political analysis, therefore, may be defined as the application of an explanatory proposition to a variety of countries or contexts. Studies whose data are drawn from a single country may be part of the comparative enterprise if their conclusions are stated in such a way that they logically could be applied to a variety of political systems. By applying our explanatory proposition to as wide a variety of contexts as possible, we can take account of the impact of the widest variety of contextual factors as possible on our explicandum.

The comparative method is a means for building theory incrementally. With each observed weakening of theory, one adds the contextual factor that was present where the theory held true and absent where it did not. This renders the theory more complex but also more accurate in the predictions it logically generates. Our explanatory theories can thus become progressively more complete and more accurate as more contextual factors are taken into account.

The idiosyncratic nation states, labeled with a proper noun, are actually repositories of contextual factors. When we say that such a particular nation state is the one place in which a generalization does not hold true, that logically halts inquiry. There is no logical basis for extrapolating from the relationship we have directly observed to cases as yet unseen. Yet, science is an inferential enterprise that is supposed to logically generate predictions. However, if we translate the proper noun name of the system in which the observed pattern does not hold to those common noun variables that distinguish that system from those in which the pattern does hold, we now have a logical basis for such inferences. We now expect that the relationship between gender and religiosity will disappear not only in Norway but also in that infinite category of other systems in which the level of religiosity is similarly low. Therefore, we may also conceptualize comparative inquiry as the translation of the proper noun names of systems to common noun variables that lend themselves to the process of generalization.

CONCEPTUALIZATION AND MEASUREMENT IN CROSS-CULTURAL INQUIRY

This commitment to cross-cultural generalization generates problems in conceptualization not encountered when one confines analysis to a single country and culture. Conceptualization refers to the forming of ideas that give meaning to the truth claims we make and the observations on which they are based. We have discussed above how the goal of making science inter-subjective requires that we ground our concepts in the world of experience, to render them empirical.

When one engages in cross-cultural inquiry, one finds that the meaning of terms is to some extent context-specific. That is, the meaning of concepts varies from one cultural context to another. We will see below, for example, that different cultures have very different understandings of the concept of democracy. Because that term has acquired a widely accepted positive normative content, some governments that we in the West would regard as clearly authoritarian or even dictatorial claim to be practicing a variety of democracy. Similarly, we would find that the specific behaviors that would be denoted as indicating a strong level of political participation in one setting might not be considered particularly strong in another setting. The widely used indicator of religiosity, frequency of attendance in a house of worship, would not apply to orthodox Jewish women who are forbidden from taking an active role in such services but rather are expected to take the responsibility for maintaining a kosher kitchen. The meaning of particular behaviors that constitute the indicators of our concepts are context-specific.

The challenge for conducting comparative political inquiry is to have one's concepts have consistent meaning across the cultures and settings in which the study is conducted. Accordingly, it may be necessary to assign different indicators for the same concept when applied to different settings. This of course means that a researcher should have a thorough knowledge and understanding of the countries or settings to which his or her inquiry is applied.

This need for consistency in conceptualization and measurement led to a preoccupation on the part of comparative politics scholars with the development of concepts and with research problems involving systems of logically related concepts—frequently referred to as *conceptual frameworks*—at a high level of generality with a wide applicability across a wide range of countries or contexts. David Easton, for example, proposed a framework for a general theory of politics based upon the concept of a system, an unspecified set of processes, institutions, and values interacting with an environment generating demands and supports.[13] The essential research question of this scheme is to determine how the system converts the demands placed upon the system from the environment, thereby maintaining a state of equilibrium between inputs and outputs. When the stress generated by inputs (demands on the system) is not ameliorated with proportionate output, the system may break down. Note here we are using concepts at the highest level of generality. The concept of conversion of inputs into outputs could refer to the wide universe of processes by which a nation state takes action. The concept of political system is not limited to nation states. When operating at that level of generality, the problems of translating such broad concepts into precise categories of observations are enormous, if not insurmountable. How, for example, does one measure stress on the boundaries of the system? How does one distinguish system breakdown from system change and adaptation? Moreover, the entire framework is beset with problems of tautological reasoning. The system breaks down because the stress has reached intolerable levels. How do you know the levels are intolerable? Because the system has broken down. Consequently, despite its popularity over five decades, Easton's system analysis has not generated a single testable proposition. That the discipline of political science spent better than a decade enthralled by claims of a scientific inquiry which it did not understand is testament to the importance of empirical falsifiability as the criterion of what is or is not scientifically useful.

Gabriel Almond and others built significant academic careers uncritically lifting a conceptual framework called functional analysis from its sister social science, sociology.[14] Aiming again at universal applicability as an overreaction to the now discredited one-country-at-a-time approach, the functionalists attempted to specify the functions that must be performed in any political system, no matter how industrialized or primitive, complex or simple, authoritarian or democratic it may be. The precise meaning of the term *function* is not consistent throughout this literature;[15] however, the term most frequently appears to refer to a role that entails a set of processes or tasks that contribute to the operation of the system. The literature does not specify indicators to determine if the system is in fact operating at an adequate level nor to determine whether the functions are being adequately performed independently of the phenomenon the functions purport to explain, the breakdown of the system or absence thereof. The presence of the functions themselves appears to be "explained" by their necessity for the maintenance of the system. Thus, the functions are performed because they are needed. The search for universal applicability has led to the renaming of processes or "functions" familiar to students of Western democracy. Thus, lawmaking is now called rule making, to account for primitive systems without a formal law-making process. Here again, we find a lack of precise empirical content and circular reasoning that plagued much of the early search for conceptual frameworks of universal applicability.[16] Familiar terms have been renamed to expand the universality of their applicability and include more of the phenomena that might affect the explicanda—the phenomena to be explained. While the focus of our analysis a generation ago was the nation state, now the literature discusses political systems. A political system includes phenomena not formally part of the state but which do participate in the basic political function of making laws or rules for that society, phenomena such as interest groups and political parties.

THE FOCUS ON SOCIOLOGICAL AND OTHER CONTEXTUAL FACTORS

The modern explanatory focus of comparative analysis has led to the analysis of factors previously ignored by political scientists as outside their domain of constitutionally designated structures. We have seen how this has included the analysis of the context in which those structures operate. Contextual factors, it will be recalled, include historical, sociological, and economic factors. When we seek to explain political behavior, we must include within our study those factors that affect that behavior. This may also include the psychological causes of political behavior. Hence, comparative analysis now concerns itself with material formerly left to other social sciences, sometimes to the neglect of the nation state and other political phenomena that were once the raison d'être of our discipline—what Roy Macridis called "the fallacy of inputism."[17] In particular, political scientists focused on the culture and social structure as if understanding them was an end in itself rather than a means of explaining political phenomena. While the rigid boundaries between the social sciences have broken down with regard to what kinds of phenomena we may include in our research project, political scientists differ from sociologists, psychologists, or economists with regard to the phenomena they ultimately seek to explain.

IMPORTANT CONCEPTS FOR COMPARISON: POLITICAL CULTURE

We have clearly moved beyond being confined to such terms relating to constitutionally designated structures in Western democracies to utilizing concepts that can be applied to less-developed systems, as well as modern ones and to authoritarian as well as democratic states.

Among the more commonly used concepts in modern comparative political analysis is the concept of political culture. Culture generally refers to patterns of mental or psychological orientations that are so pervasive in a society that they are held to characterize that whole society. Culture thus bridges the gap between the individual and whole system level of analysis. Attitudes, one element of culture, are attributes of individuals; yet, we can speak of the French (Belgian, German, etc.) attitude toward something.

When these mental or psychological orientations are directed toward political objects, we speak of the political culture. This concept, given varying empirical content by various researchers, has been posited as a major cause of variations among political systems.[18] However, there are some dimensions that are commonly included in the use of the concept of political culture: attitudes, especially attitudes toward authority, beliefs or conceptions of what is thought to be true, a conceptual style in reaching decisions that may be manifested in ideologism or pragmatism, feelings that may be manifested in affect or identification with a collectivity or alienation from or rejection of a collectivity, trust or distrust of elites and of one's fellow man, knowledge and information, and values or conceptions of good and bad.

Attitudes toward authority may be manifested as authoritarian or submissive (unquestioned and obsequious obedience to authority figures), egalitarian (a sense that people are more or less equally qualified to make political judgments and demand for close control of authority figures), and deferential (a belief that some people are more fit or qualified for the day-to-day business of governing or leading in a particular situation and therefore should be given wide latitude in their decision making; however, these leaders have an obligation to work in the interests of the governed and should be held accountable for the results of how they have governed).

Within the broad concept of culture is what Herbert Spiro called "the political style," the kinds of criteria and processes that were used in resolving issues and making policy.[19] A distinction may be made between an ideological style of decision making in which one bases one's policy choices on their consistency with broad principles as differentiated from a pragmatic style in which one makes policy in an incremental fashion—small adjustments are made to the status quo based on what works on trial and error without much reference to principle or logical consistency. Ideology is frequently distinguished from just any set of principles by a relatively closed character, that is, being insensitive to new information; hence, policy made in an ideological style is unlikely to be responsive to public needs, opinions, or changes in the context in which policy is made. An ideological style is less conducive to the effective resolution of actual issues or the solving of actual problems. Ideology, however, does provide a guide to ends or a sense of purpose and a consistency and predictability to policy making.

Pragmatism, on the other hand, in its constant adjustment to actual results, is by definition sensitive to both the public and to context. Given its focus on what works rather than what is logical, it is effective in the resolution of actual issues. However, in its eschewal of principle, pure pragmatism does not provide a sense of direction or purpose. It tends to render the direction of policy making less predictable. Most scholars think that a balance between the two styles is the most effective policy making style.

Another dimension of political culture is the realm of feeling. In this dimension, the factor of identity has received much attention in comparative political analysis in recent years. Identity has appeared in the field of comparative political analysis with the increasing emergence of the politics of multiculturalism and subcultural defense on the one hand and a growing concern for the cultural integrity of nation states in the face of increasing levels of immigration from culturally distinct sources. Identity is about such questions as "who am I?" and "what is my purpose in life?" As such, identity is in the ontological realm of being,[20] arguing that one has a need to belong to an entity greater than oneself to provide a sense of purpose and meaning in one's life.[21]

When the individuals who comprise such a system feel a part of it and perceive that they have a personal stake in its well being, sociologists call that *system affect*. Individuals who do not so identify with a system, who regard that system as "them" rather than "us," are said to be *alienated* from that system. When the predominant numbers of individuals identify with a system or experience *system affect*, we say that system is *legitimate*. A legitimate regime is widely accepted among its own subjects and by other nations. Legitimacy, which thus entails widespread support for a system or regime regardless whether one approves of its specific policies or actions, enables a system to survive over a span of time in which the actions of the system will inevitably produce both winners and losers. An aggregate of individuals based upon a common sense of identity and some sharing of values may be called a *community* or *nation*.

When the boundaries of a community or nation coincide with or are congruent with those of a state, the regime controlling that state has a better chance of effective performance or even survival over time. The boundaries of some states may contain more than one nation or community. We will see, for example, among Western democracies that the state Belgium contains two culturally distinct nations: the less urbanized, Flemish speaking, more religious Flanders and the more urbanized, French speaking, more secularized Wallonia. Among less-developed states, Nigeria contains over three hundred culturally and linguistically distinct tribal groupings. In each of these countries, these nations or communities within the state are alienated from the other nations within the state and from the state or regime itself. When a state contains such mutually isolated and alienated subcultures, we call it a *segmented society*. When tolerance of cultural and other differences evolves into a policy of resisting assimilation of a subculture into a broader sense of identification with the nation state, segmented societies are encouraged. The feelings of affect or alienation that define identity in a political culture are often expressed through symbols. The pomp and ceremonies surrounding the British royalty in its role as head of state (in contrast to the head of government, the prime minister who with his cabinet directs the policy making process) is a symbolic role. That does not mean it is unimportant. Political symbols may constitute the glue that holds a nation together as a coherent entity.

Finally, a culture contains values or preferences that may define the nature of a system. For example, Western publics generally place a high value on freedom and equality while leading Islamists striving to subvert the Iraqi government value strict adherence to Islamic law (as they interpret that law) over freedom and equality. In fact, equality for women and infidels is offensive to them. American President Bush, defending his goal to bring democracy to the Arab world, claimed any and all men, when given the choice, would choose freedom. Clearly, that is not the case with the leader of the antigovernment insurgency who states that he hates the idea of democracy.

The dimensions of the concept of political culture are shown in Table 1–1.

THE CLEAVAGE STRUCTURE OR STRATIFICATION SYSTEM

The political culture is part of the context or setting in which political behavior occurs and which may impact that behavior. As such, it is an attribute of the system itself. A related aspect of this setting is the social stratification system or cleavage structure, the criteria by which people are grouped and divided in a society. These criteria may include social class, religion or religiosity, language, race or ethnicity, and tribe. (*Religion* describes a religious grouping while *religiosity* refers to the relative importance of religion in the lives of people).

Social class is objectively present in every reasonably complex society. Some people will always be better off financially than others; there will always be salaried workers and owners and managers. The question is whether people primarily identify with their socioeconomic group or whether such identification is overridden by other identifications such as race or ethnicity. For example, it is unlikely that Flemish workers in Belgium feel much common identity with Wallonian workers; rather, it is likely that their identification with their cultural-linguistic subculture overrides any common identity or sense of common concerns among workers in these distinct subcultures. Class is therefore a latent or residual cleav-

TABLE 1–1   The Dimensions of Political Culture

Attitudes: Psychological orientation toward political objects frequently involving conceptions of how things ought to be. Especially relevant are attitudes toward authority.

   a. *egalitarian*: people are relatively equal in their capacity to assume political roles and to make political judgements

   b. *authoritarian*: some people are more qualified to rule than others whose duty is unquestioned obedience

   c. *deferential*: some people are more qualified to occupy leadership roles but these these leaders have an oblication to rule in the general interest and should be held accountable for the results of their rule

Beliefs: conceptions of how things are which may or may not be accurate. Ideology refers to a comprehensive system of beliefs that is relatively closed, that is, a belief system that does not adjust to fit new information.

   a. *ideologism*: style of policy making that holds as a criterion for decision making the consistency of those decisions with a set of principles

   b. *pragmatism*: a trial-and-error style of decision-making using results as a criterion without regard to principles.

Feelings:

   a. *affect*: a sense of belonging to a larger entity, that one has an interest in, such that one regards the system as "us" rathern than "them"

   b. *alienation*: a sense of detachment from the system, feelings that the interests of the system are distinct from one's own interests, a tendency to regard the system as "them," rather than "us"

   c. *emotional attachment* to political symbols

Values: priorities and goals (when framed in terms of particular objects, values become atitudes). Values become fundamental when they define the nature of the system, such as freedom, equality, or strick adherence to a set of religious laws.

age in those countries in which a sense of identity with ethnic, racial, religious, or tribal groupings overrides a sense of class identification. Class emerges as a significant cleavage in countries, such as was the case in Great Britain, in which regional, religious, or ethnic identification did not assume political importance. After the resolution of the conflict over Scottish nationalism in the early 1700s until recent decades, British politics revolved around class-based issues.

Robert Alford, in demonstrating that class-based cleavages had dominated the politics of both Britain and Australia as of the early 1960s, argued that the class basis of the politics of these two countries was a major factor in their success in effectively resolving the issues that they faced.[22] Class-based issues, he argued, are about *how much;*, such questions lend themselves to splitting the differences and making compromises. Issues surrounding the questions of religion or culture are not so easily compromised. There is no logical middle ground between the true faith and heresy.

CONSTITUTIONALLY DESIGNATED STRUCTURES OR THE POLITICAL FORMAT

While students of comparative political analysis in focusing on such contextual factors as culture and social structure are covering ground occupied by other social sciences (such as sociology, anthropology, or economics), political scientists are not interested in these contextual factors for their own sake. Rather, they use them as factors to explain and predict patterns in the political structures or political systems that constitute the ultimate focus of our inquiries.

In fact, we noted above how political scientists have been criticized for losing sight of the traditional focus on political systems by treating those contextual factors as if understanding them was the ultimate goal of our inquiry.[23] Modern political science, however, moved away from a focus on the state itself for reasons that are still valid. The state, the constitutionally designated structures that participate in making authoritative rules for that society, is essentially a legalist concept that grew out of the Western political experience. The concept of the political system, however, is a broader concept that includes the state but also refers to all the structures and institutions that participate in that process of making authoritative decisions. It thus includes such structures as the political party system, the interest group system, and associational life in general. Some of the political systems gaining independence in the post-World War II era have a very weak to almost nonexisting system of constitutionally designated structures. Rather they are governed by the social movement that led the struggle for independence. The leader of Libya, for example, is known officially as Colonel Muammar Qaddafi, not President or Prime Minister Qaddafi. In fact, in many systems one may note the extent to which, despite the existence of the formal institutions of the state, informal institutions and processes actually make the authoritative decisions. Interest groups, possessed of specialized knowledge in their field, may dominate the policy making for that field because of the advanced state of technology in advanced industrial societies while holders of formal political office are frequently more generally trained in fields such as law, social sciences, or humanities.

Yet, constitutionally designated political formats constitute an important focus for our field. To the extent that we include them in our enterprise of building a body of explanatory theory, we must generalize about those formats. The first step in generalizing about as complex a set of observations as the diversity of political formats is classification, grouping diverse observed phenomena under a common heading or concept based upon significant shared attributes. This is one of a number of attempts to categorize this diverse universe, a task fraught with difficulties.[24] Yet, the universe of political formats is so complex and diverse that this process of aggregating and labeling them seems essential to bring that universe within the bounds of manageable simplicity. Classification thus fills the same role as conceptualization in scientific inquiry.

This classification based upon political format (or typology since it is based upon qualitative attributes) is one way to organize and categorize the universe of political systems. These systems may also be categorized by their level of industrialization or by type of economic system they pursue. Table 1–2 represents the classification of political formats offered here. The utility of any such classification depends on three factors: One, whether each political system can be unambiguously placed in one and only one cell; two, whether there is at least one case for each cell; and three, whether a nation's category in this classification scheme relates systematically to another dimension or variable. To illustrate this, Table 1–3 offers a cross-classification of regime format on the one hand and level of industrialization on the other, a possible relationship suggested by Seymour Lipset's hypothesis that a level of economic development may be a necessary precondition for the successful establishment of a democratic format.[25] One may cross-classify regime or political format type with other variables as well, such as the level of stability (as measured by the frequency of unscheduled regime changes or changes in government). The distinction between a presidential and a parliamentary format for democracy is related to the occasional unscheduled removal of the head of government in the latter type of system.

The criterion offered here for placing a nation in the democratic category is the now classic minimal one offered by Joseph Schumpeter: more or less regular competitive elections, which leaves other more difficult-to-measure and, in some cases, arguable criteria such as level of participation, responsiveness, and accountability matters for inquiry. These criteria are considered more fully in Chapter Two.

Clearly, there is a judgmental aspect to placing a given regime in a given category. France, for example, has been characterized as a mixture of parliamentary and presidential formats, an ambiguity that resides in identifying the actual head of government in that regime. Although a premier exists who may be removed by a vote of no confidence (or censure, as they call it), the holder of that office does not function as the chief policy making official in France but remains, to a greater or lesser extent, depending on the personalities involved, subject to the will of the president. Similarly, there is considerable ambiguity regarding the competitive nature of the Russian system under President Putin. Such ambiguities can be mitigated by clarifying the criteria by which systems are assigned to one or another category.

PUBLIC POLICY AND ECONOMIC SYSTEMS

We discussed above how the search for widely applicable concepts and questions to facilitate broad-ranging comparisons led to a preoccupation in the 1950s and 1960s with the development of what have variously been called conceptual frameworks, paradigms, or models of the political process. This book, then, took note of the popularity of systems analysis as a loosely constructed model of the political process, a model that posited an equilibrium between inputs, a conversion process,

Table 1–2   Classification of Political Systems by Decision Making Format

I. Democratic Systems: important policy making roles are selected in regular elections in which the opposition is not suppressed.

  A. *Presidential systems*:   the same directly elected individual is both head of government and chief of state and may not simultaneously serve in the representative assembly or legislature.

  B. *Parliamentary system*: the head of government—variously called prime minister, premier, or chancellor—is named by the separate chief of state from among the members of the legislature. The head of government is accountable to the legislature in that the assembly can remove the head of government from office by a simple majority vote (of no confidence).

   1. *Assembly dominated system*: the outcome of the election to the assembly does not ordinarily determine who commands the support of a majority of that assembly and therefore who must be the head of government. Governments will be comprised of coalitions of several parties and are more likely to lose votes of no confidence.

   2. *Cabinet system*: the election to the assembly normally provides one party with a majority of seats: hence, the leader of that party must be named prime minister. Governments in this system rarely lose votes of no confidence.

II. Authoritarian systems: either elections are not held or the opposition is suppressed by force by the government or by the use of election fraud, intimidation, etc.

  A. *Dictatorship*: one person is able to dictate policy unrestrained by considerations external to his or her own will.

   1. *Ordinary dictatorship*: power is exercised for its own sake based upon monopoly control of the means of coercion.

   2. *Populist dictatorship*: the dictator creates a popular legitimacy based on the widely held belief that he or she embodies the will and values of the population. These values generally include a millenaristic ideology, a closed set of ideas that posit a millennium that will reshape the socioeconomic order. When a populist dictatorship attempts to reshape the fundamental values and structures of society in such a way as to eliminate a zone of privacy beyond the reach of the state, it approaches the model called totalitarian dictatorship, a model that was once important in the literature and is now regarded with a great degree of skepticism.

  B. *Bureaucratic authoritarianism*: the discretion of the political leader is constrained by an autonomous public bureaucracy and/or by the military forces.

TABLE 1–3 Cross-Classification of Systems by Regime Type and Level of Economic Development

	Presidential Democracy	Parliamentary Democracy	Ordinary Dictatorship	Populist Dictatorship	Bureaucratic or Praetorian Authoritarianism
Industrialized	U.S.A 5th Republic France	Great Britain United Germany	Kenya Central African Republic	Nazi Germany	USSR after Stalin
Less Industrialized	Argentina Phillipines	Malaysia India	Nicaragua (under Somoza) Iraq (under Saddam Hussein)	North Korea Kampuchea	Egypt Nigeria (under Sani Abacha)

and outputs. The discussion of political culture and the social stratification scheme illustrated the focus on inputs. The format of government is the mechanism for converting inputs into outputs. Outputs are concerned with what government does—in other words, public policy.

The contextual factors and the format of government are important for how they impact on public policy. Policy is, after all, the means by which government directly affects our lives. Public policy may be defined as a set of actions by the government directed at the achievement of some goal. It includes but is not limited to the passage of laws. Decisions by high-level civil servants, executive orders by the head of government, the interpretation of laws by the courts, and the implementation of rules by police or other public officials are also part of the policy making process.

Among the important policy choices for government in the modern world is the specification and operation of the economic system. The economic system determines the price and allocation of goods and services in a society. Thus, economic systems are distinguished from the type of political system which is the basis for determining how political decision makers are chosen and how political decisions are made.

In popular discourse in the United States, there has been a tendency to equate democracy (a political choice) with capitalism (an economic choice). It should be theoretically possible for each type of political system to choose and operate one of various types of economic systems. Whether certain kinds of economic systems may encourage or impede certain types of political format can thus be a question for inquiry rather than a relationship proclaimed true by definition.

One can identify three pure or ideal types of economic systems: market capitalism, welfare state capitalism, and state socialism. In practice, actual systems use combinations of these ideal types of economic systems. While the United States has been more ideologically committed to market capitalism than most other industrial democracies, it has also adopted many of the policies guaranteeing a level of material well-being associated with the welfare state model. The absence of real world manifestations of these pure economic system categories may suggest that these pure types may be unworkable in practice. The events of the 1920s and 1930s suggested that reliance on pure market economics produced unsatisfactory results in the real world, and the collapse of the Soviet Empire in 1989 was in part encouraged by a growing disenchantment with the ability of purely planned economies and public ownership to provide minimally acceptable levels of prosperity. While the formerly Marxist systems of the now-collapsed Soviet Empire and even Communist China have been moving in the direction of limited amounts of free enterprise, the United Kingdom and France unloaded most of their state-owned enterprises into the private sector in the 1980s. Yet, even under the leadership of a prime minister more ideologically committed than any other to free enterprise market capitalism, Margaret Thatcher, this move toward *privatization* of the means of production and dismantling of the welfare state was limited. The railroads, health care system, and postal service remained under government ownership. Thus, it seems that most of the modern world systems are moving toward a hybrid of an increased reliance on market forces combined with the retention of significant amounts of welfare state guarantees. The ideal types of economic systems are outlined in Table 1–4.

TABLE 1–4   Pure or Ideal Types of Economic Systems

I. **Capitalism**: the major means of production, distribution, and exchange are privately owned and operated and run for profit.

    A. *Market capitalism*: Decisions about what, where, and how much to produce are left to the individual producer and supplier of that product or service, and decisions about who gets how much of what are left to the impersonal forces of supply and demand. Goods and services are competitively allocated and material well-being is not guaranteed.

    B. *Welfare state capitalism*: While the major means of production, distribution, and exchange are in nongovernmental hands and run for profit, many aspects of material well-being are considered to be rights guaranteed by public policy. Values are allocated by rational decision making by designated actors rather than by impersonal market forces; hence, this system entails a planned economy.

II. **Socialism**: The major means of production, distribution, and exchange are owned and operated by the government and presumably operated in the public interest rather than run for profit. Values are allocated by rational decision making by designated actors rather than left to impersonal market forces. Equality of material well-being is pursued by public policy.

FORMAL MODELING AND RATIONAL CHOICE THEORY: A DOMINANT PARADIGM ?

The search for a common conceptual framework or paradigm, to facilitate cross-cultural generalization for a theory-hungry discipline, has led political scientists to co-opt such paradigms from other disciplines, sometimes uncritically—which obsequious political scientists regarded with envy for appearing more scientific. We noted above that our love affairs with David Easton's systems analysis and the functional analysis of Gabriel Almond and others failed to produce any testable propositions, not to mention any enhanced ability to predict significant political events.

A major trend in political science in recent years has been to adopt the intellectually mesmerizing model of market economics to the study of politics, an enterprise generally referred to as rational choice theory. Market theory in economics is intellectually mesmerizing because, once the assumptions are granted, the theory can deductively generate precise predictions of economic behavior, a classic manifestation of the covering law model, held by such epistemological gurus as Carl Hempel to be the essence of scientific explanation.[26] The construction of logically coherent and mathematically rigorous models has become a major subfield of economics known as econometrics. Yet, despite the logical rigor of classic market theory and the precise measurability of its concepts, economists are remarkably unable to accurately predict economic reality.

The difficulty lies in the fact that the accuracy of the predictions generated from a rationally coherent theory depends on the extent to which the assumptions that underlie any such theory describe reality. Market theory in economics assumes the following: mankind is rational; economic goals and motivations override all other considerations; mankind is afforded choices; and individuals have the information to know which choice will maximize their economic values. Clearly there is truth in these assumptions but they are clearly imperfectly accurate. The assumptions that underlie all theories like market economics and rational choice theory, which predict rational behavior from a model of human interaction, are in the goals or preferences of the actors. These goals are frequently more complex than assumed by the model. Thorstein Veblen in a classic tome describes how people spend with irrational ostentation to demonstrate their wealth and gain social status, a concept known as "conspicuous consumption."[27] If people were always motivated by rational economic considerations, there would be no public school teachers. The problem here is the simplistic specification of goals or preferences; human beings are not motivated by one set of values such as economic gain. However, one can find out the priorities assigned to various goals by the outcomes those goals are supposed to explain and predict.

The adaptation of rational choice theory in political science has gained sharply in popularity to the point where, by 1992, 36 percent of the articles in the discipline's leading journal were exercises in rational choice scholarship.[28] Some of its

proponents go so far as to argue that rational choice theory constitutes the only scientifically valid achievement in political research.[29]

The essence of the approach is to create a model of the political process in
which the actors (individuals or institutions) choose between courses of action
based upon their assessment of what would be the most rational choice or action of
competing actors, assuming all parties are rationally trying to maximize certain
values or minimize certain risks. The model is concerned with identifying the rational choice given preference priorities when the relevant probabilities are known
and the outcome is not determined solely by one's choice alone.[30] The elements of
this model should correspond in logical form to a parallel set of elements in the observable world; however, since the model is comprised of selected elements, it is a
simplification of that observable world. Applications of this approach vary between the goal of maximizing values and minimizing one's maximum risks, the
so-called "minimax" strategy which addresses the reality that the choice that could
maximize one's values would, if the other makes the rational and expected choice,
cause the first actor to suffer maximum losses. A simple example from an application of rational choice theory, game theory, will illustrate using the simplest two
person, zero-sum game. (A zero-sum game is one in which the gains of one actor
must originate from the losses of the other because values are finite.) Game theory
is more formal than the rest of rational choice theories and focuses more on the
strategic interaction of the actors. In the example, the gains of actor A are connoted
by pluses and the gains of B are connoted by minuses.

In this model, if A takes choice one by which she could gain her maximum of 5.
A would have to assume, however, that B would take choice two by which A
would lose 6. If A takes choice two, however, the worst she could lose is 4. Meanwhile, if B takes choice one, A could lose 5 while with choice two the worst she
could do is lose 4. In this scheme based on perfect information, A must assume that
B will choose the option that will lead to his best outcome. Thus, quadrant four
yields the rational minimax outcome for both players. In game theory jargon that is
known as "the saddle point." Of course, for such an approach to yield knowledge
of the real world, the numbers which are, after all, symbols, have to be translated
into observable phenomena.

An almost canonical example of the use of game theory is the so-called "prisoners dilemma." In this scenario, two prisoners are in police custody and interrogated

Figure 1–1   A Two-Person Zero Sum Game

		Actor A	
		Choice One	Choice Two
Actor B	Choice One	+5	–4
	Choice Two	–6	+4

separately. They each believe that if they both remain silent, the police can only convict them of a relatively minor charge. However, the police tell each prisoner that if he confesses and convicts his accomplice of a serious crime, he will go free while the accomplice gets serious punishment. If both confess, they will each get serious punishment although not as severe as if he or she remained silent and was convicted by his or her accomplice's confession. As one of the leading early advocates of game theory, Thomas Schelling says, "There is no independently 'best' choice that one can make—it depends on what the others do."[31]

Anthony Downs' 1957 analysis of voting and party strategy constitutes one of the more famous early applications of rational choice theory to the real world of political behavior.[32] Downs' work, framed in readable prose rather than the complex notational and mathematical language that characterizes much rational choice literature, attempts to explain political party behavior and interaction in a modern democracy.

Assume, for example, that parties will seek to maximize their votes and that interests will seek to maximize their values or policy agendas. In a situation involving two political forces, both parties can take the support of their respective extreme bases for granted—the most right wing conservative or radical leftist will be better off with the centrist wing of their own party than with a victory by the opposition. Free to ignore their bases, both parties will converge toward the uncommitted center and compete for the same centrist majority. Yet, this logic of Downs' would have failed to predict the bipolarization of the British party system during the Thatcher era when the British Labour Party fell under the control of the socialist-egalitarian wing of their party led by Michael Foot while Margaret Thatcher earned a reputation as the most ideologically pure and farthest right British prime minister of modern times. Clearly, the policy agendas of these two leaders took precedence over presumed goals of vote maximization. Rational choice will necessarily depend on goal or value priorities, which will vary among human beings, and thus cannot be assumed for all actors in a given type of situation.

In another classic piece of rational choice scholarship, William Riker explains coalition formation with the "size principle."[33] This states that actors will form the "minimum winning coalition" because there are costs to securing additional allies; hence, the larger the winning margin, the less value will be secured by winning. Just when it seems that Riker has offered a general theory of rational behavior in coalition formation, Riker qualifies his theory with the "information corollary." This refers to the fact that in a fluid bargaining situation, the precise size of the coalition that will be needed to win cannot be known in advance; hence, it is rational to make the payments and pad one's lead in order to be assured of winning. Thus, the operation of the size principle or the presence-of-information uncertainty is indicated by the results that these principles are adduced to explain. This is a classic case of "the fallacy of affirming the consequent"—a logical fallacy that one frequently encounters in rational choice literature—because the intentions and value priorities of actors are difficult to determine independently of the results they are supposed to produce. Yet, one cannot definitively infer the intentions from the behavior unless one can show that there are no other competing explanations of that behavior—a generally impossible task.

Works such as these illustrate the appeal of rational choice theory, that propositions about the real world can be logically deduced from theory, the form that scientific explanations, it will be recalled, are supposed to take. Major criticisms of rational choice theory take the following forms: In their zeal to produce universal theories, rational choice theorists have compromised the specification of empirical content and therefore the testing of the logical entailments of their theories.[34] Some rational choice advocates go so far as to reject the standard that theories should be revised or rejected in the face of disconfirming data. Rational choice advocate Dennis Chong of Northwestern University argued that "A theory cannot be rejected because of disconfirming facts. It can only be supplanted by a superior theory."[35] Yet, how can one judge a theory to be superior if the accuracy of its predictions does not matter? Rational choice theorists select those aspects of the world of politics that lend themselves to that form of analysis, especially with reference to the availability of quantifiable data, such as voting choice or coalition formation. They ignore other important considerations in the world of politics that we political scientists have an obligation to address.[36] Rational choice theorists not only make assumptions about rationality but also about the motives and goals of actors which may be imperfectly true because of the complexity of human motivation.

Yet, it is undeniable that rational choice theory has advanced our understanding of the world of politics. It has been useful, for example, in distinguishing individual and collective rationality—that what is rational for an individual is not necessarily rational for the collectivity to which the individual belongs, a proposition famously addressed by Mancur Olsen with his "free rider problem,"[37] that rational individuals will not sacrifice their individual short-term interests for the collective good. It will cost the factory owner far more to clean up his or her emissions than the value of extra clean air that this industrialist has to breathe. Moreover, rational choice theory has become much more sophisticated and complex from its early cooptation of neoclassical economics to the study of politics. Rational choice theory now, for example, considers the constraining impact of institutions and normative considerations on the availability of choice.[38] Clearly rational choice theory is appropriate for the investigation of some research questions in political science. Clearly, it is less appropriate for others. Perhaps scholars on both sides of this issue need to get past the Thomas Kuhn-initiated myth that a field of inquiry has room for one dominant paradigm only.

CONCLUDING REMARKS: CRUCIAL QUESTIONS FOR THE FIELD

This chapter has described a field struggling to emerge from a state of lacking consensus with respect to purpose and method. After decades of struggle in the early post-war period, a consensus has begun to emerge on the explanatory purpose of the field and of the importance of scientific respectability. Yet, the field remains badly divided over how to achieve these goals or on what constitutes scientifically valid research in the study of politics. From the strong critiques of the work of Gabriel Almond and his associates on the Comparative Politics Committee of the Social Science Research Council in the 1950s through the early 1960s to the controversy surrounding the growing popularity of formal theory in the 1990s into the twenty-first century, we see a field that remains divided as to theory and method.

The struggle for explanatory theory in comparative political analysis has had several important effects on the nature of research in the field. First, many scholars in the field have abandoned the early quest of scholars like David Easton for universally applicable theories of politics. With some notable exceptions, we shall see that the study of advanced industrialized democracies has become a separate enterprise from the study of social and political change in the less-industrialized parts of the world. This book is organized accordingly. Second, although the precise impact of given factors is a matter of vigorous dispute among scholars, it is widely accepted that previously neglected contextual factors must be studied as potential causes of the political phenomena we wish to explain. Accordingly, this book examines the vast literature on such factors. Finally, it will be clear from this book that there is still sharp disagreement among scholars as to the best methods to use to build this sought-after body of explanatory theory. Hence, comparative politics is still very much a work in progress.

ENDNOTES

[1]See, e.g., Roy Macridis, *The Study of Comparative Government* (New York: Random House, 1955). Harry Eckstein, "A Perspective on Comparative Politics, Past and Present," in Harry Eckstein and David Apter, eds., *Comparative Politics: A Reader* (New York: The Free Press, 1963); Lawrence Mayer, *Redefining Comparative Politics: Promise versus Performance* (Newbury Park, CA: Sage Publications, 1989).

[2]Crane Brinton, *The Anatomy of Revolution* (Englewood Cliffs, NJ: Prentice Hall, 1952).

[3]Abraham Maslow argues that his impressionistic conclusions in the field of psychoanalysis are "humanistic and holistic conceptions of science... in blunt contradiction to the classical, conventional philosophy of science that is still too widely prevalent, and they offer a far better substitute for scientific work with persons." Abraham Maslow, *Motivation and Personality, 2nd* ed. (New York: Harper and Row, 1952), p. 3.

[4]This delineation of the difference between the natural and social sciences is most eloquently found in May Brodbeck, "Explanation, Prediction, and Imperfect Knowledge," in Brodbeck, *Readings In the Philosophy of the Social Sciences* (New York: The Macmillan Co., 1968), pp. 363–397.

[5]Ernest Nagel, *The Structure of Science* (New York: Harcourt Brace and World, 1961), pp. 18–23. Nagel, a classic philosopher of natural science argues that one should be able to

deduce the necessary occurrence of the *explicandum* (the fact to be explained) from a universal law, a standard that would eliminate all social and political inquiry from scientific status.

[6]Karl Popper, *The Logic of Scientific Discovery* (New York: Harper Torchbooks, 1954), pp. 40–43.

[7]Seymour Lipset, "Some Social Requisites of Democracy: Economic Development and Political Legitimacy," *The American Political Science Review,* Vol. 53, no. 1 (March, 1959), pp. 69–105.

[8]Thomas Kuhn, *The Structure of Scientific Revolutions* (Chicago: University of Chicago Press, 1962).

[9]Imre Lakatos, and Alan Musgrave, eds., *Criticism and the Growth of Knowledge* (Cambridge, UK: Cambridge University Press, 1970), esp. pp. 115–120.

[10]A. J. Ayer, *Language, Truth and Logic* (New York: Dover Publications, 1952), p. 33.

[11]Cf. James Conant, *On Understanding Science* (New York: Mentor Books, 1958) for the argument that the building of cumulative knowledge constitutes the main criterion for distinguishing science from "nonscience" or what A. J. Ayres would call "metaphysics."

[12]Lawrence Mayer and Roland Smith, "Feminism and Religiosity: Female Electoral Behaviour in Western Europe," *West European Politics,* Vol. 8, No. 4 (October, 1985), pp. 38–49.

[13]David Easton, "An Approach to the Analysis of Political Systems," *World Politics,* Vol. 9, No. 3 (April, 1957), pp .383–400; Easton, *The Political System* (New York: Knopf, 1953); Easton, *A Systems Analysis of Political Life* (New York: John Wiley & Sons, 1968); Easton, *A Framework for Political Analysis* (Englewood Cliffs: Prentice Hall, 1965). Clearly, Easton built a career on this one unworkable idea , and an entire discipline was unable to say that the emperor had no clothes.

[14]Almond's most famous presentation of his functionalist perspective appears in his introduction to Gabriel Almond and James Coleman, eds., *The Politics of the Developing Areas* (Princeton: Princeton University Press, 1960), pp. 1–64.

[15]Sociologist Robert K. Merton lists several distinct meanings to this concept in the social science literature. See Merton, *Social Theory and Social Structure,* rev. ed. (New York: The Free Press, 1957), pp. 74–77.

[16]For a carefully reasoned and detailed critique of the functionalist perspective, see A. James Gregor, "Political Science and the Use of Functional Analysis," *The American Political Science Review,* Vol. 62, No. 2 (June, 1968).

[17]Roy Macridis, "Political Systems and Comparative Politics," in Macridis and Bernard Brown, eds., *Comparative Politics: Notes and Readings*, 5th ed. (Homewood, IL: The Dorsey Press, 1977), pp. 9–14.

[18]Ronald Inglehart, "The Renaissance of Political Culture," *The American Political Science Review,* Vol. 82, No. 4 (December, 1988), pp. 1203–1230. While traditional comparative government made impressionistic pronouncements about "national character," the first major cross-national data set on cultural attributes and political outcomes was published in the landmark tome, Gabriel Almond and Sydney Verba, *The Civic Culture* (Boston: Little Brown, 1965), utilizing data drawn from The United States, the United Kingdom, the Federal Republic of Germany, Italy, and Mexico gathered in the late 1950s.

[19]Herbert Spiro, "Comparative Politics: A Comprehensive Approach," *The American Political Science Review,* Vol. 5, No. 3 (September, 1962), pp. 577–595; Spiro, *Government by Constitution* (New York: Random House, 1959), pp. 213ff.

[20]Ashutosh Varshney, "Nationalism, Ethinc Conflict and Rationality," *Perspectives on Politics,* Vol. 1, No. 1 (March, 2004), pp. 85–89.

[21]See, e.g., Eric Fromm, *Escape From Freedom* (New York: Avon Books, 1965).

[22]Robert Alford, *Party and Society* (Chicago: Rand McNally, 1963).

[23]Theda Skocpol, "Bringing the State Back In," *Items,* Vol. 36, Nos. 1/2 (June, 1982), pp. 1–8.

[24]Perhaps the most famous effort to classify the universe of political systems is Gabriel Almond, "Comparative Political Systems," *Journal of Politics,* Vol. 18, No. 3 (August 1956), 391–401. For a critique of this scheme, see Lawrence Mayer, *Comparative Political Inquiry* (Homewood, IL: The Dorsey Press, 1972), pp. 17–19.

[25]Lipset, "Some Social Requisites of Democracy."

[26]Carl Hempel, *The Philosophy of Natural Science* (Englewood Cliffs, NJ: Prentice Hall, 1960), pp. 55ff..

[27]Thorstein Veblin, *The Theory of the Leisure Class* (New York: Vanguard Press, 1928).

[28]Donald Green and Ian Shapiro, *Pathologies of Rational Choice Theory: A Critique of Applications in Political Science* (New Haven, CT: Yale University Press, 1994), p. 3.

[29]William Riker, "Political Science and Rational Choice," in James Alt and Kenneth Schepsle, eds., *Perspectives on Positive Political Economy* (Cambridge: Cambridge University Press, 1990).

[30]Abraham Kaplan, "Mathematics and Social Analysis," in Martin Shubik, ed., *Readings in Game Theory and Political Behavior* (New York: Doubleday, 1954), p. 13 and Richard Snyder, "Game Theory and the Analysis of Political Behavior," in Nelson Polsby, Robert Dentler and Paul Smith, eds., *Politics and Social Life* (Boston: Houghton Mifflin, 1963), p. 133.

[31]Thomas Schelling, "What is Game Theory," in Charles Charlesworth, ed., *Contemporary Political Analysis* (New York: The Free Press, 1967), p. 213.

[32]Anthony Downs, *An Economic Theory of Democracy* (New York: Harper and Row, 1957).

[33]William Riker, *The Theory of Political Coalitions* (New Haven, CT: Yale University Press, 1962).

[34]The failure to rigorously subject rational choice theories to empirical testing is the central complaint in Green and Shapiro.

[35]Jonathan Cohen, "Irrational Exuberance," *The New Republic* Vol. 221, no. 17 (October 1999), p. 30.

[36]*Ibid.* pp. 25–32.

[37]Mancur Olsen, *The Logic of Collective Action* (Cambridge: Harvard University Press, 1965).

[38]Margaret Levi, "A Model, A Method and a Map: Rational Choice in Comparative and Historical Analysis," in Mark Lichbach and Alan Zuckerman, eds., *Comparative Politics: Rationality, Culture and Structure* (Cambridge, UK: Cambridge University Press, 1997), p. 22.

2

The Contextual Foundations of Advanced Industrial Democracies

Democracy as an idea appears to be a widely held value. The word has been claimed to describe a wide range of regimes that most of us in the Western world would not think of as democratic. For example, the Soviet Union claimed that it was practicing "democratic centralism," while strong man Kwame Nkrumah of Ghana claimed he was practicing "guided democracy" and Sekou Touré of Guinea claimed to be practicing "tutelary democracy," although none of these states operated with anything resembling the institutional framework that those of us in the West associate with the term "democracy." Although democracy, as that concept has been more or less understood in the West, has been spreading among the nations of the world in the past three decades, it is still practiced only by a minority of all of the recognized nation states. Indeed Sam Huntington finds that in 1990, after the most recent "wave" of transforming formerly authoritarian states into democracies, among the 129 nation states of the world with a population of at least 1 million, approximately 58 states (or 45 percent) were democratic by Western standards.[1]

This part of the book is concerned with nations that are included in the category of nation states that are democratic by Western criteria. Assuming that this category of regimes is valued, this chapter will consider research and theory regarding the question of what contextual factors promote or impede the establishment and effective operation of Western liberal democracy. However, the criteria for inclusion in this category remain imprecise. Mexico, for example, was a regime that conducted elections in which the opposition was free to contest all of the major political offices. Yet, for nearly three-quarters of a century, the ruling party, the Party of the Institutionalized Revolution (PRI), harassed the opposition parties and the voters that supported them to an extent sufficient to remain in office at the national level all that time. Finally, under severe international pressure, the main opposition party, the Party of National Action (PAN) was allowed to win the presidency in 2000. Does Mexico belong in the liberal democratic category along with Britain and the United States and, if so, when should it have been included?

Unless the criteria for inclusion in the liberal democratic category are rendered precise, any statement about the impact of contextual factors such as history, culture, and social structure will be judgmental and subjective. Unless we can agree on whether a given country belongs in the democratic category, we cannot agree on whether that country is supportive of or an exception to a proposition that a given contextual factor promotes democracy.

While the idea of democracy appeared in the writings of classical Greek philosophy, the first attempts to implement democratic regimes occur in the early modern history of the West in what was becoming the industrialized world. Until recent decades, democracy among the less-developed countries was an infrequent occurrence. The industrialized democracies are generally treated as a group distinct from democratic regimes in the less-developed world and will be treated as such in this volume. Whether or not the attributes of Western industrialized countries are a necessary precondition for the implementation and successful operation of democratic regimes is a research question that has received serious attention in recent decades and will be discussed later in this chapter.

CONCEPTUALIZING INDUSTRIAL DEMOCRACY

The indicators of industrial and postindustrial society are widely recognized and are easily stipulated. A society is considered industrialized when over half of its work force is engaged in manufacturing or the transformation of raw materials into finished products rather than in agrarian pursuits (farming and herding). Most of what we call the Western world, however, has now moved into the postindustrial era in which a majority of the population neither grows or produces food or goods but provides services, especially in the formulation and dissemination of information. This is significant because postindustrial societies operate at a high state of technology requiring massive increases in the complexity and quantity of information, a fact that we will see has a significant impact on the political processes of those countries.

There is less agreement on the indicators of democracy. Major conceptualizations of that regime type may be grouped into minimal process-oriented definitions and more elaborate definitions that include societal attributes frequently associated with democracy or values promoted by democracy.

The classic statement of a minimalist definition of democracy was presented by Joseph Schumpeter: competition for political leadership.[2] In practical procedural terms, that means countries are democratic if their political leadership is chosen in more or less regular elections in which an opposition is not suppressed by the power of the government. As long as the incumbents retain power by persuasion or effective performance, this definition does not imply any particular rate of turnover or alternation of elites in office. Some nations widely regarded as democratic experience long periods of hegemony or continuous control by one political party. In Sweden, for example, the Social Democratic Party remained in power from 1935 to 1976 because during that period Sweden enjoyed one of the highest per capita incomes in the world, low unemployment, and a lack of significant threats to the nation's security. (Sweden remained neutral through World War II.) The fragmented four-party opposition had no hook on which to mount an effective opposition. The Liberal Democratic Party of Japan controlled that government from onset of its postwar democracy to 1993, while the Christian Democratic Party of Italy provided the premier for 53 of Italy's 55 governments from 1948 to 1993. Yet, these three nations are widely regarded as among the world's democracies.

This definition focuses on political processes: the means of choosing decision makers and reaching decisions. It thus regards democracy as a political phenomenon rather than a philosophical or economic one. It is sometimes asserted that socialism is the antithesis of democracy or that capitalism is an essential part of the democratic process; yet, each of these varieties of economic systems has coexisted in a country with both democratic and authoritarian systems. Whether a given set of economic arrangements may encourage or impede democratic political systems is thus a question to be resolved by research rather than settled by definition.

The same may be said of values promoted by a system of competitive elections, values such as the propensity of a system to be responsive to the needs and demands of the voting public. Logically, one might expect greater responsiveness from elites who must face legitimate electoral opposition. The question is whether this should be declared true by definition as does Lijphart, who asserts a government is democratic to the extent that it acts "in accord with the people's preferences."[3] Aside from the problem of measuring the degree of responsiveness, Eric Nordlinger persuasively argues that modern democratic states operate with much greater autonomy from the publics they putatively serve than democratic theory would have us believe.[4] Rejecting a society-centered explanation of government actions, Nordlinger argues that government possesses the resources to mobilize public opinion and manipulate public preferences to bring them into line with government decisions. Governing a modern state, after all, is a role demanding skills, knowledge and a degree of commitment not found among the general population. Decades ago, Walter Lippman observed that public opinion is largely created from above by opinion leaders; that elites use public opinion to mobilize support rather than being constrained by it.[5]

COMPETITIVE ELECTIONS AND ACCOUNTABILITY

The criterion of regular competitive elections raises the question of whether these elections should provide clear and meaningful choices to the voting public such that the outcome of a general election should determine the policy direction for the country. When the election can be reasonably interpreted as a public authorization for the winning elites to pursue a given policy direction, we say that the government has a mandate to pursue those policies. This model of the democratic process is increasingly at odds with a reality that finds competing parties increasingly resembling one another in promoting an imprecise and centrist policy agenda. We noted in the previous chapter how Anthony Downs' model of party behavior in an aggregated party system shows how it would be rational for parties in such a system to converge toward an amorphous center.[6] Otto Kirchheimer, in an oft-quoted essay argues that parties in Western Europe are discarding their ideological baggage to attract the widest possible range of voter support, becoming what he calls "catch-all parties."[7] Both of these scholars are casting doubt on the validity of the model of elections in Western democracies—elections that purport to be competitions between meaningful policy choices. Thus, the mere fact of a competitive election, one in which the opposition is not suppressed, should—by the logic of Downs' rational choice model—be sufficient in constraining political leadership from governing in an arbitrary manner (without regard for the public interest).

It should not be expected—according to this rational model of democracy—that the major parties would differ in fundamental ways over the major issues. If it is clear which issue positions are favored by a majority of voters, both parties will move toward those positions. No set of political leaders will advocate what they know to be minority positions merely to provide voters with a choice. Thus, with a competitive election coming up, both parties will feel compelled to be able to justify their policies in terms of some reasonable conception of the public interest. In this way, democratic elites are *accountable*; their policy options are constrained by the need to justify their behaviors and choices in terms of the public interest. If they do not, they must assume their opponents will.

All elites, even those in authoritarian regimes, make some attempt to justify their rule in terms of the public interest. In fact, most modern dictatorships are populist in the sense that the rulers claim to embody the values of ordinary masses of their society. While this perceived need by modern dictators may constrain their policy options to some extent, clearly democratic elites facing competitive elections are more narrowly constrained by the need to justify their policy plans and the results of how they have governed. One may therefore say that democratic elites are *more* accountable than their authoritarian counterparts, a situation brought about by the mere fact of competitive elections.

The minimal definition has the further advantage of facilitating communication by making empirical sense—by grouping together rather heterogeneous nation states that most people in the West intuitively perceive ought to be grouped together, and separating out other states that Western publics widely perceive ought to be excluded from the democratic category. By inductively relying on those attributes the world's democracies have in common, the minimal definition makes distinctions that correspond to our perceptions of the real world of experience, rather than posing an impossible standard that no real world state can meet. Thus, the *minimal* definition can include presidential or parliamentary states, or federal or unitary states, not eliminating particular categories of regimes by arbitrary definition. Such definitions are neither true nor false; they are merely useful in facilitating scientific communication.

ACCOUNTABILITY, DEMOCRATIC FORMATS, AND THE PROBLEM OF POWER

It was shown above that the regular competitive elections that define modern democracy function to render elites more closely accountable than are elites in more authoritarian systems. Accountability was conceptualized as a situation in which elites feel pressure to be able to justify their rule and policies in terms of the public interest. Institutions and procedures in Western countries are created to encourage this perceived need to justify one's policies and goals. We will discuss below how the various institutional patterns one finds among the world's democracies create a structure of accountability.

Accountability is one means of resolving what I call the problem of power. Power entails the capacity to make decisions and impose them on others. Power wielders thus have the capacity to choose to act in the public interest or not, thereby abusing their power. The problem is how do you grant elites the power to choose among policy alternatives, the power to govern, while denying them the capacity to choose to abuse their power?

There are two styles of structuring the regime so as to render it more likely than not that elites will act in the public interest. One is to fragment power among a number of independent power wielders, each of whom could veto major policy proposals. It is believed to be unlikely that a number of independent power wielders would spontaneously agree on any specific abuse of power. Of course, such fragmented elites will also not have the capacity to resolve pressing issues, the power to govern. The American system, for example, consists of numerous independent power centers, any one of which has the power to effectively veto any proposed policy.

A second style is to centralize decision making power with clear lines of responsibility, and then create a set of structures and processes to render the elites accountable. Great Britain will be shown to epitomize a highly centralized democratic format with lines of responsibility that at times have been envied by American scholars.[8] However, it will be argued in the chapter on political parties that the British model is inappropriate for the American context.

There are therefore several options in how a given regime structures account-ability that are explored below in the treatment of regime types. The operation of any given regime, however, is a function of the context in which it operates.

PATTERNS OF NATION BUILDING

The process by which a nation state arrives out of a setting characterized by smaller and perhaps less elaborately organized political units, in other words, the nation's history, was given extensive treatment in prebehavioral work in compara-tive government. However, this historical process has been given much less atten-tion in modern comparative analysis. Yet, patterns in a nation's historical experiences are part of the context that shapes contemporary politics.

Scholars have theorized that there are a set of problems that must be addressed by all nations in the course of their building an effective nation state.[9] These may be differently defined from one scholar to another; however, there is a great deal of overlap among these scholars in identifying these problems and the sequence in which they ought to occur. This book argues that sequence is critical in the build-ing of effective nation states.

The establishment of the boundaries of the realm, the area over which the state will attempt to exert its authority, may be a prerequisite to establishing the legiti-macy of a regime or a particular constitutional format. As stated in Chapter One, legitimacy refers to widespread acceptance or support for the regime or institution in question, regardless of one's feeling about the performance or specific policies of the regime. Since no regime pleases most citizens all the time, legitimacy is cru-cial in allowing regimes last through those times of inability to resolve critical issues. Yet, one of the important ways in which legitimacy is acquired is for the re-gime or institutions in question to have been around for long periods of time. Thus, what we call *the paradox of legitimacy* is that regimes acquire legitimacy by last-ing over time but in order to last over time, they must be legitimate. Legitimacy, it appears, may also be acquired by competent performance. The Federal Republic of Germany, for example, acquired legitimacy for its newly installed democratic regime with outstanding economic and effective political performance in the post World War II era. Yet, again paradoxically, outstanding system performance is more difficult if the system has not acquired legitimacy.

Because legitimacy is acquired by performance or durability, it is difficult to achieve it when the political system is still in conflict over the extent of the realm. Subjects are more likely to accept a regime when that regime has established its control over the territory in which they reside. Hence, Henry II of England was able to extend "the king's peace"—effective control of much of his realm barely a century after the Norman conquest, partly through the spread of the "common law," because British boundaries were quickly and naturally established by Brit-ain's island status while French kings were still trying to unite a collection of autonomous feudal principalities such as Armagnac, Artois, Blois, and Limoges as late as the fourteenth century. Other fiefdoms such as Valois, Anjou, and Bourbon were controlled by relatives of the kings and only indirectly controlled by French kings. The difference between the earlier success of the English kings in establishing control of their realm and the longer, more difficult struggle by the French kings to establish theirs is thought to be a function of the naturally established insular borders of Britain, compared to the absence of such natural barriers to mark France's eastern and northern borders.

Once the extent of the realm is established, the emerging nation must settle the question of regime, what kind of constitutional format to choose decision makers and to convert political and economic issues into policy. When a regime is in place and acquires legitimacy, that regime may be employed to resolve the divisive issues that inevitably face modernizing nations: coping with the increased volume and complexity of demands from the newly mobilized masses, how to deal with the social dislocations of early industrialization and urbanization, how to settle the questions of the relationship of church and state, how to legitimate or reduce socioeconomic inequality, and how to reconcile the sometimes conflicting imperatives of national security and individual liberty.

For example, religion was, for the most part, taken off the table as a divisive issue in England when Henry VIII used his own well-established authority to defy papal authority and replace Roman Catholic influence in his country with his own creation, the Anglican Church. Clearly, Henry was an odious autocrat who serially married and disposed of young women, three of whom he had beheaded. He defied the Church in order to clear the way to marry his second wife. But the function he performed of secularizing British politics had a lasting beneficial effect of lowering the intensity of partisanship. Religious conflict tends to be framed in terms of irreconcilable differences that do not lend themselves to compromise.

Consider, by contrast, the case of France. The Catholic Church maintained an almost symbiotic relationship with the Old Regime's monarchy. Cardinal Richelieu was the de facto ruler during the youthful reign of Louis XIII. The Church opposed even the initial moderate phases of the Revolution in their unqualified support of monarchial authority. Hence, to support the Revolution meant being anticlerical. This split between the anticlerical and republican left and the pro-Catholic authoritarian right was to infect French politics for the next two centuries. This cleavage was mobilized in the Dreyfus Affair that dominated French political life for the better part of two decades at the end of the nineteenth century. Dreyfus was the first Jew to become part of the French general staff. After France's humiliating defeat in the Franco-Prussian War, the French elite looked for a scapegoat to explain the defeat away. The charge that someone in the general staff committed treason by giving French military secrets to the Prussians provided that excuse. Dreyfus, a Jew whose loyalty was automatically suspect, was the perfect scapegoat. When he was convicted and sent to Devil's Island in 1894, the country split in a vigorous and bitter debate lasting two decades. When it became known that the real culprit was an aristocratic Catholic royalist, the French right still sought to uphold the conviction for the honor of the army and the Church. Dreyfus was ultimately pardoned in 1899 but his exoneration did not come until 1906. Meanwhile, practicing Catholics were virtually excluded from the elite of the Third Republic, the regime that emerged in the wake of the Franco-Prussian War and the center was unable to govern because it was split between pro- and anticlerical forces. Loyalty to the Church among many French superseded loyalty to the republic during the Third and Fourth Republics, detracting from the legitimacy of those two regimes.

The intense partisanship generated by religious issues is just one of several divisive issues that create severe pressure on the political processes of modernizing states. That pressure derives from the significantly greater volume and complexity of demands generated from newly mobilized masses in a modernizing society. As we shall learn in discussing less-modern countries later in this volume, modernization entails urbanization, the spread of literacy, and increased exposure to mass media, all of which generate demands on the system.

The Napoleonic Wars that followed the Revolution of 1789 were a watershed event in this regard. Although Napoleon was an autocrat who led France into aggressive attacks on other countries to serve his thirst for power, the wars were fought in the name of the ideals of the Revolution: liberty, equality, and fraternity. Hence, Napoleon's forays around Europe spread what was then a heretical idea, that the masses had rights. Conservative autocrats in other European countries, such as Prince Clemens Metternich of Austria, recognized the potential threat that such ideas had on their power in their own countries. The mobilization of the masses with the idea of the rights of man would henceforth render it more difficult for European regimes that had not yet acquired legitimacy to do so.

Nations such as Great Britain and the Scandinavian countries that established the legitimacy of their regimes well before the late eighteenth century experienced stable and effective political systems into the modern era while those that were still struggling with that question—Germany, France, the principalities of the decaying Holy Roman Empire—had more difficulty resolving the divisive issues that followed the mobilization of the masses and their rising expectations.

Sequence theory refers to the idea that nation states have a better chance of developing stable and effective regimes if they can solve the issues of first realm and then regime before confronting the other divisive issues emanating from the modernization process. It does not imply any particular order in the resolution of these other issues. Obviously, many nations have built effective regimes long after the European masses were mobilized at the end of the eighteenth century. Many less-developed nations are mobilizing their masses and confronting other divisive issues of modernization simultaneously with varying degrees of success. Yet, in general, these LDCs have experienced a high degree of regime instability and poorer performance in providing prosperity, security, and order. It thus seems reasonable to conclude that resolution of the issues of realm and regime before confronting the divisive issues emanating from a mobilized public will, other things being more or less equal, be more likely to produce stable and effective regimes.

The failure to establish a legitimate regime by the time the masses have been mobilized, with their expectations of system performance in response to the socio-economic dislocations of early industrialization, may generate a compensatory sense of exaggerated national pride. The French, who were still struggling to legitimate a regime in the second half of the twentieth century, widely regard their nation as a fount of Western culture. Hence, being French connotes a higher level of civilization than other peoples; people in the French nation tend to regard their non-Gallic neighbors—the Anglo Saxons, the "rest of Canada," and the Flemish in Belgium as less cultured and civilized than themselves.

In the German nation, this phenomenon was exacerbated by the millennium long gap between a sense of a German nation and the realization of a German state. The Germans may have epitomized a sense of frustrated nationalism driving a glorification of the idea of the German state. Thus, Georg Friedrich Hegel, one of that nation's preeminent philosophers in the mid-nineteenth century could extol the idea of the German nation state preaching that "the state is the divine idea as it exists on earth…we must therefore worship the state"[10] Frustrated nationalism arose out of the millennium gap between the German nation and the German state and also led to the glorification of martial values by which the state could be realized. Hegel, again, gives voice to this glorification. "War has the deep meaning that by it the ethical health of a nation is preserved… (war) protects people from the corruption which an everlasting peace would bring upon it."[11] While such attitudes did not cause the Third Reich to emerge in Germany in the early 1930s, together with other cultural attributes, they rendered the German people more receptive to that kind of appeal.

In this lengthy period in which Germans had a strong sense of identification with a German nation before this nationalism could be expressed in a state, German nationalism was expressed in cultural, ethnic, and racial terms. Hence, the failure of German nation building contributed to the strong element of racism that was to pervade German thought and mobilize support for the systematic oppression of Jews by the Third Reich.

THE SOCIAL CONTEXT: THE CLEAVAGE SYSTEM

In order to explain contemporary politics, scholars must analyze the social and cultural context of politics, as well as the historical background. The social context here is meant to refer to the social stratification system, the criteria by which people are grouped and divided in a system of social cleavages. These lines of cleavage may be along class lines, religion, ethnicity, language, region, or a combination thereof. These cleavages may or may not override a sense of common identity for that putative nation.

Robert Alford has argued that class cleavages facilitate the resolution of issues in comparison to religious, ethnic, or other identity based cleavages.[12] Class based cleavages generate issues involving distribution of material well being, issues that lend themselves to compromise. Religious or ethnic cleavages, however, generate issues of right and wrong or true and false for which there is no logical middle ground. Accordingly, when politics is based a combination of ethnic, linguistic, and religious cleavages as in the case of the cleavage between French Canada and "the rest of Canada" (ROC), subcultures such as the *Québécois* tend to be isolated and alienated from the rest of the country. The *Québécois* have tended to regard ROC as "them" rather than "us" to the extent that a number of major French Canadian publications openly favored the Nazis in World War II and the French Canadian AWOL or fail-to-report rate among French Canadians was over 50 percent.

Similarly, the linguistic and cultural cleavage between the Flemish-speaking people of Flanders and the French-speaking people of Wallonia has caused Belgium to evolve from unitary state to what is in fact a confederation. There is little individual interaction between individuals in these two subcultures. The people of Flanders have tended to be traditionally more bucolic and more religious than the Wallonians and in recent decades the Flemish have tended to be more enterprising and more prosperous. The somewhat effete, urban, French-speaking Wallonians tend to regard themselves as culturally superior to the Flemish. Belgium, therefore, contains at least two distinct nations. (The French-speaking Brusselites and a small German-speaking community on Belgium's eastern border each have their own cultural council with virtually sovereign powers over their constituents. The isolation of the French Canadian and Belgian subcultures is exacerbated by the fact that these subcultures are geographically defined. Thus, they have their subcultural elites whose interest is in defending and perpetuating the isolation and distinctiveness of their subculture.

When subcultures become isolated and alienated from other peoples or nations within a political system, we refer to such societies as segmented. There are, of course, degrees of segmentation. The Netherlands formerly consisted of four distinct subcultures or "pillars" as they called them: the Catholic, orthodox Protestant, working class and collectivist, and liberal (secular middle class). However, the mutual isolation and distinctiveness of these pillars has been weakened by the progressive secularization of Western societies in general, although the alienation of French Canada from ROC remains strong on a cultural-linguistic basis despite the weakening hold of the Catholic Church on its French Canadian flock. Referenda on the withdrawal of Quebec from the Canadian federation have twice in recent years come within a few percentage points of passage. Meanwhile, the *Québécois* continue to insist on constitutional reforms as embodied in the narrowly defeated Meech Lake (Constitutional Amendment 1987) and Charlottetown Accords (1992) that would have accorded Quebec a virtual veto over national policy, a situation considered unacceptable to most of ROC.[13] These events are indicative of the fact that, in general, segmented societies do not fare well with regard to regime stability and political effectiveness compared to regimes that govern a relatively coherent or culturally integrated nation.

In contrast to such segmented societies, geographically defined cultural or ethnic differences ceased to be important in modern British history once the last assertion of Scottish nationalism was successfully suppressed with the defeat of Mary, Queen of Scots at the end of the seventeenth century, with the notable exception of the Irish who successfully rebelled against rule from Westminster in the 1920s. (Westminster is the borough within London in which the houses of Parliament are located.) The refusal of most Irish Catholics to accept the rule of Westminster continues to be expressed in the rebellion of the Irish Republican Army in Ulster to the present day. Clearly, the image of Britain as a society of peaceful homogeneity refers more to England, the southern part of the isle of Britain, than to the United Kingdom (currently, England, Scotland, Wales, and Northern Ireland or Ulster). Scottish nationalism has experienced a resurgence in recent decades, especially with the discovery of the North Sea oil fields, a disproportionate amount of whose revenue has been spent in and by England. A policy of devolution of political power from Westminster to the Scottish national parliament has been one response to resurgent Scottish nationalism. Scotland has never been fully integrated culturally in English-dominated Britain.

Nevertheless, from the end of the eighteenth century until well into the second half of the twentieth century, Britain was known as an ethnically, religiously, and culturally homogeneous country. The religious, ethnic, or cultural diversity as did exist were not politically important. This means that they did not form the basis of politically important cleavages. The remaining or residual factor that did form the basis of politically important cleavage was socioeconomic class. Class differences always objectively exist; there will be wage earners, professionals, and capitalist entrepreneurs or managers of industries in any reasonably complex modern society. Britain stood out in recognizing and accepting these class-based distinctions.

Class-based differences pervaded the lifestyle of British people. Working class people would frequent "pubs" and consume ale, "bitters," or warm beer while the middle to upper classes prefer sipping sherry or single malt scotch. The working classes are avid and sometimes rowdy football (soccer in U.S. terms) fans while the middle to upper classes prefer a laid back following of cricket or fox hunting (which was banned in 2005 by a working-class sensitive Labour Party government in an act of class envy). The middle to upper classes frequent West End (of London) theaters while working class people prefer movies, rock concerts, or the "telly." The professional classes buy their suits on Saville Row while working class people prefer "mod" styles of dress. Class differences are most apparent in speaking style or accent. The middle-to-upper classes speak with a mellifluous accent called Oxford. This accent varies with the region from which the speaker comes but these differences are not usually apparent to the untrained non-British ear. The working and underclass speaks with an accent called Cockney that is distinctly different from the middle-to-upper-class accent. (Middle class speech is neither Cockney nor Oxford but, to the untrained ear sounds closer to Oxford). Despite upward mobility, a person's accent will betray his or her class of origin. The class origins of these accents are not manifested in Scotland and Wales where a regional accent dominates. Class-based distinctions in lifestyle are not as apparent in Scotland and Wales as in England. In Scotland, a distinction has been made between "Clydeside" urban dwellers and rural dwellers.

The British recognized and accepted these class cleavages. One might hear of a working class person speaking of his or her "betters." This legitimacy of the class structure resulted in an acceptance of authority that will be discussed below.

This class-based cleavage system has weakened in recent decades. Scholars such as Richard Rose and Ian McCallister have presented data documenting the declining salience of class in English politics.[14] A rising egalitarianism that no longer accepts the dominant political influence or disproportionate material well being for the upper middle to upper classes, what Samuel Beer calls "the new populism," is a result of the newly mobilized sense of injustice of the old hierarchical structure of English society.[15] The confidence that the British had in their political and social elites has been undermined by the poor political and economic performance of the system in the post-World War II decades in which Britain lost its empire and became known for economic performance as "the new sick man of Europe." The declining salience of class in Britain is related to several factors.

The rising tide of regionalism is a phenomenon affecting politics throughout the developed and less-developed parts the world, not only in segmented societies such as Canada and Belgium discussed above, but in numerous venues where regional identification has been mobilized in competition with the nationalism and pan-national bases of identification such as class. The Basques and Catalonian separatists battle for secession from Spain. Umberto Bossi has mobilized regional sentiments among the population of the northern Italian provinces out of a sense of resentment that these more productive and industrialized provinces provide a disproportionate share of Italy's revenue—a disproportionate amount of which is spent in the less productive south. While it is doubtful that most supporters of Bossi's separatist party, *Lega Nord*, want to secede from Italy and form a new state of Padania, regional sentiments in Italy override any sense of pan-national class. The rising tide of regional sentiment in Britain is manifested in the demand for devolution of power from the Parliament in Westminster to the Scottish National Assembly, a movement that has already resulted in the latter body's power to tax and spend on its own initiative.

The former class basis of British society was supported by a relatively homogenous population in terms of race, language, and even, to a large extent, religion (Protestantism was clearly dominant over other faiths). However, in the post-war era, Britain experienced an unprecedented wave of immigration, much of it from parts of Britain's former empire. Britain's population became racially, ethnically, linguistically, and religiously diverse to an unprecedented degree. These bases of identification, when socially important, tend to override class consciousness.

The core support for the overtly class-based Labour Party in Britain has been the trade union movement. The almost symbiotic relationship between the party and the Trade Union Congress (Britain's major trade union federation) will be detailed below in the chapter on political parties. The decline of the trade union membership throughout the Western world has weakened the consistency of labor support for labor-based parties in these countries. The decline driven by technological change has reduced the demand for semi- and unskilled workers. Class consciousness is therefore not only weaker among the political left, but conservatives are less focused on their role of protecting private property from being assaulted by a class-conscious left.

Finally, the former class basis of politics has been weakened by the declining salience of issues of material well-being in a post-World War II era of long-term prosperity, a trend documented in the often cited large body of research by Ronald Inglehart and his associates.[16] Because Western publics could now take their material well-being almost for granted, they focused instead on what Inglehart calls "post-materialist" issues, issues involving lifestyle such as environmentalism, tolerance, and civil liberties. To the extent that that trend accurately describes cultural changes in Western democracies, a sense of class will be accorded a lower priority.

As class declines in importance in Western societies, new sets of issues are emerging, changing the bases of political cleavages—issues involving questions of identity. This politics of identity may be manifested on the nation state level in the form of chauvinistic patriotism or at the subcultural level in the form of seeking autonomy or secession from the larger nation state. The politics of identity thereby supplants class consciousness as, for example, French Canadian factory workers will identify more with French Canadian entrepreneurs than with factory workers in English-speaking Canada.

One manifestation of this emerging politics of identity has been the proliferation of movements of subcultural defense. The example of the *Québécois*, noted above, consists of French-speaking Catholics largely concentrated in the province of Quebec. Hence, the government of that province in effect becomes the representative of French Canadian separatism and the interests of those elites lie in emphasizing and perpetuating the alienation rather than the integration of that subculture. The degree of that alienation may be seen in the fact that two resolutions of secession from the Canadian federation narrowly failed (by less than five percentage points) in recent decades and in Quebec's language laws that forbid the public display of writing in English and mandated that all public education be in French. The *Québécois,* once a highly religious and very conservative people, have secularized and modernized over the past three decades with what has been called their "quiet revolution." However, their sense of alienation from "the rest of Canada" (ROC) remains deeply entrenched in their psyche.

Cultural, ethnic, and linguistic differences exist in all reasonably complex societies. They are more likely to be mobilized into an alienated and isolated subculture when they are geographically defined—located in a political subunit such as a state or province—and thus represented by subsystem elites. This is also the case with respect to Belgium's Flemish population located in Flanders and its Walloons located in Wallonia and with respect to the Basque and Catalonian separatists in Spain. Belgium's subcultural councils have demanded and acquired a veto over any national policy or law that they deem impacts the integrity or distinctiveness of the subcultures they represent. (These policies include especially housing, the environment, energy, transportation, employment, and agriculture.)

While the Flemish and Walloons constitute the main cultural linguistic group-ings among the Belgians, there are actually two other such groups: the French-speaking citizens of Brussels and a small German-speaking contingent on the east-ern border. Belgium has therefore evolved, over some three decades of constitu-tional change, from a unitary system to a loose confederation, culminating in the Constitution of 1995 with sovereignty, the final power to make and implement laws, effectively residing at the subcultural level.

Separatist sentiment has also been mobilized among Italy's northern provinces although among a minority of that population. A separatist party, the Northern League (*Lega Nord*), whose leader, Umberto Bossi advocated creating a new state, Padania, out of Italy's northern provinces, was the largest vote getter in the 1993 Italian election although many of the party's supporters were casting a protest vote against the distinct interests and culture of the southern half of that country. Aus-tralia's Irish Catholic population, in contrast, are dispersed among that country's six states. While the Australian Irish have displayed distinct attitudes and inter-ests—at one point causing a split in that country's Labor Party—they have never shown separatist sentiment or alienation from that nation. Thus, the defense of an ethnically based identity—what we may call ethno-nationalism—is more easily mobilized when the boundaries of that ethnicity are congruent with the boundaries of a political unit, creating a leadership strata whose interest lies in perpetuating and defending that ethnic identity, as shown in Figure 2–1.

The rising importance of identity in Western culture has also been manifested in nationalism in the sense of chauvinistic patriotism. This nationalist sentiment is in part a reaction to the growing heterogeneity of the populations of Western democ-racies, an increasing percentage of non-European minorities that reject assimila-

	Entire State	**Subculture**
Congruent	National Socialism National Front	*Vlaams Blok* renamed *Vlaams* *Beland Bloc* *Quebecois*
Not Congruent	Palestinians	Northern League

Figure 2–1   Political Manifestations of Ethnonationalism

tion into that dominant European culture. The most prevalent and alienated of those minorities is an Arab Muslim population, whose leaders have expressed the goal of transforming Europe into an Islamic republic rather than the converse goal of assimilation. Leaders have mobilized a populist right in response to this perceived threat to European culture, a populist right that has also attracted support from the former neo-fascist strata on that continent.[17] The underlying assumption of the literature on these emerging populist parties of identity is that they are all on the radical right, an assumption with which this author disagrees. Canada's *Bloc Québécois* is on the left regarding economic policy but it is clearly a party concerned primarily with identity. Other parties of cultural defense are difficult to classify on a left to right dimension as we shall see below with respect to the Netherlands.

The common thread among the parties of identity at the nation state or subcultural level is the protection and preservation of a nation, folk or community. Thus, the leader of France's National Front, Jean Marie Le Pen, struck a responsive chord among many voters who would normally never vote for a populist right party when he expressed the concern that his grandchildren would still speak French. The resulting protest vote vaulted Le Pen, with 17 percent of the vote, over the Socialist candidate Lionel Jospin, into second place and thus into the run off round in the French 2002 presidential election, a result that alarmed many Western people who feared that result signaled a reappearance of the fascism that engulfed the Continent in the 1930s. The protest nature of the vote for Le Pen was shown in the fact that he received only 18 percent of the vote to Chirac's 82 percent in the run-off and the Front fell to only 11 percent in the June parliamentary elections.

This fear of a resurgent fascism was reinforced and exacerbated by the emergence of Austria's populist right party, the Austrian Freedom party (FPÖ) under the leadership of a charismatic leader, Jörg Haider, a man with neo-Nazi connections. The 1999 Austrian general election saw the FPÖ receiving 27.2 percent of the vote and emerge as Austria's second strongest party. Together with the center right Peoples' Party (ÖVP), the FPÖ became part of a coalition government. The concerns of the world community were only slightly assuaged when Haider, in a largely symbolic move, stepped down as official head of the party in 2000. The fortunes of the FPÖ receded in the 2002 elections to Austria's lower house, the National Council (*Nationalrat*), when its vote fell to 10 percent for 18 seats of a total of 183 in that body as the center right ÖVP co-opted many of the concerns of the former FPÖ supporters.

We have noted that not all parties of identity are unambiguously parties of the radical right. For example, a charismatic and gay politician emerged mobilizing an antiimmigrant platform in the Netherlands in 2002, a previously almost unheard of sentiment in that country. When the young man, Pim Fortuyn was assassinated (by a Muslim who objected to his calls for restrictive immigration policies), another unprecedented event in that country, his party, Pim Fortuyn's List, stormed into second place with its antiimmigrant stance, especially aimed at that country's expanding Arab population, constituting the essence of its appeal. This stance was a negative expression of traditional white European identity. This mobilization of anti-Muslim populism was carried on by conservative Dutch legislator Geert Wilders, who angered the Muslim community by referring to Palestinian leader Yassir Arafat as a terrorist and was accordingly marked for death by members of that community. Wilders, like Fortuyn, ran on a one-issue personal Geert Wilders List. That issue, anti-Muslim immigration, netted his list 28 seats in the 2004 election to the Dutch Second Chamber (*Tweede Kamer*), about a fifth of that body, as anti-Muslim passion was readily mobilized in the wake of the killing of popular Dutch filmmaker, Theo Van Gogh, by a young Muslim man who objected to the anti-Muslim content of one of Van Gogh's films. The Netherlands had been a multicultural society with its segments called "pillars:" the Orthodox Protestant (Calvinist and Dutch Reformed Church), the Catholics, the secular middle class, and the working class). These "Pillars" have been crumbling with the erosion of religiosity and the class consciousness of a strong trade union movement, a trend we have seen across Western societies. The result has been an elite that prides itself on toleration: legalized prostitution, hashish in coffee houses, and a very liberal immigration policy. The Dutch masses, however, have reacted with a renewed assertion of Dutch national identity. Eighty percent of these Hollanders think the country is too tolerant.[18]

This emerging politics of identity at the nation state level or at the subsystem level appeals most strongly to those strata of the masses that have been marginalized by modernity: clerks, peasants or owners of small farms, and shopkeepers—the *petit bourgeoisie*. Thus, this trend takes on the attributes of the venerable concept of populism—a movement of the less educated masses that asserts a strong faith in the conventional wisdom of those masses and a suspicion of elites in general and intellectuals in particular. Populists tend to explain their grievances with a conspiratorial view of the world and a strong animosity toward those who are not accepted as part of their culturally and ethnically defined nation or "folk." Hence, these populist movements tend to be antiforeigner and had tended toward anti-Semitism. Jews, who tend to be urban, educated, and cosmopolitan, are the antithesis of the populist folk. Naziism was a classic case of right wing populism; however, the current wave of right wing populist movements in Europe are not the equivalent of the Nazis. Because of the demographics—Europe's rapidly expanding Muslim population—the current wave of European antiforeigner populism is focused on the exclusion of that group.

While the object of the exclusivist impulses of populism may have changed, with Muslims replacing Jews and Gypsies as the main group threatening the integrity of the nation or folk, the politics of identity seems to be displacing class-based politics in Western democracies. Implications for the fit of party-system cleavages formed earlier in the twentieth century to the emerging system of social cleavages will be explored below in the chapter on party politics.

SEGMENTED SOCIETIES AND THE CONSOCIATIONAL MODEL

The rising salience of identity politics exacerbates the incidence and the intensity of social segmentation. Segmented societies are those with one or more subcultures isolated and alienated from the main culture. These subcultures are isolated in that there is little personal interaction occurring between individuals in and outside the subculture; they are alienated in that members of the subculture regard the nation as a whole as "them" rather than "us." Belgium, Canada with its French Canadian subculture, and the formerly pillarized Netherlands are examples of segmented societies that have been discussed. Iraq, site of the American effort to import democracy to the Middle East, is a highly segmented society divided between the Sunni, Shiite, and Kurdish subcultures. The legitimacy of the broader nation is compromised for the subcultural segment.

Hence, in such segmented societies the conventional majoritarian model of democracy, with the political forces representing the dominant cultural segment holding power for a fixed period of time and the minority sociocultural forces excluded from the political process for that period, will not work. The minority subculture will not accept the rule of the majority forces. The once dominant Sunnis in Iraq will not accept being governed by their hated enemy, the Shiites, and the French Canadians will not accept the rule of the English-speaking "rest of Canada."

An alternative model of democracy has been proposed for such segmented societies—what its creator, Arend Lijphart calls the *consociational* model.[19] In this model, each of the major decision making institutions, including the higher civil service, are staffed with a proportionate number of people from major cultural groups, and each of these groups is given a veto over policies affecting their cultural integrity. With a virtual guarantee that none of the cultural segments will have to accept policy imposed on them against their will, the system itself becomes more legitimate in their eyes. While the consociational model has enabled several segmented Western democracies to continue a precarious existence, cultural segmentation in non-Western settings (see the discussion of Nigeria in Chapter Six) has rendered those societies virtually ungovernable.

POLITICAL CULTURE: REQUISITE FOUNDATION FOR DEMOCRACY?

The dimensions of political culture are defined in Chapter One. Attitudes regarding authority are thought to constitute one of the most important of these dimensions. One may categorize these attitudes as submissive, egalitarian, or deferential. A submissive attitude regards the duty of subordinates as unqualified obedience to one's parents, to one's teachers, to one's employer or manager, and ultimately to one's political elites. The underlying assumption is that such leaders are in that role because they are more fit to lead. An egalitarian attitude, by contrast, assumes that people are relatively equal in their ability to make judgments; hence, elites ought to be kept under close control and given narrow bounds of discretion. In the political world, the egalitarian would favor such measures as referenda on major issues of the day, provisions for the recall of elites, frequent elections, and strict constitutional limits on the discretion of elites. A strongly egalitarian attitude toward authority would not grant government the latitude to govern. Sociological theorists have suggested that elites require a degree of insulation from the passions of the masses in order to fulfill their leadership function.[20]

Between these essentially polar opposite conceptions of authority lies the concept of deference, a position that accepts the proposition that people differ in their abilities to assume leadership roles in politics as well as in other walks of life. Political authority, therefore, ought to be granted the discretion inherent in day-to-day governing and thus insulated from the shifting currents of public opinion. Unlike a submissive or authoritarian conception of authority, deference requires that authority be exercised in the public interest and ultimately accountable to the public or its representatives for the results of the exercise of authority.

One school of thought holds that the optimum conception of authority is the one that most closely fits the authority patterns dominant in that society. One learns in one's upbringing and daily life to either accept or distrust and question authority in one's relations with parents, teachers, peers, co-workers, and so forth. To shift one's orientation toward authority as one steps into a political role, for example, to obey authority unquestioningly in all other aspects of life and then to demand accountability of political authority would generate psychological strain. Social and political authority patterns should be approximately "congruent" with one another for optimum political effectiveness according to Harry Eckstein, the author of "Congruence Theory."[21] Eckstein, however, is unclear as to precisely what result would follow what degree of incongruence. Would we expect cabinet instability, regime change, political violence, or social unrest? What threshold level of incongruence would be necessary to bring one of these outcomes about? More importantly, Eckstein is uninterested in the specification of indicators to measure his key concepts. Therefore, although intuitively plausible, Eckstein's congruence theory cannot be tested, and it is therefore incapable of explaining or predicting real world events.

The intuitive plausibility of congruence theory has led some scholars to conclude that a deferential attitude in the political sphere makes for a more effective political system. In the first place, a system based on deference is able to provide elites with the insulation from shifting currents of public opinions necessary to govern. In the second place, a system based on deference will have a greater degree of congruence with authority patterns in society, which are rarely egalitarian. Parents do not run their families on an egalitarian basis, nor do teachers treat their students on an egalitarian basis, nor do employers with their work force.

Accordingly, Great Britain's vaunted success as a stable and effective democracy is widely attributed in part to its characterization as "a deferential people," a phrase coined by Walter Bagehot in his classic tome on the English Constitution over a century ago.[22] This impressionistic characterization was reinforced by survey data from the first major cross-national empirical study of the cultural foundations of democracy, Almond and Verba's oft-cited Five Nation Study (of Great Britain, the United States, Italy, the Federal Republic of Germany, and Mexico)[23], the analysis of which was published as *The Civic Culture*. This deference was manifested in a widespread acceptance of the class system by the working or manual-labor classes, an acceptance further documented in David Butler and Donald Stokes' 1963 data. They indicate 53 percent of British respondents in a national sample self-identify as working class compared to the United States, where a majority of citizens self-identify as middle class even among those in objectively manual occupations.[24] This deferential attitude provided legitimacy for a political format that we will see is more centralized with its decision making process, more insulated from day-to-day currents of public opinion, than would ever be acceptable in the American context.

Therefore, the weakening of this British deference toward authority in recent years raises serious concerns about the future of the British political system. This weakening is manifested in greater mistrust of politicians, in serious calls to modify the essential nature of such venerable British institutions as the House of Lords, in working-class assaults on such symbolic bastions of upper-class privilege as fox hunting (which was abolished in 2005 by an egalitarian Labour Government), and in the transformation of the selective basis of the government school system (what Americans call public schools) in the 1972 abolition of the "eleven plus exams."[25] This exam was a general scholastic achievement test given to all students in the state-supported school system in the fifth grade. The small minority that passed the exam were sent to "grammar schools" and given a college preparatory curriculum. These students overwhelmingly came from middle-class homes with educated parents. The majority of students, including nearly all from working-class backgrounds, failed the exam and were sent to "modern schools" in which their education was terminated after learning a trade—but which offered no prospect of higher education. Since the abolition of the eleven plus exams, most students in government schools go to a "comprehensive" secondary school encompassing the widest range of abilities. Of course, students coming out of the "comps" achieve a much lower average score on the General Certificate of Secondary Education Exams (GCSEs, which determine fitness to pursue a further study leading to possible university training) compared to the scores of students emerging from the old grammar schools. Upper-middle class to upper-class students generally avoid the government-supported school system and send their children to expensive and highly selective private secondary boarding schools (paradoxically called "public schools") which have been the main conduit to admission to Britain's prestigious universities—especially Oxford and Cambridge ("Oxbridge"). The most prestigious of these schools—e.g., Eton, Harrow, Winchester, Rugby, Marlborough—have been the source of a majority of British social and political elites in the twentieth century to the present day. These schools, full of tradition, are in fact unavailable to middle-to-working-class parents from both academic and financial considerations, thus limiting access to Britain's elite for those strata.

The decline in deference in Britain is thus a function of the mobilization of a sense of entitlements in this era of expanded literacy and media exposure, a mobilization that Samuel Beer calls "the new populism."[26] This decline in general trust in government is, of course, not limited to Britain. The mobilization of a sense of entitlements characterizes societies throughout the advanced industrial world threatening the legitimacy of regimes and institutions across the West. The popular rejection of the proposed constitution for the European Union, a strongly elite-driven project, as manifested in the decisive "no" votes in France and the Netherlands in June 2005 and in poll data elsewhere is another indicator of the declining trust in elites.

Germany has been widely characterized as having a strong authoritarian strain in their culture through the World War II period and the immediate decades beyond. This authoritarian strain in the German psyche is a second factor that rendered the German people receptive to the appeals of the Third Reich. This authoritarianism has been found to be manifested in family relations, as between parent and children or husband and wife, as well as between student and teacher, or employee and employer.[27] Moreover, data from the late 1950s presented in the aforementioned classic *Civic Culture Study* show that compared to citizens in the Anglo-American democracies, German citizens felt less competent to participate in political activity. Rather they tended to perceive that their role was to leave the business of politics to their leaders. More recent data, however, suggest that this authoritarian orientation has succumbed to the mobilization of a sense of entitlements that has characterized the Western industrial world.

Other regimes, especially those that were born out of or that express symbolic ties to a revolutionary tradition, carry a strong element of egalitarianism in their political culture. In the United States, there is a widespread feeling that ordinary people—peanut farmers, third rate actors, military officers, entertainment figures—can fill important political roles competently. Having no relevant political experience is almost a positive qualification for seeking high political office. Moreover, political figures in the United States are subjected to close public scrutiny and are frequently subjected to populist processes such as a referendum on policy matters or the recall of sitting political elites.

In France, this egalitarian sense of authority was manifested in three of its regimes (or republics) laboring under unstable and weak executives. The French have had a problem accepting direct face-to-face authority relationships stemming from the centrality of the romanticized ideal of revolution, what may be called "the barricade tradition." This concept refers to the French style of negating the firepower of a modern army by barricading the narrow streets of Paris with old furniture and spare pieces of wood, a scenario repeated in France's several nineteenth century revolutions, both successful and unsuccessful, and immortalized in Delecroix's painting "Liberty at the Barricades" (on display at the Louvre). At the same time, the French are said to value a strong, centralized but remote authority figure, a need born out of the French struggle to establish the boundaries of the realm resulting in the *Ancien Regime,* the most centralized monarchy in Europe.

These conflicting images of authority have been reflected in the French history of oscillating between strongly authoritarian regimes: Napolean, the Bourbon Restoration, the Orleanist monarchy of Louis Phillipe, the Second Empire of Louis Napoleon, Vichy, and the Fifth Republic; and regimes with a weak executive: the First, Third, and Fourth Republics. This oscillation between regime types was rendered possible by the legitimation of revolution as a solution to social and political problems. By contrast, Britain with its strong legitimation of its regime, solves problems within the context of its existing regime. Regime change has not been on the table in the modern era. France has experienced twelve coerced regime changes in the past two centuries.

These conflicting ideals of authority have also been partially reconciled in the widespread bureaucratization and impersonalization of authority relations. In the bureaucratic form of organization, authority relations are rationalized—subjected to an elaborate set of impersonal rules under which all individuals are equal under the rules; hence, the direct exercise of authority is avoided. Behavior is routinized and rendered completely predictable. Of course, this comes at a price of the loss of creativity, adaptability, and responsiveness in the formulation of public policy, creating in France what Michel Crozier calls "the stalled society."[28]

These conflicting ideals of authority are also partially reconciled in what has been until recently, a weak level of organizational life, a social structure known as a mass society comprised of relatively isolated individuals unaffiliated with secondary associations between the individual and omnipotent central authority. This absence of strong organizational life and reliance on remote central authority removes direct authority relationships. In such a mass society, the accountability of the government is lessened by the ease with which a competent modern government can mobilize an atomized set of individuals.

ENDNOTES

[1]Samuel Huntington, *The Third Wave* (Norman: University of Oklahoma Press, 1991), p. 26.

[2]Joseph Schumpeter, *Capitalism, Socialism, and Democracy* (New York: Harper and Row Torchbooks, 1950), p. 269.

[3]Arend Lijphart, *Democracies: Patterns of Majoritarian and Consensus Government in Twenty One Countries* (New Haven, CT: Yale University Press, 1984), p. 1.

[4]Eric Nordlinger, *On the Autonomy of Democratic States* (Cambridg, MA: Harvard University Press, 1981).

[5]Walter Lippman, *The Phantom Public* (New York: Harcourt Brace, 1956).

[6]Anthony Downs, *An Economic Theory of Democracy* (New York: Harper Torchbooks, 1957).

[7]Otto Kirchheimer, "The Transformation of Western European Party Systems," in Joseph LaPalombara and Myron Weiner, eds., *Political Parties and Political Development* (Princeton, NJ: Princeton University Press, 1966).

[8]E. E. Schattschneider, *Party Government* (New York: Rinehart and Co., 1942), p. 208; Evron Kirkpatrick, "Toward a More Responsible Two-Party System: Political Science, Policy Science, or Pseudo–Science?" *American Political Science Review,* Vol. LXV, No. 4 (December, 1971), pp. 965–990.

[9]Raymond Grew, ed., *Crisis of Political Development in Europe and the United States* (Princeton, NJ: Princeton University Press, 1978); Lucien Pye, *Aspects of Political Development* (Boston: Little Brown, 1966), pp. 62–67.

[10]Quoted in Karl Popper, *The Open Society and its Enemies,* Vol. 2, (New York: Harper Torchbooks, 1962), p. 31.

[11]*Ibid.,* p. 69.

[12]Robert Alford, *Party and Society* (Chicago: Rand McNally, 1963).

[13]The aborigine peoples (Eskimos) objected to The Meech Lake proposal because it did not also give them a veto. The French Canadians objected to the Charlottetown Accords because they did also give the aborigines a veto that the *Québécois* insisted should be uniquely theirs.

[14]Richard Rose and Ian McCallister, *Voters Begin to Choose: From Closed Class to Open Elections in Britain* (Beverly Hills, CA: Sage Publications, 1986).

[15]Samuel Beer, *Britain Against Itself: The Political Contradictions of Collectivism* (New York: Norton, 1982).

[16]Ronald Inglehart, "The Silent Revolution in Europe: Intergenerational Change in Post-Industrial Societies," *The American Political Science Review,* Vol. 81, No. 4 (December, 1971), pp. 991–1017; Inglehart, *The Silent Revolution: Changing Values and Political Styles Among Western Publics* (Princeton, NJ: Princeton University Press, 1977); Inglehart, *Culture Shift in Advanced Industrial Societies* (Princeton, NJ: Princeton University Press, 1990).

[17]A substantial and growing body of literature has emerged around this perceived recrudescence of radical right populism in Europe. Among the most notable are Martin Schain, Aristide Zolberg, and Patrick Hossay, eds., *Shadows Over Europe: The Development and Impact of the Extreme Right in Western Europe* (New York: Palgrave Macmillan, 2002); Herbert Kitschelt, *The Radical Right in Western Europe* (Ann Arbor: University of Michigan Press, 1995); Hans-Georg Betz, *Radical Right Wing Populism in Western Europe* (New York: St. Martin's Press, 1994); Pippa Norris, *Radical Right: Voters and Parties in the Electoral Market* (New York: Cambridge University Press, 2005).

[18]These trends in the Netherlands are detailed in Christopher Caldwell, "Holland Daze: The Dutch Rethink Multiculturalism," *The Weekly Standard,* (December 27, 2004), pp. 22–26.

[19]Arend Lijphart, *The Politics of Accommodation: Pluralism and Democracy in the Netherlands* (Berkeley: University of California Press, 1968).

[20]William Kornhouser, *The Politics of Mass Society* (New York: The Free Press of Glencoe, 1959).

[21]Harry Eckstein, "A Theory of Stable Democracy," in Eckstein, *Division and Cohesion in Democracy: A Study of Norway* (Princeton, NJ: Princeton University Press, 1966). Eckstein, "Authority Relations and Governmental Performance: A Theoretical Frame-

work," *Comparative Political Studies,* Vol. 2, No. 3 (October, 1969), pp. 269—326; Eckstein, "Authority Patterns: A Structural Basis for Political Inquiry," *American Political Science Review* Vol. LXVII, No. 4 (December, 1973), pp. 1142–1161.

[22]Walter Bagehot, *The English Constitution* (New York: Doubleday Dolphin Books, 1872), p.13.

[23]Gabriel Almond and Sidney Verba, *The Civic Culture* (Boston: Little Brown, 1965), p. 315.

[24]David Butler and Donald Stokes, *Political Change in Britain: Forces Shaping Electoral Choice* (New York: St. Martin's Press, 1969), p.67.

[25]See, e.g., Dennis Kavenaugh, "Political Culture in Great Britain: The Decline of the Civic Culture," in Gabriel Almond and Sidney Verba, eds., *The Civic Culture Revisited* (Boston: Little Brown, 1980), pp. 156–160. Samuel Beer, *Britain Against Itself: The Political Contradictions of Collectivism* (New York: Norton, 1982), Part 3, "The Collapse of Deference."

[26]Beer, *op. cit.* pp. 149ff.

[27]See, e.g., Bertram Schaffner, *Fatherland: A Study of Authoritarianism in the German Family* (New York: Columbia University Press, 1948).

[28]Michel Crozier, *The Bureaucratic Phenomenon* (Chicago: University of Chicago Press, 1964), Part 4. Crozier's book is a classic and essential to an understanding of both the administrative state and the French political culture. See also Crozier, *The Stalled Society* (New York: The Viking Press, 1970), chap. 5.

3

The Constitutionally Designated Format of Modern Democracies

The constitutionally designated structures for choosing decision makers, formulating policies, and implementing them on the realm comprise what we have traditionally called government. The preceding chapter focused on the context in which government operates because that context is thought to have some causal impact on the nature of government and its policies. The focus on contextual factors became identified with pursuing the explanatory purpose of comparative political analysis, to the extent to which the government itself, identified with a now discredited descriptive and legalistic traditional comparative politics, became virtually ignored. This fixation of political scientists on the causes of governmental structure and operation to the point of ignoring these governmental factors has been called by Roy Macridis "the fallacy of inputism."[1] This neglect of what some feel should be the focus of our scholarship led other political scientists to call for the rediscovery of the state.[2]

CONSTITUTIONS

The term "constitutionally designated structures" implies that we are concerned with constitutional government as opposed to arbitrary government or dictatorship. This latter term refers to the rule of a person who makes policy solely according to his/her will, unrestrained by any external considerations. A dictator dictates. Constitutional government, on the other hand, entails a set of fundamental rules that define the power and function of each political role. Constitutional government is not necessarily a democracy; Great Britain was a constitutional monarchy certainly after the understandings known as the Act of Settlement that brought William and Mary of Orange to the throne in 1701; but it hardly qualified as a democracy until either the First Reform Act enfranchised the middle class in 1832 or the Second Reform Act enfranchised the working class in 1867. (Here again we are confronted with the imprecision of the definition of the key concept of democracy.)

The concept of a constitution itself is imprecise. Americans think of the constitution as a set of the highest laws in a hierarchy of laws that define the essential nature of the regime and the powers inherent in each political role. A constitution in this view primarily determines how political decision makers are chosen and how decisions are reached. Yet, Americans also include in their constitutions the content of some decisions when they feel that these policy positions also define the nature of the regime; thus, the American constitution is viewed as imposing limits to what government may choose to do to individuals in its realm. The American constitution has, however, contained policies that did not define the nature of the regime but rather imposed a resolution of a partisan issue dealing with the circumstance of that point in time. The imposition and subsequent repeal of Prohibition is a classic case in point. The constitutional right to an abortion may be such an issue, a right that even some pro-choice people think should have been established in the political process. However, reasonable people disagree as to whether the right of privacy, on which the abortion right is based, is a fundamental right. The point is that circumstantial decisions—such as Prohibition—ought not to be in a constitution but are best resolved by ordinary legislation, enacted by legislators who were presumably chosen on the basis of their political preferences.

Great Britain does not have a set of fundamental laws legally higher than Acts of Parliament; yet, we speak of the British or English Constitution. The term "constitution" used in reference to Great Britain refers to those principles that most scholars believe belong in a constitution as distinguished from ordinary legislation. Constitutional principles are those that are fundamental—that define the very essence or nature of the regime. Constitutional principles should be resistant to change while ordinary legislation or circumstantial principles ought to be easily adaptable to changing needs and circumstances of that generation or point in time.

The British Constitution therefore embodies those principles that define the nature of the nation's regime and that ought to endure over changing times and circumstances. These principles may be embodied in acts of Parliament, in common law principles, in various "landmark" documents, or merely in custom or tradition. Acts of Parliament that may have constitutional significance include the Act of Settlement of 1701 that brought in the House of Orange as monarchs bound by understood limits to their power, the Habeas Corpus act, the 1999 House of Lords reform bill, and the great nineteenth-century reform bills that extended the suffrage, first to middle-class property owners and then to adult males. Freedom of speech is a common law right in Britain but certainly of constitutional significance. Magna Carta is a landmark document that has constitutional significance even though it is not a legal principle. The understanding that following an election the monarch will summon the head of the winning party to "form a government," and thereby assume the role of prime minister, is a principle that is not legally mandated but merely a matter of custom. Similarly, a bill becomes law in Britain when the monarch issues a declaration (either written or through a parliamentary clerk on Prorogation Day) that *"la reine le veut,"* which means the Queen wills it. (That this declaration is in French reflects the Norman origins of the English monarchy, a testament to the strength of tradition in that country.) The Queen may declare *"la reine s'avisera,"* (the queen takes it under advisement—or not now). The queen retains the legal power to declare or refuse to declare law irrespective of any action by Parliament (the "royal prerogative") but it is expected that this right will not be exercised (except perhaps in some extraordinary crisis barely imaginable). The last monarch to declare *"la reine s'avisera"* was Queen Anne in 1707. Therefore, were Queen Elizabeth II to withhold her royal assent from an Act of Parliament today, it would be perfectly legal but unconstitutional.

Britain is unique in the extent to which it relies on custom and tradition to enforce its fundamental principles. Sweden also lacks a single fundamental written law but the fundamental principles that define the nature of its regime are embodied in several pieces of "ordinary legislation" such as the Riksdag Act. Americans accustomed to believing that their written constitution is a bulwark against the possible abuse of governmental power tend to regard mere custom as an insufficient bulwark. Yet, there are aspects of the fundamental principles that define the American regime that are in fact customary and are not embodied in their written constitution. There is nothing in the Constitution that requires the Electoral College to vote in accordance with the popular vote. Moreover rights embodied in the written constitution have been ignored. The condition of African Americans, especially in the states of the Old Confederacy, in the century following the Civil War exemplifies systematic violation of constitutionally specified rights. A constitution does not effectively create rights that the culture of that society is not ready to grant. Rather a constitution reflects, and to some extent legitimizes, those rights that a society is disposed to respect.

PARLIAMENTARY REGIMES AND PRESIDENTIAL REGIMES

In the classification of regime types offered in Chapter One (Figure 1–2), democracies can be grouped in parliamentary and presidential formats with the former regime type further divided into assembly dominated or cabinet-dominated systems. This last type of system associated with modern Britain—and thus sometimes called "the Westminster Model" after the London borough in which the houses of Parliament are located—has been held as a model for many of the emerging democracies and is therefore also known as "the mother of parliaments." Even the former Soviet Union adopted the forms if not the essence of the Westminster model in which their Supreme Soviet (chief representative assembly—their parliament) was headed by a Council of Ministers (the functional equivalent of cabinet) whose chairman was the functional equivalent of a prime minister, a separate office from the president or head of state. Of course the real power in the USSR was exercised by the Communist Party through its First Secretary.

The presidential type of democratic regime is epitomized by the United States in contrast to the several variations of parliamentary regimes. The presidential model is based on the principle of separation of the legislative and executive roles while the parliamentary models are based on the fusion of those roles. This means in the presidential type of system, the head of government or president is chosen by a separate process from that which chooses the representative assembly or legislature. Therefore, the president may be chosen by and hence beholden to different strata of the population from those that chose the more powerful members of the legislature or assembly.

There is a built-in tension between the values and the resulting agenda of these two branches of government in a presidential system. This tension brings the possibility of a stalemate between the two branches of government, pulling in different directions, resulting in a government unable to act. Each of these branches seeks to establish its autonomy from the other by blocking the policy agenda of the other branch. Presidents may assert their independence from even appearing before the legislature or allowing senior members of the executive branch to be subpoenaed to appear before the legislature against their will. As Juan Linz argues in his polemic against the presidential format, the president, uniquely chosen by the national electorate as opposed to the local and frequently small-town or rural constituencies of the most powerful members of the assembly, has a uniquely strong claim to national legitimacy compromising his accountability to the members of the assembly.[3]

Presidents, therefore, come from outside the national political process. They are frequently former members of the military, of commerce and industry, or other professional claim to fame outside the world national politics. Their main task is to mobilize a national following rather than to build a career in the give and take of policy formulation. As Richard Rose draws the contrast, the background of presidents is in campaigning while that of prime ministers is in governing.[4]

Parliamentary regimes, by contrast, choose and groom their heads of governments—variously called prime ministers, premiers, or chancellors—by the same process by which they choose the legislative assembly. The prime minister becomes the member of that assembly who can command the passive support of a majority of it because the government—the prime minister and his/her cabinet—can be removed from office by a simple majority vote by that body at any time and for any or no stated reason. Prime ministers ascend to party leadership and the head of government role by being a member of that assembly when their party attains sufficient power in the assembly. Rose reports that postwar prime ministers in Britain spent an average of 32 years as an MP before assuming the role of prime minister.[5] Hence, prime ministers have the advantage of experience in the very political arena in which they will have to operate if they are to govern successfully, while many presidents, coming into their role from outside the political process, frequently do not fully understand the process of mobilizing power—an understanding that they would need to govern effectively. President Dwight Eisenhower in the United States was almost a classic case in point. Coming from a life entirely in the military he was used to his orders being carried out automatically by virtue of his rank. However, the president must mobilize power by persuading others it would be in their interest to do what the president wants. While the military subordinates responded to Eisenhower's directives with "yes sir," the politician would ask, "What's in it for me?' Richard Neustadt documents this variation in the ability to exercise political power among American presidents that stands in contrast to the ability of, say, British prime ministers to have their agenda enacted, as will be discussed below.[6]

SYMBOLIC AND CEREMONIAL FUNCTIONS: CHIEF OF STATE

The Westminster model of cabinet government, as in all parliamentary regimes, separates the role of head of government—the chief policy making function and leader of the executive branch of government—from the role of head of state—the ceremonial and symbolic leader of the country. In constitutional monarchies, the monarch serves as chief of state while the head of government is called prime minister, premier, or chancellor. Sometimes, prime minister is used as the generic term to refer to the office in all of its manifestations. In republics with a parliamentary regime, the head of state is generally known as the president.

Presidents of the republic in parliamentary systems are generally elected by some indirect method. For example, the German president is elected by a convention composed of party representatives from parliaments at the national and land levels (land is the German term for what we call the states). The Italian president is elected by an electoral college comprised of both houses of their legislature and 58 regional representatives. While the president serves in a symbolic and ceremonial role, he is less effective than the constitutional monarchs in the remaining monarchies. Everyone knows that the British head of state is Queen Elizabeth—whose appearances are frequently made in a context of pomp and pageantry. How many can identify the president of the German Federal Republic or of the Italian republic? (Germany's president is Horst Köhler, a bland technocrat. Italy's is Carlos Azeglio Ciampi.) Presidents in parliamentary republics generally exercise very little actual political power (although the Italian president is said to take a more active political role than other parliamentary presidents). Occasionally, a president may take a stand to promote widely held values in that society. Richard von Weizsäcker who assumed the presidency of Germany in 1984 made a then-famous speech imploring Germans to confront their responsibilities for the atrocities of the Third Reich, while the Austrians showed their lack of remorse for their role in the events of World War II when they elected as their president Kurt Waldheim, a man who had been deeply involved with the Nazis and their extermination policies.

The French have a hybrid system containing elements of a presidential format and elements of a parliamentary format. The French president is in effect the head of government as well as head of state in that country, exercising almost unchecked political power, while the premier or prime minister usually acts as a subordinate to the president and a liaison to the French National Assembly. However, the premier may exercise more independent political power when the Assembly is politically controlled by political forces in opposition to those of the president (a situation that has occurred three times since the establishment of the Fifth Republic in 1959 and called "cohabitation" after a marriage of convenience).

The potentially enormous powers of a French president with the charismatic support to exercise them include the following: under Article XVI of the constitution, the president may declare a state of emergency without any restrictions on the justification for such a declaration and to rule by fiat during the emergency; the president may bypass the Assembly by taking proposed legislation directly to the public through a referendum that presents the one policy choice and which, given the president's power to mobilize a mass public, will normally go the president's way; the president may dissolve the Assembly no more than once a year without the consent of any other actor; and the president has the power to declare that a constitutional amendment need not be subject to a popular referendum once it has been adopted by the Assembly. Charles DeGualle, the first president in the Fifth Republic, was actually the only one with the charisma to successfully use the emergency and referenda powers. Although the French presidents were originally indirectly elected for a seven-year term, they are now directly elected (since 1962) for a five-year term.

The ceremonial and symbolic role of head of state is performed by the monarch in constitutional monarchies (i.e., Denmark, the Netherlands, Norway, Sweden, and the United Kingdom among Western democracies). These monarchs may be more effective in that symbolic role than presidents in parliamentary republics because the pomp and ceremony surrounding monarchs gives them more stature than the relatively obscure presidents of Germany and Italy discussed above. This pomp and ceremony varies considerably from one monarchy to another. King Harald V of Norway conducts a rather proletarian monarchy as he appears in public in street clothes and uses public transportation. Elizabeth II of the United Kingdom and her inner circle of "royals" are surrounded by a great deal of pomp such as the state opening of parliament, the elaborate changing of the guard at

Buckingham Palace in London and at the Queen's weekend residence at Windsor Castle, and the maintenance of the huge castles and palaces that make up the royal residences. (Palaces resemble large hotels while castles were built as fortifications with parapets, draw bridges, etc.). In addition to the two mentioned above, they periodically occupy Holyroodhouse in Edinburgh, Scotland, Balmoral Castle in Aberdeenshire in the Scottish highlands, or Sandringham House in Norfolk. They also have relatives ensconced at Kensington Palace where the late Princess Diana maintained an apartment, Hampton Court Place which was the residence of Henry VIII, and the Palace at St. James. The state opening of Parliament occurs in November on the Tuesday following the Friday Prorogation (closing) of the previous Parliament. The Queen travels from Buckingham Palace to the houses of Parliament in a caravan of horse drawn carriages, complete with footmen, with the inner circle of royals. She dons the royal robes and the bejeweled crown, sits on the throne in the chamber for the House of Lords, and reads the speech, written by the inner circle of the cabinet, spelling out the government's policy agenda.

The British monarch's main function is to participate in ceremonial functions and serve as a symbol of national identity. In 1994, for example, she participated in 550 royal engagements. The ten most active of royals participated in 2,878 such functions that year. She does not reveal her partisan preferences; hence, she can serve the symbolic role for all of her subjects regardless of their politics, while American presidents, inherently partisan figures, are not viewed by all Americans as the symbol of all that America means to them. Moreover, in presidential systems such as the United States, these ceremonial duties largely fall to the president adding to the already onerous burdens of office.

The more proletarian monarchs of Scandinavia are probably less effective as symbols for their respective countries. As with the case of presidents in parliamentary systems (with the French exception detailed above), constitutional monarchs exercise very little actual political power. King Harald of Norway retains limited veto power over legislation. Queen Elizabeth II of Britain legally retains all of the power that British monarchs once had but it is power she is "constitutionally" expected not to exercise. It has been suggested that this residue of legal power, known as "the royal prerogative," could serve to check or deter an extreme case of abuse of power by Britain's highly centralized government, an unlikely scenario. In 1994, when Prime Minister John Major threatened to have the queen dissolve Parliament and call new elections over the issue of financial support for the EU, the *London Times* recommended that Elizabeth exercise her royal prerogative and refuse his request. While Major did not carry out his threat, it is notable that the *Times* thought Elizabeth still had that option.

Heads of state may still exercise some discretion and influence in the discussion of whom the president or monarch should name to form a government and become prime minister. This discretion would come into play in the event that the election of Parliament did not produce either a majority or clear plurality of seats for one party, a situation called "a hung parliament." In such an eventuality, the government would consist of a coalition of several parties built by negotiation after the election. The influence of a head of state in such a scenario would depend on the personality of that individual.

PARLIAMENTARY REGIMES: GOVERNMENTS AND THE STRUCTURE OF ACCOUNTABILITY

In Britain's Westminster model, the prime minister and his/her cabinet and other ministers constitute "the government" and are understood to be the source of virtually all of the policy making initiatives in that system. Recent cabinets have contained a little over twenty ministers, a number too unwieldy to function as a coherent policy formulating body. Hence, the actual policy formulating function of the government is performed by an inner circle of various combinations of around a half dozen of the most influential and important ministers: the secretaries of state (foreign and home), the chancellor of the exchequer (a combination of the secretary of the treasury and chairman of the FED in the American context), the minister of trade and industry, the Lord President of the (Privy) Council and leader of the House of Commons, and the Lord Chancellor (presiding officer of the House of Lords). Policies are then presented or announced to general cabinet meetings that have now been reduced to about four hours a week, hardly sufficient for cabinet to function as a policy creating body. Yet, the cabinet is collectively responsible to the House of Commons.

The preeminent role of the head of government in policy formulation is formally stipulated in the Federal Republic of Germany in their constitution (known as the Basic Law). Article 65 of the Basic Law stipulates that the chancellor (the German title for the prime minister's role) is the actor who "determines and is responsible for general policy." Unlike the British procedure of collective responsibility of the cabinet to Parliament, the chancellor alone is responsible to his/her lower house, the Bundestag. The remainder of the cabinet is appointed by and responsible to the chancellor. The autonomous power of the chancellor is compromised to some extent by the fact that the German government is normally comprised of one major party and one junior coalition partner, a smaller party needed to make up a governing majority. The demands of this junior coalition partner must be given some considerations to preserve the majority of the governing coalition. It was, for example, the defection of the small Free Democratic Party from the Schmidt government in 1982 that resulted in the passage of Germany's sole successful post-World War II vote of no confidence.

In Germany, in reaction to the ruinous cabinet instability of the Weimar Republic, the vote of confidence is further hedged by the requirement that such a vote be accompanied by agreement on the replacement government, the so-called "constructive vote of no confidence." In Weimar, the far left Communists and the far right fascists and ultranationalists, unable to agree on any policy or government, nevertheless teamed up to repeatedly vote centrist governments out of office, destroying whatever opportunity Weimar might have had to govern.

The procedure or structure of the government's responsibility to parliament lies in the threat or availability of a vote of no confidence, a vote that if passed by a simple majority of those MPs who are present and voting requires the resignation of the entire cabinet including the prime minister. No grounds or reasons need be offered for such a vote in contrast to the impeachment and removal of an American President, a procedure that must be justified by "high crimes and misdemeanors" by the president. The failure to convict and remove President Clinton from office despite the establishment of the facts that he committed grossly inappropriate sexual acts in the Oval Office and lied about it under oath and to the American public indicates that the standards for removing a president are rigorous indeed. No such requirements exist for a vote of no confidence. It used to be understood that defeating the government on major pieces of legislation constituted expressions of no confidence requiring cabinet resignation, but governments apparently no longer regard an occasional legislative defeat as the equivalent of a no-confidence vote. It is unclear if repeated government defeats, in effect an inability of the government to govern, would constitute a de facto no-confidence vote.

With such relaxed standards for a no-confidence vote, one might expect the removal of governments at frequent intervals. That has been the case, as we will see, in some assembly-dominated parliamentary formats. However, in cabinet systems such as Great Britain's, successful votes of no-confidence are extremely rare. In the entire postwar era, there have been one such removal of a government each in Great Britain, Australia, the Federal Republic of Germany, and Canada. The reason they are so rare is that, by definition, the government's party has effective political control of the lower house of the legislature (usually a majority of seats or at least a strong plurality). Without such control, the head of that party would not be asked to form a government (assume the role of prime minister). Moreover, in Western democracies, as we will see in the next chapter on parties, governments are able to exercise considerable control over how the MPs in their party vote, especially on confidence questions. Therefore, in a parliamentary system in which the political arena is dominated by two parties (the Westminster model) and except for the infrequent cases of a minority government made up of a coalition of two or more parties, it would take a rebellion of the ordinary MPs of the government's own party for a vote of no confidence to pass.

Since it is so rare, it would seem that the availability of a no-confidence vote is irrelevant in imposing accountability on the government. However, one of the reasons it is so rare in cabinet systems along the Westminster model is that governments, aware that the vote is available, act in such a way as to not offend their party members beyond understood limits of tolerance.

In Britain, the government and the would-be government of the leading opposition party—called the shadow cabinet—sit on benches facing one another on opposite sides of a table. Ordinary MPs who are not members of the cabinet or shadow cabinet sit in four additional rows of benches behind their party leaders; hence, they are called "back benchers." (The implications of the unique structure of the House of Commons are discussed below.) The cabinet leaders are in regular communication with their back bench. In fact, there are some ten individuals—Lords Commissioners of the Treasury popularly known as whips and assistant whips—whose function it is to act as liaisons between the front and back benches. Cabinets will normally resolve differences with their back bench before the issue comes to a vote.

By contrast, some parliamentary regimes operate with fragmented party systems, systems in which no one party obtains a majority or even a clear plurality of seats in the lower house of their parliament. In such systems, the government is formed by negotiations among party leaders after the election. Thus, the election to the parliament in such a system does not determine the composition of the government. Occasionally, such a governing coalition may consist of a number of weaker parties while the party with the most seats is excluded. Obviously, the lines of accountability between the government and the voting public are weakened when the composition of the government and its policies are not determined by the outcome of the only national election. This scenario has frequently been the case in the Netherlands where as many as fifteen parties have had seats in the *Tweede Kamer.* (In the 1998 elections, 23 parties offered candidates and 9 parties actually won seats.) In such systems, the government is comprised of coalitions of several distinct parties to make up the legislative majority on whose sufferance the existence of the government depends. Leaders of the government will have less control and influence over MPs who are not members of the same party (a consideration known as party discipline discussed in Chapter Four); hence, the reliability of the legislative majority supporting the government is considerably weaker than in the Westminster model, in which the government is supported by a cohesive majority party. Successful votes of no confidence may be rather frequent in parliamentary systems that rely on fragmented coalition governments, governments comprised of several parties of comparable strength. In such systems, the government may not be able to govern coherently over a range of controversial issues as majorities shift with each new issue. Italy, for example, suffered 55 successful votes of no confidence between the establishment of the postwar Italian republic and the watershed election of 1993 (discussed in Chapter Four). The Netherlands has fewer such votes but may take up to a year to resolve a cabinet crisis (the challenge of reconstituting a government after a vote of no confidence). Frequent votes of no confidence are a phenomenon known as cabinet instability (distinguished from regime instability—the frequent replacement of the constitutional order).

A no-confidence vote in countries operating with the Westminster model will almost certainly be accompanied a dissolution of parliament and a new election. Hence, a vote against one's party leadership by members of the cabinet's party is a vote to stand for reelection before one's term has expired, with the possibility that the rebellious MPs may find themselves out of a job. In France during the Third

Republic, the power to dissolve the Chamber of Deputies (lower house of their legislature) became politically unusable due to its abuse by one of the early presidents of the republic, monarchist Marshall MacMahon. In the Fourth Republic, the power of dissolution was constitutionally restricted to occasions when a no-confidence vote passed by an absolute majority (of all the members of the Assembly present or not). Yet, governments regularly fell by relative majorities (of those voting) and were reconstituted without ascertaining the will of the electorate. In these systems, a vote against the government was risk free and the rebellious deputy or member of the Assembly might hope to land a new or better ministry in the reconstituted government. It seems logical that the effective power of dissolution in a parliamentary format will make cabinet instability in the form of relatively frequent successful votes of no confidence less likely. However, if avoiding the plague of cabinet instability that robbed numerous European parliamentary regimes their effectiveness and hence legitimacy were that simple, why did such regimes eschew that power of dissolution? The power of dissolution may be less of a direct cause of cabinet stability and more of a symptom of a culturally driven support for an executive with the power to govern. The French Third Republic had that power but it became politically unusable.

The government in a parliamentary system therefore does not directly answer to the national electorate but to the lower house of its legislature. (In Italy, both houses participate in the confidence mechanism). Normally, the MPs in government party, who normally in the Westminster model comprise a majority, will oppose a motion of no confidence; hence, the government will survive such votes as long as they keep their own back bench in line. The government accountability is really to that back bench rather than to parliament as a whole or to the national electorate. The structure of accountability in democratic regimes is schematically shown in Figure 3–1.

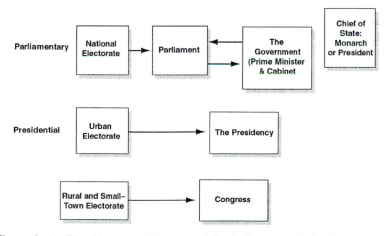

Figure 3–1   The Structure of Accountability in Democratic Regimes

DEBATE AND QUESTION TIME IN PARLIAMENTARY REGIMES

The government does answer to the House as a whole in another mechanism begun in Britain and now found in some form in most Western parliamentary systems—what is called in Britain "Prime Minister's Question Time." Each Wednesday that Parliament is in session and the prime minister is in town, the prime minister is required to appear in the House at the opening of the day's session to answer questions from the MPs for 30 minutes. The questions are submitted in writing one day before in order to allow the prime minister and his advisors to gather data and formulate responses. Every other question comes from the opposition side of the House, forcing the prime minister to defend his policy choices and their impact in terms of Britain's public interest. These sessions are frequently quite lively and draw a capacity of visitors (called "strangers") and full coverage by the print and electronic media. It is possible that the prospect of having to defend one's policies in terms of the public interest in that public venue may temper one's policy choices. Other cabinet members field questions about their areas of responsibility at the beginnings of the sessions on Monday, Tuesday, and Thursday. Because of question time and the fact that the major political conflict occurs in the lower house, it is now constitutionally settled in Britain that most of the important members of the cabinet must also have a seat in Commons. (The notable exceptions are the Lord Chancellor and the Lord Privy Seal, the presiding officer of the House of Lords and nominal head of the Privy Council respectively.) The government and the legislature are in effect chosen by the same election; therefore, the Westminster system is a far cry from the concept of the separation of powers claimed in the American presidential system.

The executive in the Westminster model is thus part of the legislative process and participates in debate on the issues of the day both in question time and in the discussion of the merits of particular pieces of legislation. Debate in the House of Commons is sometimes a lively exchange of ideas as opposed to the debate in most other representative assemblies in which "debate" is frequently a series of unrelated speeches. Some people think this level of debate in Britain may be reinforced by the physical structure of the House. Having evolved from the old Anglican Chapels in which benches along the side walls faced one another, MPs also sit on benches with the government to the right of the speaker facing its "loyal opposition" to the speaker's left, with a table in the middle with two "dispatch boxes" that serve as mini-podiums for the prime minister and leader of the opposition. A line runs in front of each set of benches behind which the occupants of each set of benches are expected to remain. The benches are slightly more than two sword's lengths apart, a tradition that originated in the time when such a violent encounter was thought possible.

In contrast members of most other assemblies sit in individual chairs behind individual small desks in a semicircular fashion facing a raised stage and podium. A person standing behind a podium on a stage facing an audience in individual seats may be more likely to make a speech than someone standing in front of a bench with only a few note cards. The opposing political forces who are facing one another are close enough to be heard in a strong conversational tone, possibly promoting the give and take that often characterizes debate in Commons. There is actually insufficient room to seat all 651 members of the House of Commons producing a crowded but intimate chamber. Winston Churchill was so convinced that this physical structure of the House of Commons contributed to what he felt was the superior level of debate in that chamber that when the House was destroyed by a German bomb during the war (fortunately when it was not in session), Churchill ordered it rebuilt almost exactly as it had been.

ACCOUNTABILITY IN PRESIDENTIAL REGIMES

While the accountability of the government in the Westminster model is to the lower House, the accountability of a president in a presidential system is directly to the voting public. The voting public in Britain never gets to vote directly on who will become prime minister, although it is likely that their vote for MP in their election district is heavily influenced by party label and by the identity of the respective head of the party who would assume that role if their party won. Given the fact that the voting public even in the most literate democratic society is largely apathetic, uninformed, and thus easily mobilized by opinion leaders, it may be argued that the MPs are better equipped to hold a government accountable than voting publics. Presidents, with stature inherent in the office and with access to the media, are able to a considerable extent to shape public opinion rather than public opinion seriously constraining the policy options for the president. It has long been understood that public opinion in a modern society is shaped to a large extent by opinion leaders—the media, political and economic leaders, and other famous and respected individuals.[7] By contrast, since politics is their primary occupation and since they have access to sources of information unavailable to the general public, MPs are apt to be much more well informed of the affairs of state than the average voter. Because of their better understanding of politics, MPs are better equipped to assess and evaluate the political information they receive.

Moreover, it is arguable that the fusion of power in which both the government and the legislature are chosen by the same electoral process promoting a centralized government provides clear lines of responsibility compared to presidential systems. In the presidential system, the head of government and the legislature are chosen independently of one another, frequently producing an outcome in which the legislature and the government are controlled by opposing political forces. This inherently invites a stalemated political system in which it is difficult to adopt any controversial policies and to resolve issues confronting that country. The creation of independent veto groups throughout the system—political forces with the power to say "no" to any policy proposal while no one power center has the power to adopt a policy—protects against the possible abuse of power but does not allow the use of the power to govern.

In a parliamentary system, a situation in which the legislature falls under the control of political forces opposed to the government is resolved by the government being replaced by one that can govern. A presidential system has to endure that kind of political stalemate for a fixed term of office, a period of time in which pressing national issues go unresolved. Moreover, with power fragmented among independent veto groups in a presidential system, it is difficult to assess responsibility for the failure to resolve such issues.

Juan Linz, in his forcefully argued critique of the presidential model, is particularly concerned with the lack of flexibility built into presidential systems with their fixed terms of office.[8] Divided government is built into the presidential system in which the legislature, chosen by a political process that is independent of the one choosing the presidency, may represent a different set of values than that represented by the presidency. Congressional leadership has traditionally been more sensitive to less urban and more one party hegemonic constituencies than are represented by the presidency, whose constituency has been the urbanized and industrialized swing states; hence, even when the same party controls both the presidency and congress, political tension may still exists between these two branches of government.

Given the failure to remove President Clinton from office in the United States and the unresolved question as to what level of malfeasance in office "rises to the level" of adequate grounds for such removal, it is far from certain that President Nixon would have ultimately been impeached had he not resigned. Yet, it is clear, reinforced by his own admission, that he had lost the power to govern while three more years remained in his term. Hence, the United States could have been saddled with three years of a totally ineffective presidency. The likelihood of a stalemated political process in which no actor or institution possesses the power to govern is built into the presidential model. That impasse appeals to those who fear the power of government. This built in inability to act, however, is not seen as an undiluted good by those who view government as a force for good in society.

Donald Horowitz responds to the Linz critique with the observation that the impasse created by divided government is the alternative to a winner-take-all system in which the losing minority may not be able to accept total exclusion from the political process.[9] Such exclusion is particularly problematic in highly segmented societies in which isolated subcultures are alienated from and do not trust the rest of the country. Of course, parliamentary regimes only produce a winner-take-all government in the Westminster model; it was discussed earlier that power in parliamentary systems with fragmented party systems is proportioned among an array of political and social forces.

The likelihood of the abuse of power is probably constrained by cultural factors that do not tolerate such abuse rather than by a particular set of constitutional structures. One may find such abuse in either presidential or parliamentary format.

THE ROLE OF LEGISLATURES AND REPRESENTATIVE ASSEMBLIES IN THE POLICY PROCESS

All modern democracies have a national representative assembly that votes its approval or disapproval of proposed laws. These proposed laws are generally known as bills. Despite a simplistic impression in some quarters that these bodies, frequently called legislatures, legislate or make laws in the sense of creating public policy while the executive or head of government executes or implements these laws, these representative bodies have never actually functioned as their country's chief policy making body.

As implied in the discussion of the structure of accountability above, policy making in advanced industrial societies originates with the political executive to an overwhelming extent, for reasons that are structural and historical. In countries characterized by legislative dominance over the executive—e.g., the Third and Fourth Republics of France, the Weimar Republic of Germany, Italy until the early nineties, the Netherlands—the policy making process has been immobilized by an inability to resolve pressing socioeconomic problems with effective policy solutions.

Structurally these legislatures are collegial bodies and collegial bodies do not function efficiently as actors. Policy making bodies become unwieldy when their membership grows beyond a certain point. That is essentially the reason why the policy making function in Great Britain passed from the Privy Council to the cabinet and then to a not-yet-institutionalized inner circle within the cabinet. The Privy Council evolved as the number of lords in the Great Council grew beyond the point where they could effectively consult with the monarch, a group within the lords met in the monarch's private chambers and became privy to the ear of the monarch. These Privy Counselors take an oath to respect the private matters of the monarch and thus have a top security clearance. They are designated by the title, "the right honourable…." Since this was a desirable position, the ranks of the Privy Council grew to the point of being unwieldy. There are now about 300 members. It no longer functions as a body but selected MPs including the entire cabinet are named to this honorific post, a practice that helps Britain maintain its highly valued link with tradition. It also insures the high security clearance for the cabinet. Meanwhile the Council remains the official advisory body to the monarch; the cabinet still has no legal standing.

Modern legislatures tend to be comprised of people trained in the law or other liberal arts while modern policy making tends to require specialized knowledge in fields such as science, engineering or agriculture. This kind of knowledge tends to be concentrated in government in the administrative sector. The resulting political role of the administrative sector is discussed below.

Historically, the so-called mother of parliaments evolved out of the practice of English monarchs, hard pressed to finance their 130 year marauding in France in the fourteenth and fifteenth centuries, gathered the baronial council or old Anglo-Saxon Wittan. Because of their independent financial base growing out of the enclosure movement and the wool trade, the barony had the ability to force a modification of the monarch's decisions.[10] It was never doubted, however, that the policy decisions were initiated by the monarchy. Rather, the barony and landed gentry acquired the capacity of checking or constraining the policy making discretion of the monarch—the then effective political executive—through the power of the purse. This ability to check the discretion of the political executive through the power of the purse remains the classic role of the representative assembly. L. S. Amery in his classic commentary on the English constitution put it this way:

> Parliament is not, and never has been, a legislature, in the sense of a body specially and primarily empowered to make laws... .The main task of Parliament is still what it was when first summoned, not to legislate or govern, but to secure full discussion and ventilation of all matters... as the condition of its giving its assent to bills.[11]

It is doubtful if representative assemblies ever functioned as policy formulating bodies, even during the so-called "golden age of Parliament." The bargaining position first of the landed gentry then of the rising middle class among the commoners with the growth of capitalism contributed to a process of power flowing "out of court" from the monarch to the increasingly autonomous parliament or to legal magistrates in the case of common law pronouncements although the power, exercised by others, was exercised in the name of the monarch. This process led to several centuries of tension between the forces of the monarch striving to retain actual power and the forces of parliament, culminating in the civil wars of the seventeenth century which resulted in the decapitation of Charles I in January, 1649. Despite the atavistic claims of James II resulting in the Glorious Revolution of 1688 bringing William and Mary of Orange to the throne, Charles' defeat in the civil wars of the seventeenth century was the effective end of any serious threat of royal absolutism in England.

In Catholic France, on the other hand, capitalism developed more slowly. Added to this, the fact that the Hundred Years' War was fought on French soil resulted in their aristocracy being more dependent on the court. The French monarch developed as the most centralized and absolute in Europe, culminating in the reign of Louis XIV who could claim, "*l'etat c'est moi*" (I am the state) as the French monarchy strove to subordinate competing forces to its control.[12] It took the Revolution of 1789 and the destruction of the French monarchy for a French Assembly to have independent power.

The victory of Parliament over Charles I meant that policy making passed not to Parliament as a whole but to the inner circle of ministers within Parliament, the Privy Council and then to the cabinet as described above. The point is that policy formulation has always been an executive function. While there is a provision in the House of Commons for the introduction of private members' bills, such bills are never enacted. In the United States, individual senators and congressman introduce bills but these bills normally originate with interest groups who have the specialized knowledge needed to write modern legislation.

Scholars have decried the declining influence of representative assemblies and their being dominated by political executives.[13] There have been proposals to reform parliaments to better enable them to cope with the task of policy making in the modern world, proposals such as increasing the level of specialization and technical competence among MPs.[14] Such proposals are oriented toward transforming parliaments into something they never have been, policy making and hence governing bodies.

THE REPRESENTATIVE FUNCTION OF PARLIAMENTS

Parliaments also function as representative assemblies which means that MPs represent something. That is, they are presumed to speak for some segment of the population as well as for the broader national interest. There is a potential conflict here that was addressed by the great nineteenth-century English statesman, Edmund Burke. The interest and demands of that segment of the population the MP is ostensibly supposed to represent may conflict with what the MP judges to be the interest of the nation as a whole. Burke argued in his famous "speech to the electors at Bristol" (the constituency that elected him) that when there was a conflict between the interests and desires of the geographically finite electoral district that elected him and the interests of the realm as a whole, the statesman's duty is to the realm. While he is directly elected from one finite district, the statesman "virtually represents" the entire nation. Moreover, Burke argued in that speech that the statesman owed his constituents not only his presence to follow their orders and wishes on parliamentary votes but rather he owes them his reasoned judgment as a statesman who is presumptively more astute on matters of public policy than the ordinary citizen. Clearly, this is not a formula for popularity among one's own constituents, and Burke eventually finished his career representing a "rotten borough" (one that had been physically swallowed by the North Sea but still sent an MP to Parliament). It is still not settled whether the concept of representation requires the member of the legislature to ascertain and follow the public opinion of his constituents or if it requires him/her to exercise his/her best judgment. Scholars generally agree with Eric Nordlinger that modern democracies act with a good deal more autonomy from the publics to whom they are theoretically accountable than democratic theory would suggest.[15] Hence, the concept of representation probably means protecting the interests of one's constituents and balancing them when they conflict rather than to ascertain and promote their specific policy preferences.

Also unsettled is the question of whose interests and desires require representation. Should given numbers of a randomly chosen group of citizens have their spokesmen in parliament or should functionally defined segments of society each have their spokespersons such as labor, the entrepreneurial middle class, the landed gentry, and so forth? In the former case, each representative should represent approximately the same number of constituents as the other representatives. That would not necessarily be true in the latter case.

Geographically defined subdivisions of a polity such as states, provinces, or länder in a federal system, or culturally distinct regions such as Scotland and Wales in the United Kingdom, may claim the need for its spokespersons in a parliament. This is typically the function of upper houses in a bicameral legislature (containing two houses) in federal systems. Thus, in the United States Congress, each state, large or small, has two senators to balance off the larger representation of more populous states in the House of Representatives. Similarly, the Australian Senate has the same number of senators from each state. The original number of six senators from each state was expanded in 1948 to ten, each still equally distributed among the states. Today it has twelve senators from each of the six states plus two from each mainland territory for a total of seventy-six. In the Federal Republic of Germany, the members of the upper house, the Bundesrat, are chosen by the governments of each of the several länder with each land delegation voting as a bloc and presumptively representing the interests of their land. The Canadian Senate consists of 105 members appointed by the governor general on the recommendation of the prime minister. Canadian Senate seats are divided equally among Ontario, Quebec, the Maritime Provinces (Newfoundland, Nova Scotia, Prince Edward Island), and the Western Provinces (Alberta and British Columbia). The Canadian Senate's role in representing distinct provincial interests is weakened, however, by the fact that it rarely rejects bills passed by the House of Commons. The upper house in the Netherlands is elected by provincial councils even though the country is not actually a federal system. The provinces had had autonomous status until the nineteenth century.

The representation of subunits in a federal system is not the only justifiable function for upper houses in bicameral legislatures. However, upper houses are hard to justify if they do not represent something different than the constituency defined by raw numbers, normally represented in the lower house, although that situation may occur. In Norway, the upper house, the Lagting, is chosen from the Storting or lower house (which is then called the Odelsting) in the same proportional party composition, rendering policy confrontations between the two houses very unlikely; hence, the logic of the division of the Storting into two houses is hard to discern. The House of Lords in Britain, by contrast, has represented the landed gentry in that system which, although less numerous than the population at large, was perceived to constitute a distinct and important role in the history and traditions of that society. The movement to "reform" the House of Lords, driven by the claim that it was intolerable to have a house not chosen by popular election, culminating in the 1999 House of Lords Reform Act constituted a compromise with egalitarian forces of the left who demanded either the abolition of that house or its transformation into one that was popularly elected. By the terms of this act, 92 hereditary peers chosen by the previous universe of such peers will retain their voting membership as do the specialized peers: the Lords Spiritual (Anglican bishops) and the Law Lords (the Judicial Committee of the Privy Council, Britain's highest court of appeals). Fifteen of these ninety two shall hold leadership posts and the other 77 proportioned as to party strength in Commons. The remaining peerages are life peerages, commoners appointed to Lords by the Prime Minister and whose peerage does not pass to their heirs. These provisions are meant to counter the traditional Conservative advantage in Lords. Some feel it makes little sense to have a second house chosen the same way as is the lower house. Two houses make sense when each represents a different segment or set of interests of that society. Thus, while the American House of Representatives and the German Bundestag (lower house) represent groups of individual voters, the American Senate and German Bundesrat represent territorial subunits of the system. Accordingly, some nonfederal systems have taken the step of abolishing the upper house and going with a unicameral legislature. Sweden's Riksdag and Denmark's Folketinget are unicameral legislatures.

Because the accountability of the government in Britain through the confidence mechanism is exclusively to the House of Commons, the House of Lords is outside the structure of accountability. Moreover, by the terms of the Parliament Act of 1949, its actual power over legislation has been curtailed to the power to delay the enactment of an act of parliament for one year. Hence many Brits, especially those on the political left, argued that this hereditary and antidemocratic body had outlived its usefulness and should be abolished. The aforementioned House of Lords Reform Act of 1999 was a response to this criticism. Yet, Lords—referred to by members of commons as "the other place"—has performed useful functions. Because it does not have to debate every bill, it can and does engage in serious and thoughtful debate on matters the Commons does not have time to fully explore. Moreover, Lords will defeat the government on a number of bills forcing the government to rethink or revise sometimes hastily conceived policies. From 1979 to 1994, Lords rejected bills passed by commons 233 times, forcing the government to amend its bills to avoid the one-year delay. Usually this results in improvements in the writing of the bills. To the extent that the role of legislatures in modern democracies has become one of constraining to the policy-making head of government through public and informed critique of that policy, the role of the two houses of Parliament are not really that different from one another.

LEGAL SYSTEMS IN ADVANCED DEMOCRACIES

The idea of laws as confined to principles enacted by the lawmaking body of that political unit is not entirely accurate, depending on whether one is talking about the legal system used on the continent usually called "Civil Law" or the system used in most of the Anglo-American democracies known as "common law." These legal systems reflect the culture and political style of their respective countries.

In common law jurisdictions, principles of law evolved inductively out of the practice of resolving actual disputes.[16] Thus, the great jurist Oliver Wendell Holmes, in oft quoted words, phrased it this way, " ... the life of the law has not been logic; it has been experience."[17] The process began in the twelfth century when Henry II was concerned with extending his effective control over the breadth of the realm, a process known as extending the "king's peace." The king, and then ministers acting in his name, advanced that cause by resolving the many disputes generated by feudal rights and obligations in various communities in the realm. Even the forms of action at common law, such as tort, were devised to accommodate actual disputes. The form of action, *asumpsit*, was devised to deal with the reality of indirect injury when that situation presented itself. The key at first was to seek the most viable resolution of the dispute, that which was in accord with the customs of that community as opposed to seeking abstract principles of justice. Thus, from the outset, common law was a harsh but pragmatic system in which custom and practice had legal force. This concern with the resolution of disputes in common law as contrasted to a concern with dispensing social justice or finding the truth, is reflected in the principle of adversary jurisprudence by the terms of which each party in common law litigation is responsible for presenting its own best case while the court or judge remains a neutral arbiter whose role is to ensure that both sides play by the rules of procedure. If the defense attorney is, for example, too incompetent to object to hearsay evidence, it is not up to the court to take that step for him/her. The rather harsh emphasis on the resolution of disputes limits the rewards at common law to monetary damages for wrongs already incurred. Hence, this harshness of common law was ultimately mitigated by a corollary system called "equity" by which anticipated wrongs could be prevented by a court order or injunction, and other compensations may be dispensed when monetary damages are inadequate.

Eventually, it became obvious that the principles of law needed to be consistent and thus predictable over time and space. Somehow, a consensus was reached among the law ministers that insofar as the circumstances of the dispute remained the same, the pattern of earlier decisions should be followed. Thus, "the multitude of manorial courts where local magistrates dispensed justice whose custom and character varied with the customs and temper of the neighbor..." would be replaced by royal courts administering legal principles *common* to the realm—hence the term common law.[18] This became a fundamental principle of common law, "*stare decisis*" or let the decision stand. There is, of course, room for interpretation or inference as to whether the circumstances of a particular case are in fact consistent with those of a given precedent. There is room for flexibility in the development of the principles of law.

By contrast, the countries on the continent operate under a system known as civil law in which legal principles are limited to those enacted by a duly constituted law-making body in advance of any dispute to which it might be applied. The standards for such a legal code are interpretations of justice and logical consistency. The court in a civil law system takes an active role in discerning the just solution to the dispute or the true facts in the case. Thus, on the one hand, students of the law in a common law jurisdiction read opinions from past cases trying to discern the turning point on which the case was decided from extraneous discussion or *obiter dicta* in the opinion. The brief or legal presentation of the attorneys in a common law dispute consists of the citation of precedent and arguing why particular precedents should apply to the case at hand. Civil law students, on the other hand read law codes discussing their internal logic and the abstract principles of justice they imply.

While most of the Anglo-American world operates under common law reflected in their pragmatic cultural orientation, pockets of civil law exist in that world where continental heritage prevails as in, for example, Louisiana with its French Creole heritage and in parts of Scotland.

FEDERALISM, CONFEDERATIONS, AND UNITARY GOVERNMENT

The strategy of resolving the aforementioned problem of power by dividing it among independent power centers finds expression in the institution of federalism in a number of Western democracies. Federalism will be shown to be more appropriate for some systems than for others.

Much of the work on federalism has focused on the legal distribution of power between the central and constituent governments, conceptualizing that each level of government has its sphere of power.[19] However, particular activities of government are usually not so neatly classifiable. For example, is a factory that refines 95 percent of the sugar sold in America engaged in interstate commerce, an activity whose regulation is delegated to the national government, or in manufacturing, a sphere of regulation not so delegated? Obviously, it is both. Therefore, the idea of dividing the activities of government into two autonomous and sovereign spheres of power runs into difficulties when applied to the real world.

Federalism, it is universally agreed, involves a national or whole system government and constituent or subsystem governments ruling over the same territory. This, however, describes virtually all political systems. In a unitary system, the constituent or subsystem governments can legally be abolished by the central government regardless of how much independent power these constituent governments may be authorized to wield. Thus, despite the considerable amount of "devolution" of power from the government at Westminster to the Scottish parliament, the government at Westminster could theoretically abolish all of the Scottish political institutions. In a federal system, however, the existence of the constituent units and right to exercise their power are guaranteed by a fundamental law independent of the will of the central government.

Federal governments differ from confederations in that confederations place sovereignty—the final power to make and enforce law over individuals—with the constituent or subsystem units. In confederations, the central government cannot directly command individuals but rather must act through subsystem governments. The relationship between the constituent units and the central government in a confederation is rather like the relationship between the United Nations and the nation states that belong to it. The American Articles of Confederation (1776–1789) constitute another well-known example of this form of government. Belgium, with its cultural segmentation between the Flemish and Wallonian regions described in Chapter Two, has been transformed over the past three decades from a unitary system to what is in fact a confederation. The final power over any matter affecting the cultural integrity of that region is left to the subcultural councils who define which matters that includes. The European Union has for the most part been a confederation with its member states retaining their sovereign power over most matters. However, with adoption of the common currency, the Euro, the member states have surrendered sovereign control over their money supply and hence of their ability to regulate inflation and unemployment. With the concept of "perforated sovereignty," the EU has been claiming some other specified powers over individuals in its member states. However, the rejection of the proposed EU constitution by the voters of France and the Netherlands in the summer of 2005 cast doubt about the further evolution of the EU into a European federation.

In a federal system, the central government has the final power to regulate and exercise power over individuals. This means that in the event of a conflict between a valid exercise of national power and an otherwise valid exercise of subunit power, the national power takes precedence and the subsystem activity is thereby rendered void. The much misinterpreted tenth amendment to the American constitution does not reserve to the states exclusive or final power over any matter in a way that would limit the exercise of national power. It merely says that the states may act on any matter that does not conflict with a valid exercise of national power.

In some federal systems, the boundaries of the subunits or of groups of subunits are approximately congruent with cultural or economic diversities that are geographically defined.[20] In such systems, the leaders of the subsystems become guardians of and spokespersons for the protection of interest growing out of those diversities. In Canada, for example, most of the segmented French Canadian subculture lives in the province of Quebec (with a significant minority spilling over into western New Brunswick). The Quebec elite becomes a defender of the resistance to assimilation in the broader English-speaking Canada. The elites of the states of the old Confederacy became defenders of the interests of the antebellum South as they perceived them. Congruent federalism therefore resists the assimilation of these geographically defined diversities into the broader national economy or culture. In extreme cases, it may lead to the breakup of the nation state as in the case of Czechoslovakia which broke up into the Czech Republic and the republic of Slovakia.

On the other hand, the range of social, ethnic, religious, and economic diversities in one political subsystem may be close to the range in the other subsystems in that federal system. Australia has six states in each of which the range of these aforementioned diversities is similar. Hence, there is not a clear set of distinct interests that the elites of Australia's states are expected to promote or distinct demands to which they are expected to respond. Australia, of course, has diversities in its population; they are not, however, geographically defined. The subsystems in the Federal Republic of Germany , called *länder,* (singular: *land*) used to represent some culturally distinct former principalities with distinct histories such as Prussia or Bavaria. However, these were abolished after World War II by the allies because of their roles in supporting German militarism and Naziism leading up to World War II. The redrawn federal map shows *länder* that are artificial creations without any distinct history or culture producing much in the way of distinct interests and demands.

Although the United Kingdom—the nation state that is comprised of England, Scotland, Wales, and Ulster or Northern Ireland—legally is a unitary system with the government in Westminster retaining sovereign power over its entire realm, it has many of the attributes of a federal system. It has geographically defined distinct cultural and economic diversities within its realm. Scotland, which has a history of armed struggle against England in a vain effort to retain its national independence, has a distinct accent, a distinct legal system, a distinct educational system, and distinct economic interests stemming from its North Sea oil. Wales also has a distinct history and language. Up to the end of World War II, a majority of Welshmen spoke Gaelic rather than English and the language is still widely spoken among the Welsh population. The longtime struggle of Northern Ireland's Catholics to free themselves from British rule is widely known. These geographically defined diversities have resulted in substantial devolution of power from Westminster to subsystem political units with varying amounts of power. A Scottish Parliament, with the power to tax and spend independently from Westminster, exercises considerably more independent power than does the Welsh Assembly. Both units were set up by the Scotland Act and Government of Wales Act in 1998.

The difference between this degree of devolution to these regional assemblies and federal government is that these regional institutions exist at the sufferance of the government at Westminster, which could legally abolish them at any time. Practically and politically, however, the government at Westminster could no more retract devolution than could the state of New York rescind the official incorporation of New York City, although it has the legal power to do so. Whether the growing autonomy of Scotland will eventually lead to a significant volume of demands for Scottish independence from Westminster remains to be seen.

PAN-NATIONAL INTEGRATION: MAASTRICHT AND THE EUROPEAN UNION

Federalism and regionalism are concerned with demands for autonomy by subnational government. However, in the other direction, perhaps the most significant trend in European politics is the effort to recast the structures of European politics on a pan-national basis. Beginning with functional cooperation, cooperation based on the convergence of interests in a specifically defined set of issues, the aims of the prophets of pan-national integration in Europe have evolved to a federation of Europe that would effectively eliminate the sovereignty of such traditional nation states as France, Germany, etc. The sovereignty of the nation state—their final power to make and enforce law—had been central to European politics since the writings of Jean Bodin in the sixteenth century.[21] This agenda of European integration is driven by a widespread assumption that one of the causes of the two world wars in the twentieth century was excessive nationalism, the mobilization of political identity around the exalted concept of the nation state. The drive toward pan-national integration is further driven by globalization, the belief that political, social, and economic forces operate in what Immanuel Wallerstein identified as a worldwide system beyond the effective control of the governments of nation states.[22]

Functional integration began with the Bretton Woods Agreements of 1944 which pursued the goal of free trade and stable exchange rates; it continues through the North Atlantic Treaty Organization, a collective security response to the threat posed by the Soviet Union and the Cold War, and the Treaty of Paris of 1951 that set up the Coal and Steel Community. Devoted Europeanists such as Jean Monnet, Jacques Delors, and Robert Schuman, who probably had the broader goal of European federation in mind, counted on the concept of *spillover,* the idea that when states cooperate in one area such as coal and steel, the pressures and skills for cooperating in other areas will increase.

The Treaty of Rome in 1958 led to the establishment of the European Economic Community, which committed its six signatories to a tariff free "common market." The original six expanded to twelve in the 1980s as the EEC sought further integration of their economies setting up the Exchange Rate Mechanism to stabilize and standardize exchange rates. Affiliation with the ERM led to the collapse of the British pound sterling in September, 1992, an indicator that the persistence of national identities and their resistance to displacement by a European identity is based upon the reality that these national identities develop from real differences of interests. The eradication of tariff barriers will benefit strong and efficient industries and threaten those that are less strong. The trend toward closer integration of European economies continued with the signing of the Single European Act in 1986 committing the signatories to the elimination of physical barriers to trade (custom and passport controls), fiscal barriers (taxes and tariffs), and technical barriers (standards and regulations).

The Maastricht Treaty (Treaty on the European Union) of 1993 signaled the attempt to move from economic to political integration. In fact, a draft form, removed at the insistence of Great Britain, stated that the goal was federal union. Maastricht set up the structures out of which a European federation could be formed; however, the hopes of the Europeanists were dashed in the summer of 2005 when the populations of the first two member states to put it to a vote, France and the Netherlands, soundly rejected a draft constitution for a European federation. Indications were that other voting publics within the EU were also prepared to reject the constitution but their referenda were cancelled as moot.

The effort of the pan-European idealists to move from economic cooperation to political integration and ultimately to a federation of Europe has been fraught with two major difficulties. First, there has been a widespread perception among a large portion of European publics that the power and control over matters of major importance in their lives was being further removed than they already were. If their national governments often seemed powerful and remote, that perception was exacerbated several times over with respect to the EU institutions based in Brussels. This perception was further strengthened by a built-in insulation of the EU decision making structures from democratic accountability and control—what EU critics call "the democratic deficit." The European Parliament is directly elected by voters of member states on the basis of proportional representation; although it debates issues and makes recommendations, it has little actual decision making power. The European Council consists of the heads of the member governments meeting twice annually to consider broad policy questions and to set the agenda for the Council of Ministers. This latter body consists of ministers of member states who are relevant to the issues being considered and thus has a variable membership and approximately two dozen technical councils that meet as needed. The Council is the EU's key decision making and policy formulating body; yet, its permanent representatives meet and make decisions in a closed door and nonaccountable environment. The European Commission is a bloated bureaucratic structure of some 16,000 employees based in Brussels and seeking to protect its own positions and interests.

The second major difficulty is that the European idealists are trying to construct a state before the widespread development of a European identity or nation. The differences of interest among member states are real and important, and survey data show that the citizens of the member states still perceive of themselves as Frenchmen, Norwegians, Swedes, or Germans before they see themselves as Europeans. The resistance to abandoning national identities for European identity is stronger in some places, such as England, than in others. The analogy of the success of the federating of the thirteen American colonies is misplaced. The American colonies not only spoke a common language and came from a common English heritage, but they had enough of a common bond to have successfully fought a war together. This author witnessed the bitter opposition of citizens of Dover to the completion of the cross-Channel "Chunnel" bringing the prospect of being inundated by Frenchmen, and the disdain expressed by segments of French society toward the Anglo-Saxon culture, just two indicators of how far the Continent is from a common identification with a European nation. The growing strength of an anti-European orientation known as "Euroskepticism" in a number of member states suggests the difficulty facing the pan-European idealists. [23]

The question is whether the creation of the institutions of a European federal state will, in and of itself, generate the cultural and social basis of that state—a European nation. The record of the attempt to create states in Africa and Asia in the post-World War II era that were not congruent with a nation is not encouraging.

THE ADMINISTRATIVE STATE

The foregoing material dealing with the structure of accountability in advanced industrial democracies is based upon a key assumption: that policy is made in these politically accountable structures of government while the administrative parts of the government—the higher civil service—are confined to the implementation of these policy decisions. The politically accountable parts of the government, i.e., parliaments and presidents or prime ministers, are supposed to reflect a set of values that are desirable for the policy making process: responsiveness to public needs and demands, adaptability to changing circumstances, and creativity in producing innovative policy solutions.

Meanwhile, the civil service, theoretically confined to the implementation of these policies, is designed to reflect a different set of values. The civil service comprises what is known as the governmental bureaucracy. Bureaucracy is actually the form that all large organizations tend to take for the purpose of rational efficiency in carrying out its functions. Rational efficiency here means the attainment of goals with a minimum expenditure of resources (such as capital, time, energy, etc.). Thus, large corporations, the military, and large universities are also bureaucracies.

The association of the concept of bureaucracy with rational efficiency is counterintuitive to a widespread populist image of bureaucrats as clerks needlessly complicating the just and reasonable solutions to problems with needless forms and regulations, popularly know as "red tape." This disparagement of bureaucrats appeals to those segments of the population that fear and resent the complex interdependence of the postmodern world and yearn for simpler solutions of a largely apocryphal past.

The frustration with bureaucracies stems from the fact that in modern societies the assumed separation of the functions of politics and administration that is at the heart of classic organization theory does not conform to reality. Increasingly, in advanced or postmodern societies there has been a devolution of the policy making function from the political to the administrative sector, a function for which bureaucracies were not designed.

The properties that provide rational efficiency in the implementation of policies were spelled out by the early twentieth century German sociologist Max Weber, who offered a model or "ideal type" of organization as the essence of organizational modernity.[24] Weber's ideal type consists of the following characteristics:

1. A comprehensive set of impersonal rules. (The response to each eventuality is spelled out regardless of who occupies that role.)

2. A hierarchical structure—a chain of command with each lower office under the supervision and control of a higher one.

3. Allocation of tasks on the basis of specialization and division of labor.

4. Members subject to authority only with respect to their official roles.

5. Selection of those who occupy offices on the basis of the possession of credentials or demonstrated competence.

6. Tenured office holders providing insulation from public pressure.

7. Compensation of officials by fixed salary. (This allows bureaucrats to implement policies on the basis of expertise rather than financial gain).

These characteristics relate to the ideal purpose of the bureaucratic organizational form. Hierarchy permits the coordination of numerous office holders with disparate specialties in common purpose such that their activities and skills complement each other in a coherent whole. Specialization provides the organization with access to a greater body of knowledge and skills than could be possessed by a single individual allowing it to cope with the technological imperatives of the postmodern world. The attributes of impersonalization and routinization provide predictability. Tenure of office allows office holders to act in accordance with their specialized expertise rather than being hostage to the current fluctuations and passions in public opinion. It is notable that the values embodied by the classic model of bureaucracy to promote efficient policy implementation are diametrically opposite from those values desired for those who are charged with the function of policy making. The Weberian ideal type of bureaucracy promotes routinization, impersonalization, and insulation from public opinion. For political leaders one desires adaptability, creativity, and responsiveness to public opinion.

Moreover, the attributes in the Weberian model are internally inconsistent. The specialization of function and impersonal rules effectively isolate each office and strata from one another. This undercuts the coordinating function of hierarchy. One cannot be responsible for office holders whose tasks one does not understand.

The basic problem, however, with the administrative sector in advanced democracies is the aforementioned role of the civil service in the policy making process. The presumed clear separation of politics—setting goals and values and determining who gets how much of what—and administration—the application and implementation of policy does not conform to reality because of the technological imperatives of policy making in the postmodern world. Policy making requires specialized knowledge generally not possessed by the people who occupy politically accountable roles such as members of parliaments or governing cabinets or presidencies. For example, policies to protect air quality involve decisions as to how much of what gases can be safely emitted into the atmosphere, decisions that require knowledge of chemistry not possessed by these politically accountable officials who typically are trained in law, business, or other nonscientific fields. Hence, modern governments set up specialized agencies, such as America's Environmental Protection Agency, to make the appropriate rules that have the force of law. It is usually in the public bureaucracy, after all, that one finds the technical expertise needed for policy making in the modern world. Government by such technically trained people is sometimes referred to as *technocracy* and the officials are called *technocrats.* Laws passed by parliaments, therefore, are typically vague and general enough to allow for a great deal of bureaucratic discretion as to how to interpret them.

In fact, the higher civil service in Western democracies generally plays a major role in policy making. There normally are four distinct levels in the civil service in the European democracies; one does not work his or her way up from a lower to higher strata in the organization. Policy making occurs at the highest level. Positions in the higher civil service in these countries carries a great deal more prestige than do civil service positions at any level in the United States, and they attract the very best graduates of the most prestigious institutions. In France, for example, members of the political and administrative elites overwhelmingly are "enarchs," graduates of the prestigious and highly selective ENA (*Ecole Nationale d'Admininstration* or National School of Administration). Graduates of this prestigious postgraduate school overwhelmingly have parents who were "enarchs," making this key policy making elite a "semi-closed caste." The political role of the higher civil service has been particularly strong in countries such as France with a history of weak or unstable political institutions.[25] Members of Britain's higher civil service come from a public school such as Eton or Harrow and then from "Oxbridge." (See the discussion of British education in Chapter Two.)

The political role of the civil service or administrative sector in modern democracies, referred to by the term "the administrative state," means that policy making in these systems will be characterized by the lack of imagination, creativity, responsiveness to public needs and demands, and adaptability that are inherent in the bureaucratic model. The administrative state detracts from the ability of modern democracies to protect the public interests and resolve unfolding and complex issues in the fast moving postmodern world.

CONCLUSIONS: THE STATE MATTERS

In the transformation of the field discussed in Chapter One from an enterprise focused on descriptive summaries of legally or constitutionally designated structures (meaning the state) to one that is focused on the scientifically valid explanation of political behavior, it became fashionable to focus on the contextual factors—culture, social cleavages, historical background, demographics—in which these structures operated. Ignoring these legalistic and constitutionally designated structures of government became almost a sign of being at the cutting edge of the field. It became popular to consider the state as an arena in which social forces competed to influence policy. Policy or outputs were regarded in this view as balancing the pressures of demands and supports from the societal context.[26] It was widely assumed that these constitutionally designated structures were the result of the contextual factors in which they operated. Doubt was cast on the ability of the state to act independently of its context. One of the leading scholars in the comparative field, Ronald Inglehart, has over a period of three decades published a large body of research devoted to the importance of culture and cultural change as the causal foundation of political outcomes.[27]

Other scholars, however, have emerged to argue that this neglect of the independent power of the state to act and produce policy is as much a distortion of reality as the earlier neglect of contextual factors.[28] Thus, it may be possible for a regime or political format put into place by the decisions of a set of political leaders, as the democracies installed by the Allies in the nations of the defeated Axis powers at the close of World War II, to shape the context into one that is more supported of that regime type.[29] Eric Nordlinger's thesis, cited above, that modern democratic states act with a good deal more autonomy from their publics than democratic theory would suggest reinforces the idea that modern governments are not simply the product of socioeconomic factors.[30] In this view, the modern state can shape the cultural and social context as much as the context can shape the state.

ENDNOTES

[1]Roy Macridis, "Comparative Analysis: Method and Concepts," in Roy Macridis and Bernard Brown, eds., *Comparative Politics: Notes and Readings,* 7th ed. (Pacific Grove, CA: Brooks Cole, 1990), pp. 6ff.

[2]Theda Skocpol, "Bringing the State Back In," *Items,* Vol 36, Nos. 1 & 2 (June, 1982); James Caporaso, ed., *The Elusive State* (Newbury Park, CA: Sage Publications, 1989).

[3]Juan Linz, "The Perils of Presidentialism," *Journal of Democracy,* Vol. 1 (Winter 1990), pp. 51–69.

[4]Richard Rose, "Presidents and Prime Ministers," *Society,* Vol. 25, No. 3 (March-April, 1988), pp. 61–67.

[5]*Ibid.,* p. 62.

[6]Richard Neustadt, *Presidential Power: The Politics of Leadership* (New York: John Wiley and Sons, 1976).

[7]Walter Lippman, *Public Opinion* (New York: The Macmillan Company, 1922 and Penguin Books, 1956) and Lippman, *The Phantom Public* (New York: Harcourt Brace, 1956).

[8]Juan Linz, "The Perils of Presidentialism," pp. 51–69; Juan Linz, "Presidential or Parliamentary Democracy: Does it Make a Difference," in Juan Linz and Arturo Valenzuela, eds., *The Failure of Presidential Democracy: Comparing Perspectives* (Baltimore: Johns Hopkins University Press, 1994), pp. 3–87.

[9]Donald Horowitz, "Comparing Democratic Systems," *Journal of Democracy,* Vol. 1, No. 4 (Fall, 1990).

[10]These developments, especially with respect to the impact of the Enclosure Movements in England, are discussed in Barrington Moore Jr.'s classic, *The Social Origins of Dictatorship and Democracy* (Boston: The Beacon Press, 1966), p. 28.

[11]L.S. Amery, *Thoughts on the Constitution,* 2nd ed. (London: Oxford University Press, 1964), pp. 11–12.

[12]This centralizing tendency on the Continent is compared to the decentralizing tendencies in the Anglo-American world in Samuel Huntington, *Political Order in Changing Societies* (New Haven, CT: Yale University Press, 1968), pp. 95–102.

[13]Karl Bracher, "Problems of Parliamentary Democracy in Europe," *Daedalus* (Winter, 1964), pp. 179–198.

[14]E.g., Bernard Crick, *The Reform of Parliament* (New York: Doubleday Anchor, 1965).

[15]Eric Nordlinger, *On the Autonomy of the Modern Democratic State* (Cambridge, MA: Harvard University Press, 1981).

[16]Benjamin Cardozo, *The Nature of the Judicial Process* (New Haven, CT: Yale University Press, 1921). Cardozo's book is a classic exposition of the spirit of the common law.

[17]Ibid., p. 33.

[18]Winston Churchill, *The Birth of Britain; Volume 1 of A History of the English Speaking Peoples* (New York: Dodd Mead, 1956), p. 216.

[19]K. C. Wheare, *Federal Government* (New York: Oxford University Press Galaxy Editions, 1964); William Riker, *Federalism: Origin, Operation and Significance* (Boston: Little Brown, 1964), p. 6.

[20]The concept of congruent federalism is discussed and applied to Australia and Canada in Lawrence Mayer, "Federalism and Party Behavior in Australia and Canada," *Western Political Quarterly* Vol. XXIII, No. 4 (December, 1970), pp. 795–807.

[21]Charles McIlwain, The Growth of Political Thought in the West (New York: The Macmillan Co., 1932), p. 286.

[22]Immanuel Wallersteein, *The Modern World System: Capitalist Agriculture and the Origins of the European World Economy in the Sixteenth Century* (New York: Academic Press, 1974).

[23]The arguments for uniting Europe are collected in John Van Oudenaren, *Uniting Europe: An Introduction to the European Union* (Boulder, CO and New York: Rowan and Littlefield Publishers, 2005). The critical case is summed up in Noel Malcolm, "The Case Against Europe," in Ronald Tiersky, ed., *Euroskepticism: A Reader* (Boulder, CO and New York: Rowan and Littlefield, 2001), pp. 177–190.

[24]Weber's essential writings on this subject, originally published in the early twentieth century under the title *Wirtschaff* and *Gesellschaff,* may be found in *From Max Weber: Essays in Sociology,* edited and translated by H. H. Gerth and C. Wright Mills, (New York: Oxford University Press Galaxy Books, 1958), pp. 196–255.

[25]See Michel Crozier, *The Bureaucratic Phenomenon* (Chicago: University of Chicago Press, 1964) esp. pp. 145ff. for a classic treatise on the impact of this bureaucratization of the policy process especially as manifested in France but applicable to other advanced democracies.

[26]This was the essence of systems theory popularized by David Easton, *The Political System* (New York: Knopf, 1951); Easton, *A Systems Analysis of Political Life* (New York: Wiley, 1968).

[27]The culmination of this corpus of research is Ronald Inglehart and Christian Welzel, *Modernization, Cultural Change and Democracy* (New York: Cambridge University Press, 2005). See note 16, Chapter Two for additional titles in this research tradition.

[28]Skocpol,"Bringing the State Back In." She discusses instances of autonomous state actions.

[29]Edward Friedman, *The Politics of Democratization: Generalizing From the East Asian Experience* (Boulder, CO: Westview Press, 1994) is one of the most notable and forceful rejections of the thesis that for democracy to be successful, certain cultural "requisites" must be in place. The example of Japan is Friedman's main case in point.

[30]Nordlinger, On the Autonomy of the Modern Democratic State.

4

Political Parties and
Party Systems

The discussion in Chapter Three of the structure of accountability in Western democracies was necessarily incomplete because the operation of the constitutionally designated structures of any modern democratic state is affected by the attributes of its political party system. The political parties and party systems of these modern democracies play critical functions that allow these states to govern and to respond to the needs and demands of their societies. Indeed, despite major differences in regime format among Western democracies, universal patterns seem to exist in this category of political systems with regard to the functions more or less performed by their party systems. These patterns, plus the fact that many of the attributes of parties, such as voting support and behavior, are rigorously quantifiable and thus amenable to rigorous empirical research, have produced a large body of research in the area of political parties.

Political parties in democracies are essentially different from the structures that are called "parties" in authoritarian systems. In the latter, parties exist alongside the structures of the state to mobilize the population and carry out policies to serve the purposes of the leadership of that state. In the former, parties are structures formed to promote principles, protect the interests of certain segments of the population, and consolidate and transmit the demands of those segments to the decision making authorities by nominating and promoting candidates for office. In this regard, parties in democratic systems perform functions that overlap those of interest groups (groups formed to promote the interests of certain segments of society by bargaining with and seeking to influence government and other groups). Interest groups do not, however, nominate candidates for political office, although they may support or oppose those selected by parties. While parties may perform some of the functions also performed by interest groups, they generally do so at a higher level of generality. Thus, parties may head a coalition of and derive support from a number of interest groups. While an interest group may, for example, promote the interest of farm laborers, a center-left party must balance the claims of that group against the interests of, say, industrial labor or the environmental movement. Therefore, where there is a well-developed set of interest groups promoting the specific demands of their segment of society or the economy, parties will tend to consolidate demands and policy proposals at a higher level of generality; in systems where the interest groups system is relatively weak, parties represent the more specific demands of specific groups. Thus France, which until recently had a weak level of associational life, had a party system with a number of smaller parties with specific clienteles and agendas.

PARTY SYSTEMS

Political parties function within the context of a party system. A party system is defined by the number of parties operating in the political arena of a particular nation state, their relative strength, and the patterns of interaction among them. Party systems may therefore be classified according to those foregoing characteristics. The different types of party systems are a product of their nations' particular history, culture, and electoral system. The electoral system is the set of rules by which votes are translated into the allocation of legislative seats or political offices among parties and their candidates for office. The different types or categories of party systems determine the effectiveness with which they perform the functions that constitute a vital contribution to the performance of a modern democracy.[1] While the explanatory power of functional analysis has been brought into serious question, the stipulation of the functions a set of institutions is expected to perform constitutes a useful descriptive device in the quest for cross-national patterns.[2]

THE FUNCTIONS OF PARTY SYSTEMS

Political party systems represent the array of ethnic, religious, socioeconomic, and cultural groups in a society and the interests that emanate from them. The term *represent* entails the identification of demands, their consolidation, and their transmission from society to the state decision making processes. Consolidation here means grouping a number of specific demands under a broader label. A. N. Holcombe says that parties sublimate private interest by finding principles that merge them with a general interest.[3]

To the extent that demands are consolidated, purity or accuracy in the transmission function is necessarily compromised. However, this consolidation (or, in Gabriel Almond's term, aggregation) of demands permits party systems to present to the voting public manageable choices with regard to alternatives of public policies. These choices should also be meaningful, that is, based upon real differences. In this consolidation function, party systems also perform the functions of educating the voting public and mobilizing or recruiting that public into the political process. In educating the public by presenting policy proposals and critiquing the proposals of competing parties, parties structure the public debate over issues.

Parties are not only expected to present clear and meaningful choices of policies, but also of political leaders to create and implement those policies. Thus, parties perform the function of selecting and training candidates for political leadership. As with all of these functions, actual party systems perform them to a greater or lesser degree of effectiveness. Thus, the political leaders of the major parliamentary democracies of Europe emerge from long careers as members of their parliaments through numerous posts at lower level and ultimately highest level cabinet positions. When they finally emerge as party leaders in their parliaments, they are experienced in the exercise of political power in the system, a skill generally acquired and honed through experience in the arena. In the United States, by contrast, candidates for political office are chosen in primary elections independently of the policy making political arena. Combined with the American penchant for preferring political leaders from outside the political process (post-war American presidents have included a peanut farmer, a movie actor, a career military officer, and an oil company executive), that country's political leadership may emerge without relevant experience in the mobilization and exercise of the kind of power needed to govern.[4]

By coordinating and in some cases controlling the political behavior of their members, parties may provide a majority in the legislature able to govern, as well as a viable opposition to keep the system competitive. In countries with weak party systems unable to exercise such control, each legislator or parliamentarian is elected on the basis of his/her individual appeal and majorities shift from issue to issue. In such a scenario, governments are not able to enact a coherent legislative program over time.

TYPES OF POLITICAL PARTIES

Scholars have identified different types of parties, a typology based upon the goals or *raison d'être* of the parties. Here we are talking about individual parties rather than party systems. ("Systems" refers to the parties in a nation state arena with respect to the number of parties, their relative strength and the pattern of interaction among them.)

Among individual parties, there are parties of principle. The purpose of these parties to their leadership is the articulation and promotion of a set of principles or values, usually through the promotion of policies that advance them. When the principles are maintained impervious to any unfolding evidence to the contrary, that set of principles becomes an ideology. Obviously, by definition ideological parties do not adapt to unfolding realities and events since we have defined ideology as a closed system of thought, one that is insensitive to unfolding events and new information. Ideological parties tend to perpetuate old conflicts the way that parties in France fought the pro-and-anticlerical issues through the Dreyfus Affair and through the Fourth Republic, long after the Revolution that generated the issue had passed. Marxist parties and some clerical-based parties exemplify this type of party. Some of the policy choices made by Marxist parties may have a detrimental impact on the short-term well-being of the industrial working class in whose interests these parties are ostensibly acting in order to mobilize the workers' revolutionary class consciousness. Here the proletarian revolution becomes an end in itself rather than one means of improving the lives of the working class.

Other parties may promote a policy or legislative agenda to promote the material well being of the strata of the population they represent without much reference to principle. Not all parties whose electoral base is the industrial working class are Marxist or even socialist, for example. The leadership of a number of parties labeled either labor or social democratic with a trade union base is primarily concerned with policies to protect the economic well-being of trade union labor—policies such as higher minimum wages, protecting worker safety, or protecting the right to strike. The programmatic goals of such parties are tactical and, as such, they adjust to the contingent situation. Such parties lack the rigidity of parties of principle. The British Labour Party has, by and large, exemplified this type of party except for a period from the late 1970s to mid 1980s when control of the party was seized by a Fabian Socialist and pacifist faction, a faction that had up until then always been a backbench minority within the party. The moderate and generally mainstream faction of the party had an almost symbiotic relationship with the trade union movement as represented through the Trade Union Congress. The Congress was guaranteed a percentage of seats and votes at the party conferences, and Labour Party dues paying membership automatically accompanied trade union membership unless the trade unionist formally requested otherwise. The party therefore generally pursued the policy agenda of the T.U.C. without much regard for principle or consistency. This type of party pursuing the policy agenda of the industrial working class, rather than a Marxist overthrow of the capitalist order, is also manifested in the Swedish Social Democratic Party, the Norwegian Labor Party, and the Social Democratic Party of Germany (since its 1959 Bad Godesburg Convention).

A third type of party is not wedded to either a clear set of principles or a policy agenda. Rather these parties seek to maximize their electoral support and political power as ends in themselves rather than the pursuit of any policy agenda or principled objectives. Political machines that governed many American cities in the first half of the twentieth century epitomized this type of party. Decisions about the allocation of public values—the awarding of government contracts, the hiring of personnel, etc.—were done to obtain or solidify political support without consideration of the public good entering into these decisions. The major American parties are characterized by the absence of any coherent policy agendas let alone any set of principles coherent enough to be called an ideology. Some scholars have argued that political parties throughout the Western world have been moving in the direction of seeking the broadest, largest, and most diverse electoral base at the expense of any clear or coherent set of principles or policy agenda, toward what one oft-cited article calls "catch-all parties."[5]

Such scholars relate this trend to "the end of ideology" thesis, the idea that the problems addressed by the great ideologies that have shaped Western political discourse for most of the modern era have essentially been resolved.[6] Thus, Francis Fukuyama pronounced that we have reached "the end point of man's ideological evolution and the universalization of liberal democracy as the final form of human government."[7] Clearly, the ideologies that had defined the major political parties of the first half of the twentieth century have been rendered atavistic by the processes of modernization. The declining political relevance of religiosity has already been discussed. The Marxist claim that an oppressed proletariat will mobilize to overthrow capitalism is impossible to reconcile with unionized labor living middle- to upper-middle class lifestyles. The declining relevance of the ideologies that defined the political parties of the first half of the twentieth century results in a lack of correspondence between the cleavages of the traditional party system and the cleavages that are emerging in today's postindustrial world. New parties are therefore emerging to reflect these new issues, principles, and cleavages, where the institutional structure of the political system does not impede the emergence of new parties, a phenomenon discussed below. Ideologies are not disappearing so much as new sets of principles are emerging to replace the declining relevance of the classic ideologies or principles that shaped political discourse in the modern world through the end of World War II. The traditional cleavage structure that Lipset and Rokkan found "frozen" in the post-World War II decades has thawed.[8]

Hence, the phenomenon of cultural change that was discussed in Chapter Two, the emerging importance of postmaterialist values replacing the traditional class-based and religious-based values, is significant because, among other things, the cleavages that defined the traditional or existing party systems in Western democracies are no longer congruent to the emerging social cleavages of the postmaterialist era. Therefore, existing parties have often had to redefine themselves to compete with emerging new parties that better reflect the emerging postmaterialist values. The difficulty faced by traditional parties in redefining themselves is manifested in another trend, partisan dealignment among the voters. Research showed that in the earlier post-World War II era most voters psychologically identified with a particular party.[9] However, it became clear by the late 1970s, the percentage of voters developing those long-term partisan attachments was down sharply.[10] Russell Dalton offers several factors in explaining this dealignment, such as the failure of parties to adequately deal with contemporary issues.[11] This book suggests an additional and related factor, the lack of congruence between the traditional party-system cleavages that Lipset and Rokkan found "frozen" and the new social cleavages of a postmaterialist or postmodern age.

These new ideologies are often being represented by the emerging new parties. The traditional or mainstream parties have therefore become parties of expediency in which the acquisition of power for its own sake or for the enrichment of its politicians trumps the defense of principles or the pursuit of a policy agenda. Epitomizing parties of expediency were the French Gaullist Parties known under various names from the Fourth Republic to recently in the Fifth Republic (Rally for the French People [RPF], Union for the New Republic [UNR], or Rally for the Republic [RPR]). The defining essence of these parties was following and supporting General De Gaulle who, while generally on the right, was hardly a model of ideological consistency (for instance, unpredictably betraying the nationalists and the military who were fighting a war to keep French West Africa within the decaying French empire). Finally, in 2002, the former Gaullist Party was renamed the Union for a Presidential Majority, which was in turn renamed the Union for a Popular Movement (UMP), the purpose of which was to unite the moderate right to capture the presidency.

Perhaps the classic example of this putative trend toward catch-all party status is the "embourgeoisement" of the formerly Marxist Social Democratic Party of Germany. Formed in the nineteenth century as the original policy of Marxism, the party maintained all the symbols of a Marxist party through the end of World War II, waving the red flag and singing about "the Workers' International," a stance which netted them the loyal support of, perhaps, one-third of the electorate who were either committed Marxists or sympathizers from the industrial working class. In an emerging two-and-a-half party system discussed below, this failure to attract middle-class votes kept the party in permanent opposition status. Finally, at the party's Annual Conference in 1959, a group of party rebels led by the maverick Willy Brandt captured control of the party and issued a new Basic Programme (platform) designed to woo that middle class. This document praised the socially responsible use of private property and the profit motive, positions that signaled the complete abandonment of Marxism and the transformation of Marx's original party into a bourgeois organization. A year later, the party entered a "grand coalition" with the Christian Democrats, and two years after that the country had its first Social Democratic chancellor.

German Social Democracy had a long history of internal struggle between those who sought ideological purity and those who sought legitimacy to govern the country. Programs designed to ameliorate the social or living conditions of the working class were excoriated by Marx and his associates as weakening the revolutionary consciousness or zeal of the workers.[12] Finding itself in power during the crisis of World War I, the party discovered nationalism trumping its commitment to the Workers' International; hence, its slogan, "to this system, no man and no penny" became modified into the slogan "in the hour of need we will not leave the Fatherland in the lurch."[13]

These expediential or catch-all parties are weak in performing the functions of structuring debate so as to provide manageable and meaningful alternatives of public policy to the voting public. They may be quite strong, however, in providing a majority able to govern. How stable and effective that majority is over time will depend on the coherence of the party and the discipline it exercises over its members.

The emergence of new parties to reflect the new ideologies alluded to above varies from system to system depending on the "opportunity structure," the extent to which institutions such as the electoral system impedes the successful establishment of new parties, a question discussed below. As implied in the discussion of cultural change in Chapter Two, a major transformation in the culture of Western countries is not only the emergence of postmaterialism as demonstrated by Inglehart and others—a concept with somewhat imprecise content—but the emergence of a politics of identity. This identity may be manifested in a concept of a nationhood or "folk" at the national level or in the preservation and autonomy or independence of a subculture. New parties have been emerging to represent this politics of identity.

Because these parties focus on identity with a folk or nation and primarily appeal to a less-educated segment of the population, they become a manifestation of the venerable concept of populism, as explained in Chapter Two. Parties such as France's National Front, Austria's Freedom Party, and Canada's Reform Party (before it merged with the remnants of the Conservatives) exemplify populist right parties asserting national identity at the level of chauvinistic patriotism for the nation state as a whole. Parties such as Italy's Northern League, *Vlaams Bloc* in Belgium (recently renamed *Vlaams Belang* (Flemish Interest)as the old party was banned as being neofascist), The Basque Nationalist and Republican Left of Catalonia in Spain, and Canada's *Bloc Québécois* exemplify parties of subcultural defense. Both the patriotic nationalist parties and the parties of subcultural defense focus on a sense of identity with a community or nation to the point of sharply distinguishing those who are or could possibly become part of that community and those who necessarily and permanently are outsiders, who are not nor could ever be one of the folk. The less-educated strata to whom such parties appeal feel alienated from a set of outgroups, a feeling we call "the bigotry factor."

In Europe, the outgroup traditionally consisted of the usual suspects: people of color, Jews, Gypsies, and homosexuals. In the last decade or so, the attention of the bigotry factor has focused on the growing and unassimilated Muslim Arab population that now numbers over ten percent of the French population. A growing Muslim population in the Netherlands produced the perpetrators of two high-profile assassinations on the streets of that heretofore exceptionally tolerant country: that of charismatic and gay politician Pim Fortuyn and popular filmmaker Theo van Gogh. Fortuyn's assassination was prompted by the popularity of his party list that called for substantial restrictions on Muslim immigration. When Van Gogh was killed for his filmed critique of Muslim treatment of their women, conservative politician Geert Wilders picked up Fortuyn's standard with the Geert Wilders list, a party whose sole *raison d'être* was to shut down Muslim immigration. On his one issue, Wilders' list won 28 seats, about a fifth of the Dutch Second Chamber. The perceived threat to European culture posed by the Muslim subculture, a sub-culture that beyond refusing assimilation especially among its younger members has its leaders claim that Europe will in this half century become an Islamic repub-lic. This has produced a reactionary populist movement directed at preserving the Western and Christian character of Europe. This movement for cultural defense has produced a category of populist parties where the opportunity structure per-mits the emergence of new parties.

The seriousness of the perceived Muslim threat was brought to the forefront in November 2005, with the outbreak of riots and widespread arson in the virtually autonomous Muslim enclaves surrounding major cities (into which European au-thorities almost dare not enter), riots that quickly spread to over 200 French cities and towns and even into Germany and Belgium. These riots, which lasted around two weeks, were not perpetrated by French youths over high unemployment. Rather, they were perpetrated by Muslim youths driven by a widespread hatred of the West and its values. President Jacques Chirac and foreign minister Dominique de Villepin of France initially tried to accommodate the supposed grievances of the rioters while the minister of the interior, Nicolas Sarkozy, and the populist right National Front took the lead in articulating the anger and frustration of the general population toward the rioters.

TYPES OF PARTY SYSTEMS

In addition to a literature on the attributes of individual parties, there is a literature on party systems referring to the number of parties, their relative size, and the pat-tern of interaction among them. At the simplest level, this literature relied on the number of parties in a system to characterize that system. The simplest classifica-tion in this regard is to divide democratic party systems into a two-party system and a multiparty system (meaning more than two). The significance of this differ-ence is that a two party system will automatically provide a majority under the con-trol of one party as the outcome of any general election. It was noted in the previous chapter that when a single party controls a majority of seats in a legisla-tive chamber, a parliamentary government will experience much less cabinet in-stability than if the government is composed of a coalition of several parties. Thus, Leslie Lipson could label the United Kingdom as the paragon of the two-party sys-tem supporting a stable and effective regime despite the fact that, as of 1994, nine distinct parties had some representation in the British House of Commons.[14] The same number of parties won seats in the May, 2005, election, an election in which the two "major" parties, the Conservatives and Labour, won just 67.5 percent of the vote. However, due to the major party bias of the electoral system, discussed below, the two major parties controlled just under 80 percent of the seats in the House of Commons. The results of the 2005 British general election are shown in Table 4–1.

Canada's party system is even more difficult to classify. Only two parties have come close to heading a government in the postwar era; yet, normally at least five parties get significant representation (ten or more seats) in the Canadian House of Commons and one of the two parties that have at one time governed was reduced to two seats in the 1993 election, an election in which the second strongest party and hence "the loyal opposition" had secession from the Canadian federation as its goal.[15] In the following election in 1997, the Reform Party, a party of the populist right, became the second strongest party and hence the loyal opposition, a result that further illustrates the trend away from the formerly dominant parties of interest to parties of identity. Subsequently, the Reform Party, seeking to broaden its support, became an Alliance with the remnants of the Progressive Conservatives, and by the 2004 election these two parties ran as the Conservative Party of Canada. This union meant that the former populist right orientation of the Reform Party has now been substantially modified and the new mainstream appeal has resulted in

TABLE 4–1   Results of The May 2005 British General Elections

	% of Vote	Seats
Labour	35.2	356
Conservative	32.3	197
Liberal Democrat	22.0	62
United Kingdom Independence	2.3	0
Scottish National	1.5	6
Green Party	1.0	0
Democratic Unionist	0.9	9
British National Party (far right)	0.7	0
Plaid Cymru (Welsh)	0.6	3
Sinn Fein (Irish Republican)	0.6	5
Scottish Socialist	0.1	1
Kiddermaster Hospital Concern	0.2	0
Non Partisan	0.1	1
Vacant		1

steady growth of support for the Canadian conservatives from the 1993 debacle of two seats. The Alliance received 66 seats in 2000 and the new Conservative Party won 99 seats in 2004. In that election, four parties still received significant levels of support but that support was regionally distributed. The results of the 2004 elections are shown in Table 4–2. Meanwhile, the Liberal Party, with only 43.8 percent of the seats, was relying on support from the New Democrats, a curious amalgam of small farmer populism with strength in just two provinces on the Canadian prairie, as a junior coalition partner.[16] The New Democrats, however, withdrew their support of the government beset with corruption scandals in late 2005. Canada's first successful vote of no-confidence (earlier governments had been brought down when a legislative failure was interpreted as an expression of no-confidence) brought down Liberal Prime Minister Paul Martin's government and enabled Conservative leader Stephan Harper to form a Conservative-led minority government in early 2006, the first Conservative government since that party's electoral collapse in the 1993 elections.

In Sweden, one party, the Social Democrats, steadily received either a majority or close to a majority of seats in the *Riksdag* (their lower house) while four parties—the Moderate Party, the Center Party, the Christian Democrats, and the Liberals—split the opposition. Two additional parties representing the emerging postmaterialist values (see the discussion of Inglehart's work on value change in Chapter Two) attained seats in the *Riksdag* as of 1994, further splintering the opposition.

In the Federal Republic of Germany, two major parties dominated the electoral arena from around 1960 to the late 1980s controlling around 90 percent of the votes and seats in the Bundestag with a small classical liberal party, the Free Democrats, often acting as a balance of power with about ten percent of the seats; hence, the system was characterized as an emerging two-party system.[17] However, as discussed earlier, the major parties have been losing vote share to emerging parties of identity or postmaterialist values. The pragmatic wing of a Green Party

TABLE 4–2   Results of the 2004 and 2006 Canadian Elections

	Seats		% of Vote	
	2004	*2006*	*2004*	*2006*
Liberal	135	103	36.7	30.22
Conservative	99	124	29.6	36.25
Bloc Québécois	54	51	12.4	10.48
New Democratic	19	29	15.7	17.49
Unaffiliated	1	1		.52
Others	0	0	5.6	5.05
	308	308		

(called "*realos*") finally subdued its anticapitalist West factions (called "*fundis*"— fundamentalists) and became an electoral force in the 1990s, securing Bundestag representation along with a Communist party and a populist right party, the Republicans. The formerly dominant Christian Democrats and Social Democrats hung between 75 and 78 percent through the 1990s. By the 2005 election, the Social Democrats and Christian Democrats now could muster slightly more than 70 percent between them. As Table 4–3 shows, neither of the two major parties, even with their traditional junior coalition partners, can provide a majority able to govern. A new Left Party comprised of "former" Communists and the disaffected left fringe of the SPD received 54 seats; yet, both of the major parties have ruled out an alliance with them. Moreover, both major parties insist that their leader head any "grand coalition": hence, the Bundestag appeared deadlocked until a tentative grand coalition of the two main parties that normally oppose one another was slapped together in October, 2005. Meanwhile, the National Democratic Party, a nearly moribund party that some identified as neo-Nazi, was resurrected in the September, 2004 land election in Saxony to obtain 9.2 percent of the vote, further illustrating inroads on the vote share of the major parties. The Federal Republic, for most of the postwar era the model of stability and effective government, seems now immobilized. Such failure to produce a majority able to govern may be an increasingly common occurrence as the formerly dominant parties of interest lose vote share across the world of advanced democracies.

Austria is another European party system in which the once dominant two major parties have been losing vote share to an emerging party of identity .The major parties—the Austrian Peoples' Party (ÖVP) and the Social Democratic Party (SPÖ)—received just under 90 percent of the vote in 1962 and 157 of 165 seats in the lower house. In 1974, the two major parties had 173 of 183 seats. However, the Austrian Freedom Party (FPÖ), a party of the populist right headed by the charismatic Jörg Haider—a man with ties to a Nazi past—emerged riding a rising wave of chauvinistic nationalism manifested in opposition to a growing unassimilated

TABLE 4–3   Number and Percentages of Seats to German Bundestag 2005 Election

	Seats	% of Vote
Christian Democrats (CDU/CSU)*	226	37
Social Democrats (SPD)	222	36
Free Democrats (FDP)	61	10
Left Party	54	9
Greens	51	8

Source: Adopted from BBC News, Sept. 22, 2005
*The CDU's Bavarian Branch is called the Christian Social Union and maintains a semiautonomous status.

immigrant population while the vote share of the former major parties had declined by the mid nineties to around two-thirds of the vote. This is, of course, a manifestation of the growing importance of identity politics discussed in Chapter Two. The FPÖ received a 22 percent vote share in 1995 and peaked at 27 percent in 1999, making them the second strongest Austrian party, surpassing the SPÖ. However, internal conflicts within the FPÖ and a coopting of part of its antiimmigrant stance by the ÖVP led to the FPÖ dropping to 10 percent in the 2002 election to the *Nationalrat* (Austria's lower house). Nevertheless, the FPÖ is still part of the governing coalition. The recent Austrian election results may be found in Table 4–4.

Given that the Greens will only ally themselves with the Socialists, that the Freedom Party will only ally itself with the Peoples' Party, and that the Liberals have faded into insignificance, the Austrian system has become an arena with two political forces and will function essentially as a two-party system.

Italy functioned for most of its postwar history as a multiparty system with a dominant party. The Christian Democrats (DC), strongly supported from the pulpit by the Church, regularly won about one-third of the votes and seats while the second strongest party was the Communists—an unacceptable alternative to most Italians for governing the country. Hence, the DC led 53 of the 55 governments from the founding of the postwar Italian republic to 1993. Despite the cabinet instability, the personnel and policy orientations of Italian governments remained quite constant throughout this period, allowing a large measure of continuity in the policies and personnel during this period.

The DC appeared to be an exception to the declining electoral fortunes of explicitly church-based parties, a decline that is a product of the secularization of Western Europe.[18] Compared to the United States, a small and declining fragment of the European population reports regular church attendance or belief in core Christian doctrine. Europeans are less inclined over time to have their religion determine their vote.

The Catholic Party in the Netherlands, for example, used to be one of the leading parties in the lower house of their legislature (*Tweede Kamer*), drawing over 30 percent of the vote through the mid 1960s and forming or playing a leading role in

TABLE 4–4   Austrian Elections to the Nationalrat (Pct. of votes)

	% of Votes		
	2002	*1999*	*1995*
ÖVP	42.3	26.9	28.3
SPÖ	36.5	33.4	38.3
FPÖ	10.0	27.0	22.0
Greens	9.4	7.4	4.6
Liberal	1.0	3.6	

most Dutch governments.[19] However, by the early 1970s it was drawing less than 20 percent of the vote. By the end of that decade it had merged with the two Protestant parties—the Christian Historical Union (Calvinist) and Anti-Revolutionary Party (Dutch Reformed Church)—to form the Christian Democratic Appeal (CDA). The CDA, first in coalition with the Liberals and then with Labor, had returned to the government from the late '70s to 1994 when both Labor and the CDA suffered major losses of vote share and found themselves back in the political wilderness. While the Catholics were dominant in the Netherlands in the 1960s, they also provided an element of continuity despite a highly fragmented party system. Twenty-six parties offered candidate lists in the 1994 election and twelve of them actually won seats. In the 2002 election, ten parties won seats. With this many parties, constructing a coalition that has at least the passive support of a majority of the *Tweede Kamer* is a difficult task that may take months. While a "caretaker government" (usually the previous cabinet) conducts essential business, obviously the country is not going to come up with bold and creative policies during this period of political stalemate.

The Italian DC kept its vote share as long as it did, less because of Catholics voting their faith, but rather because the DC was perceived as the bulwark keeping the Communists out of power. While the Italian Communists claimed to be a nationalist form of Communist Party, they were perceived by many Italians as an antisystem party that could not be trusted in a government coalition. Their leader coined the phrase "polycentrism," meaning there were numerous centers of Communism assuring Italians that he would not take orders from Moscow. Upon the collapse of the Soviet Union in 1989, the DC lost that claim for support and accordingly in the 1993 election, the DC—now even changing its name to the Italian Popular Party to escape its former religious connection—fell to only 11 percent of the vote.[20] Meanwhile, the formerly fragmented party system has been consolidating toward two political alliances or coalitions seeking to capture the post of premier or head of government: the center-right oriented "House of Freedoms" dominated by media magnate Silvio Berlusconi's *Forza Italia* (Go Italy), and the center-left oriented Olive Tree Coalition. These two alliances controlled 84.4 percent of the votes in the 2001 elections to the Italian Chamber of Deputies. The remnants of the former DC have been blended into the House of Freedoms Alliance. This Alliance also contains *Lega Nord,* a populist party of subcultural identity. While their leader, Umberto Bossi, professed a goal of pulling the northern provinces of Piedmont, Lombardy, Veneto, Tuscany, and Emilia Romagna out of Italy and forming a new state of Padania. Most of its supporters are protesting that the productive north creates most of Italy's wealth and the source of tax revenue which is disproportionately spent by a government dominated by the bucolic south. The Italian system also has a fascist party, the National Alliance (formerly called the Italian Social Movement and attracting former supporters of Benito Mussolini). The results of the 2001 Italian elections to the Chamber of Deputies are summarized in Table 4–5.

TABLE 4–5   Italian Election to the Chamber of Deputies 2001

	Seats		% of Vote	
	PR Seats	% of Vote	District Seats	Total Seats
House of Freedom	86	49.5	282	368
Olive Tree	58	34.9	184	242
Communist Refounded	11	5.0	0	11
Others	10	10.5	9	9

The French party system resembles the Italian system just discussed in that the French also went from a rather fragmented party system, consisting of six or seven parties of relatively comparable strength, to a aggregated system of two alliances or political forces. This consolidation was driven by the importance of competing for the majority needed to control the powerful presidency. The French system also resembled the Italians in that the French also had a strong Communist party pulling support from other parties that perhaps could have helped form and maintain a government. Moreover, the French Communist Party was unabashedly a pro-Soviet party, even a Stalinist one. On the French right one also finds a populist party of identity; however, unlike the Italian populist right which is manifested in a party of subcultural identity, on the French right one finds a strongly nationalistic party of identity, the National Front led by Jean-Marie Le Pen, a man who had displayed some neofascist attitudes and connections earlier in his career. Yet, in the 2002 presidential election, Le Pen placed second in the first round of France's two ballot system because with his nationalism, he was the only major politician to propose seriously confronting the problem of France's growing and alienated Muslim population, a concern that rang true to many French voters who normally would not support the populist right. For example, Le Pen got the vocal and financial support of Paris' leading Jewish restaurateur who saw the militantly anti-Semitic Muslims as a greater threat than France's dwindling neofascist population. This concern proved prescient in November, 2005 when the Muslims, now alienated and isolated in semiautonomous enclaves and under the influence of increasingly radical clerics, erupted into an orgy of rioting, arson, and violence that lasted two weeks and spread to over 200 cities or towns and even on to Belgium and Germany. Meanwhile the French president Chirac and his foreign minister Dominique de Villepin appeared impotent in their futile attempts to appease the Muslims, whose grievance appears to be the existence of the West. Only Le Pen, who expressed the concern that his "grandchildren still spoke French," appeared to take the radical Islamist threat seriously enough for many French voters. While some of the media and other analysts portrayed the events of November, 2005 as a riot of French youths driven by high French unemployment, French speaking Christian youths were not rioting. The Muslims were largely living off of France's generous social welfare system, did not speak French, had few marketable skills, and were not actively seeking jobs. Rather, this appeared to be round one of Huntington's "clash of civilizations."[21]

Rather than taking on the nearly impossible task of neatly categorizing hybrid party systems, it makes sense to view party systems on a continuum, ranging from highly fragmented with a larger number of smaller parties of roughly comparable strength with no one party clearly dominating that system to a relatively aggregated system with fewer larger parties, each with a more diverse body of supporters or voters. It further makes sense to note the distinction between a hegemonic system in which one party, whether or not it has a majority of seats in the legislature, has such a clear plurality that it will dominate every government and a system in which there is approximate parity between at least two parties. The hegemonic or dominant party system is at best weakly constrained by a concern with keeping power, while politicians in a two-party system are concerned with keeping power; hence, representatives of the major parties court those sectors of the voting public not permanently committed to one of the parties, rendering at least a modicum of accountability. It is not the frequency of alternation in and out of power for major parties that renders a government accountable so much as a viable opposition. The lack of accountability in Italy that allowed corruption to run rampant through the ruling Christian Democratic Party was not a matter of the infrequency of the time the party spent not running the government; the only party able to provide a viable alternative government, the Communists, was not acceptable to the majority of Italians. Party systems may therefore be classified along the following continua: fragmented to aggregated, and turnover or alternating to hegemonic, as suggested in Figure 4–1.

This variation in types of party systems is not thought to be a chance occurrence but rather a product of attributes of the political systems in which they occur. We now turn to analyses of the literature purporting to offer competing explanations of the variation in party systems.

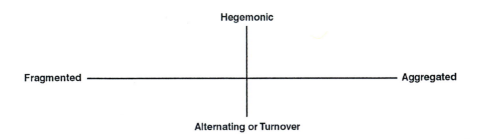

Figure 4–1   Classifying Party Systems Along Two Continuous Dimensions

EXPLAINING PARTY SYSTEMS: CULTURAL EXPLANATIONS

A school of thought among students of comparative politics is that ultimately political culture is the root cause of variations in political science with respect to a number of key attributes such as, for example, the rate of modernization or level of modernity.[22] Such cultural determinists would be inclined to argue that the institutional factors that encourage or discourage attributes of a party system are adopted to reflect the cultural imperatives that ultimately determine the party systems. We will present the argument that certain types of electoral systems produce certain types of party systems.

A highly aggregated party system approaching a two-party system is nearly always found in an environment of a largely homogeneous population characterized by a propensity to compromise and a tolerance of social, ethnic, and ideological differences. Such an environment permits the forming of alliances grouping a range of interests under the same party label. By contrast, a society rent by rigid ideological cleavages renders difficult and unlikely the compromises necessary to build broad alliances that can support an aggregated party system. It may therefore be the case that a system dominated by two parties may only work well when there is *not* a great ideological distance between the parties. When there are strongly felt political positions or grievances that are not able to be represented in the decision making process, the legitimacy of that process and the system itself may suffer.

For example, in 1968 the politically active portion of the American population was about evenly and bitterly divided over the Vietnam War. The presidential election campaign of that year posed a contest between Richard Nixon, the Republican who was strongly and clearly supportive of the war effort and Hubert Humphry, the Vice President under Lyndon Johnson, during whose presidency the escalation of the American role in that war occurred. Hence, the election was widely perceived as between two supporters of the war and the strongly felt antiwar position seemed to be shut out of the political process. This perception generated an unprecedented amount of political radicalism among some of our brightest and most promising young people, many of whom dropped out of the system. Our two-party system was under challenge, a stress that would have been exacerbated had the situation continued through subsequent elections. Fortunately for the American party system, that country's withdrawal from Vietnam in 1972 eased the crisis and a pacifist wing under George McGovern emerged to control the Democratic Party.

Another example occurred in Britain in the late 1970s. Margaret Thatcher emerged as a Conservative Party prime minister leading the party in a more ideologically right wing position than the party had ever been in modern times. Meanwhile, Michael Foote led the pacifist and socialist wing of the Labour Party into control of that party. Hence, the normally dominant pragmatic center had no place to go in the British electoral arena. A number of the centrist Labour leaders dropped out of the party and formed a Social Democratic Party which went into alliance with the centrist Liberal Party to represent the pragmatic center. Some scholars were predicting the end of the British two party system.[23] This crisis of the party system resolved itself in the mid 1990s as the centrist Tony Blair replaced the former pacifist leftist Neil Kinnock as leader of the Labour Party and the principled conservative Thatcher was replaced by John Major, who asserted his independence of his former mentor, Thatcher. He sided with the pragmatic old boy network Conservative leadership in supporting further British involvement in the EU. The British "almost" two-party system was probably saved when Major lowered the ideological distance between the major parties, a concept that Sigelman and Yough demonstrated to be measurable.[24]

A broad ranging illustration of the impact of cultural factors on the party system is in the theory of cultural change proposed by Ronald Inglehart and his followers discussed in Chapter Two. Simply restated, Inglehart claims that the dominance of class-based issues among Western publics has been waning in the context of the widespread and long-lasting postwar prosperity in the Western world. While Inglehart himself is not specific as to what will replace class-based politics, various scholars have characterized the "post-materialist" world as dominated by life style issues such as environmentalism, feminism, gay rights, and nationalist and subcultural identity.

However, the major parties in Western societies are essentially defined on class-based or religious lines: Labor or Social Democratic versus Conservative or Christian Democracy with a smaller classical Liberal party oscillating between them. These party system cleavages have not easily adapted to the changes in social cleavages driven by the cultural changes suggested by Inglehart. Hence, the party system cleavages will not be congruent to the changing social cleavages. Under the pressures to reform a party system that no longer represents the issues and interests of the society, new sets of parties are emerging in the countries in which such new parties are able to find a measure of legitimacy and electoral success.

In each of these situations, however, the tyranny of the electoral system (discussed below) prevented the successful emergence of new parties. Each of the mainstream parties was forced back to the center in order to compete for political power. However, had these crises perpetuated themselves, the pressures to modify the electoral system and permit representation of excluded, important groups might have increased and become irresistible. Thus, while the basic cause of the nature of the party system is viewed by this school as cultural, even they will admit that the institution of the electoral system is the proximate factor causing or at least supporting the result that the culture requires.

EXPLAINING PARTY SYSTEMS: THE ELECTORAL SYSTEM

The concept of an electoral system refers to the set of rules whereby the vote tabulation is translated into the allocation of seats in the legislature among parties or translated into who controls the post of head of government. A literature claiming a direct causal analysis between the choice of electoral system and the type of party system and attributes of the successful political parties constitutes some of the earliest attempts at comparative causal inference in the comparative field. In this literature, a causal inference between the electoral system and a simplistic characterization of the party system is logical and intuitively plausible; the inference between that type of party and the ability to govern or inability resulting in the collapse of democracy is a broader inference not universally self-evident; to some it borders on the polemical. This literature, whose chief advocates were Ferdinand A. Hermans and Andrew Milnor, appears to blame proportional representation (PR) for the collapse of parliamentary governments across western Europe (in Weimar Germany, Austria, France, and Italy), paving the way for their replacement by fascist dictatorships.[25] Hermans appears to have the following causal model in mind in his excoriation of PR. Electoral systems are to Hermans the root cause of political outcomes. Hermans does not consider how cultural factors affect and constrain the choice of what electoral system to adopt.

Specifically, this literature divides the universe of electoral systems into two types: the single member district plurality system that virtually compels a highly aggregated party system dominated by two parties, and proportional representation that encourages (some would argue causes) a highly fragmented party system with no party having the strength to govern.

It is evident that the plurality system is strongly biased against third and weaker parties and that it exaggerates the strength (in seats won) of the strongest party. That strongest party will tend to win most districts whether by a large or small margin. In this winner-take-all format, they get the seat from that district regardless of the margin of victory and all the other parties will get nothing. A third strongest party coming in a close second with a surprisingly strong showing in a district still gets nothing. Because voting support is not evenly distributed among districts, the

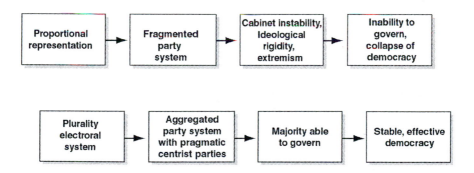

Figure 4–2   Hermans' Implicit Causal Model

second strongest party will win a few districts, especially those in which their support is concentrated, but the percentage of districts actually won by that party will always be less than their percentage of the national vote. The bias against weaker parties by the plurality system is so pronounced that Maurice Duverger in his classic comparative analysis of party systems proclaimed that "an almost complete correlation is observable between [that election system and a two party system];" so that the connection is a "sociological law."[26] The rare exceptions to this law can be explained away as the result of special circumstances. The use of the plurality electoral system in federal elections in Canada has resulted in at least five parties getting significant representation in the Canadian House of Commons seemingly violating Duverger's sociological law; however, the support of each of Canada's parties is restricted to specific regions of provinces. No party receives nationwide support and the *Bloc,* Canada's second strongest party in the wake of the 1993 election, had virtually all of its support concentrated in a single province.

Proportional systems by contrast, are often strongly biased against stronger parties and grant small parties disproportionately large representation. PR in theory works toward the principle that the percentage of seats won by a party in the national legislature should approximately equal the percentage of the national vote won by that party. In practice, PR refers to a number of specific electoral systems that have a proportional impact to varying degrees. These systems generally are not based on a national vote percentage but rather use multimember districts. For example, one of the commonly advocated proportional systems is the one devised by Thomas Hare, known as the single transferable vote or STV. Parties submit candidate lists for each of the multimember districts and the voter ranks these lists as first choice, second choice, etc. A quota is tabulated for each district, known after its creator as the Droop Quota, by this formula: the number of votes cast divided by the number of seats from that district plus one. When a party reaches that quota in a district, it is awarded the first seat from that district and on all subsequent votes for that party list, the voter's second choice is counted. Hence, the party is in fact penalized by being the strongest party. This process is continued until all the votes for that district are allocated.

Under this electoral system, a party with a narrow base of support can not only get representation in the lower house of the legislature; it can be included in a coalition government exercising power and influence far out of proportion to its size. Such parties, therefore, are under no pressure to moderate their demands or principles to attract a broad base of support. Rather, their strategy is to mobilize their base by emphasizing their distinctiveness from parties that are ideologically similar. Hence PR seems to encourage extremism and ideological rigidity among parties.

Israel, for example, illustrates the shaky status of coalition politics in a country with a highly fragmented party system. In that country after the 2001 election, 13 parties had seats in the lower house of their legislature or *Knesset.* The country was governed by a coalition of right-oriented parties led by the Likud Party since the 1973 War. This coalition included the National Religious Party, a party with 4.3

percent of the vote and 5 seats in the *Knesset*. However, the Likud has a plurality of only 29 percent of the vote and 38 seats in a 120-seat house; hence, the coalition was in danger of falling were the National Religious Party to withdraw from it. Therefore, that party was able to impose its narrow brand of religious Orthodoxy on a much more secularized population. When the National Religious Party and the National Union Party bolted the coalition over Israel's withdrawal from Gaza, Likud was forced into a "grand coalition" with its normal rival Labor. A second religious party representing Sephardic Jews (from the Iberian Peninsula or Africa rather than central and eastern Europe), the Shas, had 11 seats and also could wield disproportionate influence. When Prime Minister Ariel Sharon failed to get support from his Likud Party for a unilateral withdrawal from Gaza, he formed a new centrist party, Kadima (Forward). The March 2006 elections saw Kadima winning despite Sharon being removed from the political scene with a stroke that left him in a coma at this writing. Ehud Olmert, a former mayor of Jerusalem and deputy to Sharon, became the new Prime Minister. The new head of Likud, former Prime Minister Benyamin Netanyahu, opposed to any pullback from the territories, fell to an embarrassing fourth. Kadima will form a government; probably in coalition with Labor, favoring additional withdrawals from the West Bank. Israel is unilaterally drawing defensible borders behind a security fence. The party composition of the *Knesset* is shown in Table 4–6.

Fourteen other parties received 4 percent of the total vote but none of these passed the 2 percent threshold to get a seat. Until it broke up over Gaza, Likud's coalition included Shinui, the National Religious Party, and the National Union.

A third type of electoral system utilizes the Anglo American system of single member electoral districts but requires that the candidate win a majority of the votes cast to be awarded the electoral prize at stake in that election. With more than two candidates in most elections, normally no one gets that majority in the first round; hence, the top two candidates vie against one another in a second round. Since all parties know that one needs majority support, in majority system elections negotiations and tactical maneuvering normally occurs to build electoral alliances. These alliances may involve several smaller parties agreeing to support one another's candidates on a rotating basis, thereby freezing out the party with a plurality of votes in those districts. Hence, the majority system with runoff elections, used in France in the Fourth and Fifth Republics, is far friendlier to smaller parties than the plurality system, despite its single member district format and its lack of direct proportionality.

Scholars such as Hermans and Milnor who excoriate PR as having caused the collapse of democracies implicitly assume that the most important function of an electoral system is to produce a majority able to govern and that the most important values for political system are stability and effectiveness. Other scholars such as Lakeman and Lambert, who excoriate the plurality system and advocate that Britain scrap that system for Hare's STV, implicitly regard accurate representation of

TABLE 4–6A   Party Strength in the Israeli *Knesset* (2001)

	% Of Vote	Seats
Likud	29.4	38
Labor (Avoda)	14.5	19
Shinui (change)	12.3	15
Shas (Sephardic Orthodox)	8.2	11
National Union	5.5	7
Meretz	5.2	6
Yahadot Hatorah (National Religious)	4.3	5
Mfdal (Miflafa Datit Leumit)	4.2	6
Democratic Front for Peace and Equality	3.0	3
One Nation (Am Ehad)	2.8	3
National Democratic League	2.3	3
Yisrael BaAliyah (Sharansky's party)	2.2	2
United Arab List (Raam)	2.1	2
		120

TABLE 4–6B   Party Strength in the Israeli *Knesset* (2006)

	% of Vote	Seats
Kadima	22.02	29
Ha-Avoda (Labor)	15.06	19
Shas (Sephardic Orthodox)	9.53	12
Likud	8.98	12
Yisrael Beytenu (Our Home Israel)	8.98	11
National Religious	7.94	9
Gil-Pensioners	5.92	7
United Torah (Aqudat Israel)	4.69	6
Meretz Yachad	3.77	5
United Arab List	3.02	4
Hadash	2.74	3
Balad	2.30	3
		120

the spectrum of interests and public opinion and hence fairness to each such segment of a society to be the most important functions of an electoral system.[27] Other critics of Hermans claim that he overstates the causal impact of electoral systems. They point out that countries such as Sweden and Belgium remained quite stable for years after the adoption of PR. Belgium, from the early part of the twentieth century until the exploding salience of subcultural defense in the 1970s (discussed in Chapter Two) maintained a stable three party system.[28]

It may be fair to say that when a fissiparous cleavage structure demands the accurate representation of many strata or interests in the political decision making process, PR permits narrowly based parties to emerge. The emergence of new political forces—such as populist parties of identity—to succeed as political parties thus depends on the opportunity structure in that context of which the election system is a major factor. However, in a country with a stable cleavage structure, the introduction of PR will not by itself cause the fragmentation of an otherwise stable party system. Neither will the introduction of a plurality electoral system guarantee the total dominance of the electoral process by two dominant parties. The Canadian example of regional party systems belies that myth as asserted in Duverger's "sociological law." However, it seems reasonable to conclude that the plurality system does constitute a serious impediment to the successful emergence of new parties. Therefore, in such systems, the existing major parties tend to coopt the policy agendas and basis of appeal of promising new parties. For example, the American Democratic Party adopted most of the agenda of the Progressive Party in the 1920s after the Progressives showed surprising levels of success; similarly, the Republican Party absorbed much of the support of Pat Buchanan's right wing populism in the 2000 election. The British Conservative Party has similarly taken on the nationalistic antiimmigrant sentiment that might otherwise have gone to the British National Party.

PARTY ORGANIZATION AND BEHAVIOR

Individual parties vary with respect to organization and these organizational differences have an impact on aspects of party behavior such as legislative voting and rank and file control of party leadership.

The relationship of party leadership to party rank and file is a function of three factors: party ideology or principle, the constitutional format in which the party operates, and the nature of leadership in any large organization. The impact of party ideology may be seriously limited by the other two factors. Such party principles or ideology may have more of an impact on the structure or role of party leadership in theory than it does in practice.

One would expect that a party with strong egalitarian ideological baggage—meaning parties on the political left—would retain close control and tight rein on party leaders compared to parties on the political right that, in principle, accept a natural hierarchy in human skills. Hence, the parties on the right are more willing to accord leaders more discretion to lead and to grant them a degree of insulation from the day-to-day fluctuations in the passions of the rank and file. The British Labour Party had a specific and formal rule that their leadership in the House of Commons had to be reelected annually by the parliamentary party while for years the Conservative Party (a.k.a. Tories) chose their leadership by much more informal means and assumed that he or she could remain in the leadership post until resigning. It was said sarcastically of the Conservative method of choosing its leader, "You just looked around and there he was." However, after some confusion in the process of elevating Sir Alec Douglas-Home to party leadership in 1963, the party decided to formalize its procedures of choosing its leader, and Ted Heath was the first Tory leader to be elected.

This putative difference is also related to the origin of the parties. While some parties on the right or center such as the British Conservatives originated as factions within the House, others, especially those with a trade union or industrial labor base of support, originated as socioeconomic movements outside of Parliament. Hence, these labor-based parties were originally regarded as the political arm of the trade union movement. Leaders of these parties were expected to be under the control of the trade unions. In fact, the members of the parliamentary Labor Party in the early years in New South Wales, Australia, were required to sign a pledge that they would be bound by the policies developed in Party Conference. (Australia formerly used the British spelling for their Labour Party but in the postwar era, while moving to closer relations with the United States, they adopted the American spelling for the Labor Party but continue to use British spelling elsewhere.)

R. T. McKenzie in his classic tome on British parties concludes that Labour Party leaders are not as subject to rank-and-file control as their egalitarian ideological baggage would suggest and that the Tory leadership is not as autonomous from rank and file control as their hierarchical ideological baggage would suggest. Rather the imperatives of the constitutional system are a major determinant of the structure of its major parties rather than the ideological orientation of the party.[29] No Labour Party leader has been opposed for reelection since 1922 while a sitting Tory Prime Minister, Margaret Thatcher, was denied reelection by her own party when she failed to get the required majority plus 15 percent of her party's vote. The party currently chooses its leader by a three ballot process among the 198 MPs of the parliamentary party; the candidate list is whittled down to the final two candidates who then are voted on by the national party membership.

By national party membership, we refer to the fact that the major British parties are both mass parties in the sense they have a mass membership that pays dues and may attend meetings. This differs from parties in the United States where identification with a party merely means you are somewhat more likely to vote for that party label in a given election than for a candidate without that label. The Labour Party, originating as an arm of the trade union movement outside Parliament has a larger mass membership than the Tories because membership in a union in the

Trade Union Congress (Britain's major labor federation) automatically enrolls one as a dues paying member of the Labour Party, unless the individual in question formally requests otherwise (a procedure known as "contract out"). When a Tory government changed the rules so that inaction left one as a nonmember ("contract in"), party membership was cut in about half. When Labour changed it back to contract out, membership doubled again. This mass membership is a major source of funding for Labour since it gets little support from British industry.

The constitutional system presumes that the party leader who is prime minister can act on day-to-day policy concerns with a fair degree of autonomy from strict rank-and-file control. Winston Churchill opined, for example, that insofar as the Labour Party is merely the political arm of the TUC, it cannot fill its constitutional duty to protect the interests of the nation as a whole. The relative autonomy of the leadership of the major parties from close rank-and-file control may also be due to the nature of large organizations themselves.

Italian sociologist Roberto Michels, in an oft-cited work on large political organizations including parties, argues that leadership in such organizations becomes a specialized role entailing skills and knowledge esoteric to the leaders. This renders close rank-and-file control of that leadership nearly impossible, regardless of any egalitarian ideological baggage. Michels labels this inevitable autonomy of the leadership of putatively democratic organizations "the iron law of oligarchy."[30] Based on an early twentieth-century study of the supposedly egalitarian Social Democratic Party of Germany, Michels' book argues that the leaders of labor-based parties have more in common with management in terms of dress, lifestyle, interests, and stake in the organization than with the working class they allegedly represent.

Yet, the autonomy of the leadership of parties can be overstated. The front bench of British parties stays in touch with back bench sentiment, avoiding motions of no confidence in advance. They even have institutionalized roles to facilitate this interaction between front and back bench—party officials known as whips. The last Tory government had a chief whip, a deputy chief whip, twelve government whips in the House of Commons, and seven whips in the House of Lords. Moreover, the Conservative Party has institutionalized an organization of backbenchers, the 1922 Committee, who meet to debate and mobilize backbench sentiment which is then communicated to the front bench via the whips. While Labour does not have a parallel organization of back benchers, Labour MPs communicate regularly among themselves and to their front bench.

The militantly egalitarian German Green Party, in order to prevent entrenched leadership from being established, require regular and frequent turnover of leadership personnel. This ostensibly environmental party was in the hands of its *Fundi* (fundamentalist) wing for years and was obsessively anti-Western. More recently the party has turned to its realist *Realo* wing and was hence in the recent governing coalition with the Social Democrats. However, its rotating leadership principle inevitably detracts from the party's effectiveness.

The key organizational difference between the American parties, which seem to stand for very little in the way of principle, and many of the parties in other Western democracies is that in many other countries, the members of the parliamentary parties vote as a bloc while in the case of the American parties, party label has frequently been a weak predictor of how a member of Congress will vote on a given issue or bill. While still imperfect, party label has become a better predictor in recent years as to how American Congressmen and Senators will vote. The degree of voting cohesiveness varies a great deal from one country to another and even from one party to another; however, greater levels of cohesive voting behavior among the parties in parliamentary systems, in which governments can be forced to resign after losing a key vote in the legislature, are one of the main reasons for keeping the levels of cabinet instability within manageable bounds. Obviously, the advantage in holding a majority of votes in a house of parliament would be lost if each MP voted his or her individual conscience on each legislative vote. More importantly, it is very difficult to specify what a party stands for in the way of either a policy agenda or set of principles if each party member is free to vote or express policy preferences solely according to the way she/he decides as an individual.

Cohesive legislative voting is often referred to as party discipline. Party discipline is quite strong in Great Britain and the Federal Republic of Germany; it is much less strong in France with their individualistic political culture. Moreover, a lack of party discipline in France is of much less significance than in the other two nations because the effective head of government in France, a directly elected president, cannot be removed by the legislature on a vote of no confidence. Party discipline is also weak in America, another country in which the tenure of the head of government is fixed.

The presence of absence of party discipline, however, is not simply a function of whether it is needed to provide cabinet stability in a parliamentary system. We have examined a number of parliamentary systems with weak party systems exacerbating a high level of cabinet instability as was the case in Third and Fourth Republic France, Italy, and the Weimar Republic in Germany. As with the case of explaining the variation in party systems, the level of party discipline is a function of cultural and structural factors. Countries with a strong egalitarian or individualistic strain in which individuals have a more difficult time accepting authority will be less likely to follow the lead of party leadership. France, Italy, and Israel may be cases in point. Other countries with a tradition of greater acceptance of authority may develop a tradition of accepting the direction of party leadership, permitting a great degree of party-line voting.

The institutional factor that impacts on the degree of cohesiveness in party voting is ultimate control over nominations. In the United States, parties have had virtually no control over who carries the party banner since the "McGovern Reforms" subjected the nominating process to primary elections. Anyone with the right combination of charismatic appeal and sufficient financial backing can secure a major party nomination regardless of whether the candidate accepts or overtly rejects the principles that had defined the party.

In Britain, the constituency organization generally chooses their party nominee for their district; however, that choice must be acceptable to central party leadership. When Theresa Gorman led a group of Euro-skeptics to cross the floor in 1994 and vote against the party proposal to send additional contributions to the EU, she and her seven rebels were "de-whipped." That means the eight dissidents would no longer receive the party "whip," a document sent to every member of the parliamentary party announcing upcoming divisions and urging support of the party positions. In effect, they were drummed out of the parliamentary party, and their constituency associations were duly informed not to renominate them. Had those associations chosen to defy the national party leadership, the party leader reserved the right to replace the constituency associations. As independents without a party label, the political careers of the rebellious eight would likely have been over.

As one see from the actual whip displayed in Figure 4–2, the announcements of upcoming divisions are accompanied with pleas for support stated with varying degrees of urgency. Those divisions (the British style of legislative voting) that decide critical issues (such as a confidence question), and especially when the outcome is in doubt, are expressed with greater urgency. The number of underlines emphasizes that urgency. One may occasionally abstain where support is merely requested or perhaps up to a one-line whip. Crossing the floor in defiance of a four-line whip almost certainly will result in expulsion from the parliamentary party. It is not necessary to articulate a threat to carry out this consequence of defying party leadership; the possibility is well understood by MPs which is why it rarely needs to be invoked.

Ultimately, Gorman's eight caused the government to lose a crucial vote on part of the budget, an increase in the value added tax (VAT) on home heating oil. Sensing that he would need those eight votes on some critical upcoming divisions, Prime Minister Major admitted the rebellious eight back into the party fold a few months after their expulsion. Perhaps that was long enough for the lesson to be learned. Britain has not experienced a serious and overt backbench rebellion since, despite some obvious unhappiness on the part of the Labour backbench with the policies of the hawkish and centrist Prime Minister Blair.

Whenever there is a system of strong party discipline, the unique importance of the individual MP is sharply diminished because they generally do not exercise much independent discretion. Hence, interest groups would rarely lobby individual MPs the way they aggressively lobby Congress in the United States.

In a parliamentary system with geographically defined diversities (e.g., federalism), the MP is put in the difficult position of reconciling two conflicting imperatives: the centralizing imperative of a parliamentary regime in which

PRIVATE & CONFIDENTIAL   PARLIAMENTARY LABOUR PARTY

TUESDAY 11th January, 1994,   The House will meet at 2.30pm.

1. Defence questions,   tabling for Health.

2. CRIMINAL JUSTICE BILL: SECOND READING.
   (Tony Blair & Alun Michael)

   YOUR ATTENDANCE BY 9 P.M. IS ESSENTIAL.

   ▬▬▬▬▬▬▬▬▬▬▬▬▬▬▬
   ▬▬▬▬▬▬▬▬▬▬▬▬▬▬▬
   ▬▬▬▬▬▬▬▬▬▬▬▬▬▬▬

3. Money resolution relating to the Non-Domestic Rating Bill.
   (Doug Henderson)

   YOUR CONTINUED ATTENDANCE IS REQUESTED.
   ▬▬▬▬▬▬▬▬▬▬▬▬▬▬▬

WEDNESDAY 12th January   the House will meet at 2.30pm.

1. Trade & Industry questions,   tabling for Scotland.

2. NON-DOMESTIC RATING BILL: PROCEDINGS
   (Jack Straw & Doug Henderson)

   YOUR CONTINUED ATTENDANCE IS ESSENTIAL.

   ▬▬▬▬▬▬▬▬▬▬▬▬▬▬▬
   ▬▬▬▬▬▬▬▬▬▬▬▬▬▬▬
   ▬▬▬▬▬▬▬▬▬▬▬▬▬▬▬

3. Motion on the Insider Dealing (Securities and Regulated Markes) Order.
   (Alistair Darling)

   YOUR CONTINUED ATTENDANCE IS ESSENTIAL.

   ▬▬▬▬▬▬▬▬▬▬▬▬▬▬▬
   ▬▬▬▬▬▬▬▬▬▬▬▬▬▬▬
   ▬▬▬▬▬▬▬▬▬▬▬▬▬▬▬

THURSDAY 13th January,   The House will meet at 2.30pm.

1. Home Office questions,   tabling for MAFF.

2. Opposition Day   1st allotted day.

3. There will be a debate on BUREAUCRACY AND WASTE IN THE
   NATIONAL HEALTH SERVICE, on an Opposition Motion
   (David Blunkett & Dawn Primarolo)

   YOUR ATTENDANCE BY 9 P.M. IS ESSENTIAL.

   ▬▬▬▬▬▬▬▬▬▬▬▬▬▬▬
   ▬▬▬▬▬▬▬▬▬▬▬▬▬▬▬
   ▬▬▬▬▬▬▬▬▬▬▬▬▬▬▬

Figure 4–2   A Labour Party Whip

strongly disciplined parties provide the stable majority needed to govern and the decentralizing imperative of representing these diversities or regions. Party discipline presumes individual MPs follow the whip or the dictates of party leadership while federalism presumes MPs follow public opinion among the electorate of their district. Of course, this principle will apply only to the extent that in the federal system, the geographically defined subunit (e.g., state, land, province, etc.) actually speak for the demands of a geographically defined distinct set of interests or identity.

Given the strength of subsystem identity in Canada represented by the provincial elites in Quebec, one might expect a greater impact of the decentralizing imperatives of federalism on party cohesion in that country than in Australia, another older Commonwealth country without the geographically defined subculture congruent with state borders. However, although a comparative roll-call analysis of the two countries does find lower levels of party cohesion in Canada than in Australia, the differences are not great, due undoubtedly to the pressures for party discipline inherent in the Westminster model of cabinet government.[31] Cohesion may be seriously undermined in such systems by issues of deeply felt emotional and symbolic importance to particular regions, states, or provinces.

Such a case was the design for a new Canadian flag debated in the 1964–1965 parliament, a debate in which the *Québécois* wanted something with a *fluer d'lis,* the symbol of prerevolutionary France, while the "rest of Canada" wanted the Union Jack, a symbol of Canada's Commonwealth connection. Prime Minister Pearson, head of the Liberal Party, realized the pressures placed on his substantial Quebec contingent to support the *Québécois* position and reject the Union Jack while the Liberals from ROC would be under pressure to reject that position; hence, Pearson simply removed the whip for votes on that issue (meaning every MP can vote his her/his own conscience or community preference without regard for party cohesion). At the same time, Pearson let it be known that he was not about to resign over a vote on that issue. A free or whipless vote, with the no confidence issue removed, may be the obvious way to lessen the tension inherent in combining federalism with cabinet government.

PARTY STRATEGY AND TACTICS

Based on the rational choice model discussed in Chapter One, scholars such as Anthony Downs have produced theoretical models design to explain and predict the behavior and tactics of a political party in a given type of party system. Like all rational choice models, these models presume rationality, information needed to ascertain the rational choice, and a stipulated set of goals. Downs' model, for example, presumes the goals of vote maximization and implementation of the party's policy agenda.[32] Parties, therefore, might be criticized by idealists for not providing clear and meaningful choices to the voting public, while these parties, with the goal of winning elections, may conclude that providing such clear choices does not maximize their electoral support.

Downs argues, for example, that in a two-party scenario, parties in a democratic system can normally take their extreme wings for granted. The far left in a trade union-based labor or social democratic party will not be entirely happy with the centrist policy agenda of a Tony Blair, but they will be better off with a government headed by him than one headed by his Conservative or Christian Democratic opposition. Similarly, the far right will be better off with a center-right government than with the leftist opposition. While there is a deal of overlap between the parties on a right to left dimension (less now than a generation ago), the center of gravity or fulcrum in the labor-based or social democratic party will be to the left of that for any conservative party or party of Christian democracy. Therefore, it is rational for both parties to compete for the area of overlap, the less-committed center. Otherwise put, it is rational for parties to compete for the same majority that is normally in the center rather than take a minority position to provide an alternative.

On the other hand, in a fragmented system consisting of numerous parties with smaller differences between them, it is rational for parties to stress those differences to mobilize their base and perhaps attract a few votes from the adjacent parties. Normally a party on the left to right dimension is not going to attract support from several places over on that dimension. Hence, rationality for parties in this situation will be to take a more rigid, harder-line position to distinguish themselves from the parties immediately to their right or left.

When addressing rational behavior for the voting public, Downs takes account of information uncertainty. Information is not cost-free and the cost of the information needed to make the rational choice between competing candidates may exceed the benefits of making the rational best choice. In this scenario, ideology may allow a quasi-rational choice without the cost of the information to know which candidate is most likely to maximize your interests. It may, paradoxically, be rational to remain irrational.

As discussed in the section on rational choice research, this is one of several efforts to use rational choice models to explain or predict party tactics. Riker's work on coalition formation is another discussed in that section.[33] The problem lies in the validity of the assumptions, especially the assumption of information as to which is the rational choice. In the case of Downs, the assumption that parties seek to maximize their votes is overridden in some cases by ideological or programmatic goals. That clearly seemed to be the case discussed above of the British Labour Party being taken over by its egalitarian and pacifist backbench in the 1970s while Margaret Thatcher led to Tories to the ideological right. Riker, it will be recalled from Chapter One, admitted that his "size principle" lacked predictive power because of uncertainty about the necessary size of the winning coalition, his "information corollary." These works identify tactical choices and rob these models of their potential explanatory and predictive powers.

CONCLUSIONS

This chapter has critically reviewed a representative portion of the vast literature on political parties with respect to the putative functions of parties in a modern democracy, with respect to the types of individual parties, types of party systems, attempts to explain variations in these two sets of phenomena, and trends and patterns in party systems and voting behavior. While the attributes of a political system impact the attributes of a party system and of the individual parties it contains, the relationship is undoubtedly reciprocal. The attributes of the party system have an impact on the operation of the political system in which the party system operates. Yet, we have shown that despite the existence of patterns and trends in the behavior of parties across Western democracies, the specific form that parties and party systems take is very much a product of the culture of those societies. Thus, while a literature claimed a causal impact of the electoral system on party systems, we saw that the electoral system is more of an intervening variable between the culture and the party system.

Because many of the factors relating to the broad topic of parties are more precisely delineated and accurately measured than in other areas of inquiry, political science has produced an impressive body of literature on party and voting behaviors. These works gather an impressive body of data denoting such interesting patterns and trends as the dealignment or realignment of voter support discussed above. However the causes and significance of such patterns remain matters of debate among scholars. The relative importance of the various roles ostensibly played by parties is obviously a matter of debate as well and clearly varies from system to system. We have a collection of data on various aspects of the broad topic of political parties without any theoretical integration of these data into a coherent theory on the requisite roles of parties in a modern democracy.

ENDNOTES

[1] The stipulation of the functions of a political institution was one offered as a framework for an explanatory theory of politics. A classic statement of this perspective is Gabriel Almond, "A Functional Approach to Comparative Politics," in G. Almond and James Coleman, eds., *The Politics of Developing Areas* (Princeton, NJ: Princeton University Press, 1960), pp. 3–64. This had its roots in theoretical sociology. For these roots, see Robert K. Merton, *Social Theory and Social Structure* (Glencoe, IL: The Free Press, 1949, rev. ed., 1957); Talcott Parsons, *Toward a General Theory of Action* (Cambridge, MA: Harvard University Press, 1951).

[2] A strong critique of functionalism as a putative explanatory theory is A. James Gregor, "Political Science and the Use of Functional Analysis, *The American Political Science Review,* Vol. 62, No. 2 (June, 1968), pp. 425–439. For the argument that functional analysis as an explanatory theory is tautological, see Lawrence Mayer, *Comparative Political Inquiry* (Homewood, IL: The Dorsey Press, 1972), chap. 8, esp. pp. 145–146.

[3]A. N. Holcombe, *Toward a More Perfect Union* (Cambridge, MA: Harvard University Press, 1950), p. 93.

[4]This variation in the political skills of modern America's presidents is described in detail in Richard Neustadt, *Presidential Power: The Politics of Leadership,* rev. ed. (New York: John Wiley, 1976).

[5]Otto Kirchheimer, "The Transformation of Western European Party Systems," in Joseph LaPalombara and Myron Weiner, eds., *Political Parties and Political Development* (Princeton, NJ: Princeton University Press, 1966), pp. 117–200.

[6]Seymour Lipset, "The End of Ideology," Postscript to Lipset, *Political Man* (New York: Doubleday Anchor Books, 1963), pp. 439–456. Daniel Bell, *The End of Ideology* (New York: The Free Press, 1962). Cf. Joseph La Palombara, "The End of Ideology: A Dissent and Interpretation," *The American Political Science Review,* Vol. LX, No. 1 (March, 1966), pp. 5–16.

[7]Francis Fukuyama, "The End of History," *The National Interest,* Vol. 16 (Summer, 1989), pp. 3–18.

[8]Seymour Lipset and Stein Rokkan, eds., *Party Systems and Voter Alignments: Cross National Perspectives* (New York: The Free Press, 1967), pp. 50ff.

[9]For a concise summary of this body of research, see Russell Dalton, *Citizen Politics,* 3rd ed. (New York: Chatham House, 2002), pp. 174–183.

[10]Russell Dalton, Scott Flanagan, and Paul Beck, eds., *Electoral Change in Advanced Industrial Democracies* (Princeton, NJ: Princeton University Press, 1984).

[11]Ibid., p. 198

[12]Karl Marx, *Critique of the Gotha Program* (New York: International Publishers, 1935), p. 14.

[13]Karl Schorske, *German Social Democracy, 1905–1917: The Development of the Great Schism* (New York: Wiley Science Editions, 1955). Schorske's book is a classic account of the recurring struggles of Marxist parties between the emotional commitment to an eschatological ideologism and a realistic quest for political power in a democratic system.

[14]Leslie Lipson, "The Two Party System in Great Britain," *The American Political Science Review,* Vol. 47, No. 2 (June, 1953), pp. 337–358; Vacher's *Parliamentary Companion,* No. 1075, (August, 1994), p. 78.

[15]For a detailed analysis of the Conservative collapse in the 1993 Canadian election, see Lawrence Mayer, Erol Kaymak, and Jeff Justice, "Populism and the Triumph of the Politics of Identity: The Transformation of the Canadian Party System," *Nationalism and Ethnic Politics,* Vol. 6, No. 1, Spring 2000, pp. 72–102.

[16]Seymour Lipset, *Agrarian Socialism* (Berkeley: University of California Press ,1950) is an analysis of this curious party in Saskatchewan. It used to be called the Cooperative Commonwealth Federation.

[17]F. R. Alleman, "Germany's Emerging Two Party System," *New Leader,* Vol. 41 (August 4 and 11, 1958).

[18]Michael Le Roy and Lyman Kellstedt, "A Reassessment of the Role of Religion in Western Politics." Paper presented to the Annual Meeting of the American Political Science Association in Chicago, September, 1995.

[19]Herman Bakvis, *Catholic Power in the Netherlands* (Kingston and Montreal: McGill-Queen's University Press, 1981).

[20]Mark Gilbert, *The End of Politics Italian Style* (Boulder, CO: Westview Press, 1995).

[21]Samuel Huntington, *The Clash of Civilizations and the Remaking of World Order* (New York: Simon and Schuster Touchstone Books, 1996).

[22]See, e.g., Ronald Inglehart, *Modernization and Postmodernization: Cultural, Economic and Political Change in 43 Societies* (Princeton, NJ: Princeton University Press, 1997); Ronald Inglehart, "The Renaissance of Political Culture," *The American Political Science Review,* Vol. 84, No. 4 (December, 1988), pp. 1203–1230.

[23]See, e.g., Richard Rose and Ian McCallister, *Voters Begin to Choose: From Closed Class to Open Elections in Britain* (Beverly Hills, CA: Sage Publications, 1986).

[24]Lee Sigelman and Syung Nan Yough, "Left-Right Polarization in National Party Systems: A Cross National Analysis," *Comparative Political Studies,* Vol. 11, No. 3 (October, 1978), pp. 355–381.

[25]F.A. Hermans, *Democracy or Anarchy: A Study of Proportional Representation* (South Bend, IN: University of Notre Dame Press, 1941). Andrew Milnor, *Elections and Political Stability* (Boston: Little Brown, 1969).

[26]Maurice Duverger, *Political Parties* (New York: Wiley Science Editions, 1963), p. 217.

[27]Enid Lakeman and James Lambert, *Voting in Democracies* (London: Farber and Farber, 1955); Enid Lakeman, 'The Case for Proportional Representation," in Arend Lijphart and Bernard Grofman, eds., *Choosing an Electoral System: Issues and Alternatives* (New York: Praeger, 1984).

[28]Keith Hill, "Belgium: Political Change in a Segmented Society," in Richard Rose, ed., *Electoral Behavior: A Comparative Handbook* (New York: The Free Press, 1974),

[29]Robert T. McKenzie, *British Political Parties,* rev. ed. (New York: Praeger, 1963), p. 635ff. His thesis is summarized in McKenzie, "Power in British Parties," *British Journal of Sociology,* Vol. 6, No. 2 (June, 1955), pp. 123–132.

[30]Roberti Michels, *Political Parties,* Eden and Cedar Paul, trans. (New York: Dover Publications, 1959), esp. Part 6, Chap. 2

[31]Lawrence Mayer, "Federalism and Party Behavior in Australia and Canada," *Western Political Quarterly,* Vol XXIII, No. 4 (December, 1970), p. 805.

[32]Anthony Downs, *An Economic Theory of Democracy* (New York: Harper and Row, 1957).

[33]William Riker, *The Theory of Political Coalitions* (New Haven, CT: Yale University Press, 1962).

5

The Third Wave of Democratization

Despite what seems to the people in the West the obvious superiority of their conception of the democratic system of government, that form of government did not emerge until relatively late in human history and was not widely seen outside the West until recent decades. Samuel Huntington conceptualized democracy appearing in three waves: the first wave appearing almost exclusively in the West in the nineteenth century driven by the ideals of the British, French and American revolutions and the intellectuals such as Locke, Rousseau, and Jefferson who articulated and spread the idea of human rights. A second wave followed the end of World War II, driven by the ideals of the triumphant Western democracies and imposed by those victorious powers on the defeated Axis countries, and a third wave in the early 1970s began spreading democracy widely for the first time among the less-developed countries.[1]

The first two waves of democratization were followed by a wave of reversals, countries that had become democratic reverting back to a previous autocratic format. The reasons for these reversals were varied and to some extent idiosyncratic to individual cases. Yet, it will be argued below that patterns may be discerned regarding the causes of democratic reversals in each of the two waves of reversals. These patterns can shed light on the important question of the factors that enable democratic systems to achieve legitimacy and to weather challenges over time.

Another debate regarding democratization and reversals is whether the democratization process is in the long run linear, moving almost inexorably toward a greater prevalence of democracy as the world increasingly realizes the superiority of that format. Pop futurist and philosopher Francis Fukuyama experienced an epiphany that the world is moving in such a linear and inexorable fashion toward liberal democracy that we are coming to the conclusion of political evolution.[2] While it is true that the number of democratic states has steadily increased since World War II (from 12 in 1942 to 58 by 1990), so has the total number of states and in fact the percentage of states that are democratic in 1990 is almost the exact percentage of states that were democratic in 1922.[3]

A third question that the examination of these waves of democratization can address is the one discussed at various points in this volume—the question of whether there are contextual factors such as culture that are essential for democratic regimes to flourish. This will be reexamined in the conclusion of this chapter.

THE APPEAL OF THE LENINIST MODEL IN EMERGING NATIONS

While many countries used the language and symbols of democracy to legitimize what the West would call authoritarian regimes, most of the nations emerging in the post-World War II decades out of the collapse of the empires of the Western powers chose a version of the Marxist-Leninist model as their path to modernization. The appeal of that model has been thoroughly discussed elsewhere: hence, the factors underlying that appeal will be only briefly outlined here.[4] First, Leninism focuses on economic redemption which takes on a higher priority than abstract political and human rights for societies struggling to rise above a subsistence level of material well-being. Second, by claiming to predict the eventual triumph of the downtrodden with scientific certainty, Leninism offered hope to the hopeless. Third, Leninism purports to explain the economic marginality of underdeveloped nations in terms of oppression by the industrialized West, thereby shifting the blame for underdevelopment away from the people of the less-developed nations (LDCs) and enhancing their self-esteem. Fourth, the Soviet Union went from a peasant society to a major nuclear power in a generation, compared to the two centuries it took the West to complete that process, giving peoples of the LDCs hope that they could enjoy the benefits of an advanced industrial society in their lifetime.

Because of the compelling logic of the appeal of Leninism to people of the LDCs, this model—which entails some kind of authoritarian format—was the regime of choice among the newly independent nations in the decades following World War II. This was true despite the fact that socialism at its best provides for equality of distribution. Yet, what these countries need is not redistribution when they have little or nothing to distribute. They need economic growth which means incentives to invest, create, and take economic risks, the attributes of capitalism. When the most recent or "third wave" of democracy began with the events in Portugal in 1974, only 39 of 191 sovereign nations were operating under a democratic format.[5] A high percentage of the countries that installed a democratic format in the first two waves of democratization reverted back to an authoritarian format. It remains to be seen how many of the new democracies of the third wave will remain so in the coming years.

CONSOLIDATING DEMOCRACIES

This chapter will examine the causes or patterns in the transitions from autocracy to democracy in each of these waves. That requires a specification of from what to what? This book has already discussed the conceptualization of democracy as it is found in the modern world. Yet, as the number of first and second wave reversals indicates, it is one thing to install or establish a democratic format, that is, the more or less regular, competitive-elections format which some scholars call "electoral democracy"; it is quite another for it to last over a number of years and through the crises that political systems inevitably face. A democratic system that is able to withstand the ravages of time and its accompanying crises is said to be "consolidated."

Scholars have debated the utility of the concept of consolidation. A couple of them have tried to give a definition. One that makes intuitive sense without any indicators to determine precisely when consolidation has occurred is Juan Linz and Alfred Steppan's suggestion that a democracy is considered consolidated when it has become "the only game in town."[6] This implies that the regime has acquired sufficient *legitimacy* (widespread popular acceptance) to be valued for its own sake apart from its performance or policies. It implies that when a crisis does occur, solutions are only sought within the framework of the democratic format; alternative formats are not considered by any significant portion of the population. The losers on important policy debates do not consider replacing the regime as a solution.

A second attempt to specify indicators for the consolidation of democracy was Samuel Huntington's two turnover rule.[7] By this rule, a democracy is considered consolidated if it transfers power from one set of leaders or one political force to their opponents in two separate elections. Since in the history of human affairs the peaceful transfer of power on the basis of a mere electoral outcome has always been rare, it is assumed that when it occurs on two separate occasions, the rules of the democratic game have become more important than winning office. The precedence of the rules of the electoral game over policy outcomes or the successful resolution of issues indicates that these rules have become legitimate, that the system is valued for its own sake, allowing it to survive the crises that all political systems inevitably face.

The Huntington two turnover test assumes that a commitment to the democratic rules of the game will necessarily result in the incumbents' electoral defeat with some stipulated frequency in a given time frame. The example of Sweden suggests that this might not always be the case. Although almost no one questioned the legitimacy of the democratic regime in Sweden, the Social Democratic Party did remain in power for 47 years. Moreover, the two turnover criterion may be stringent for emerging democracies less than two decades old.

Guillermo O'Donnell is among the scholars who question the utility of the concept of consolidation to increase one's ability to predict the longevity of democratic regimes.[8] The concept may be regarded as a tautology: a regime lasts because it is consolidated but you know the regime is consolidated because it has lasted. The concept could only have predictive power if it were precisely measured independently of the result it is supposed to bring about.

AUTOCRACIES OR AUTHORITARIAN REGIMES

The conceptualization of democratic regimes has been discussed earlier in this volume; however, its antithesis, autocracy, has not been directly addressed. Briefly, autocracy refers to any regime that does not meet our criteria for being a democracy. Some scholars limit autocracy to rule by one person; others use it as interchangeable with authoritarian regime.[9] As with the case of democracy, the concepts of autocracy and authoritarian system include several specific regime types.

Many people equate authoritarian government with dictatorship. A dictatorship is, however, just one type of authoritarian regime. The term refers to a system in which one person rules unrestrained by any other forces or institutions in that society. In other words, a dictator dictates. Such a system is inherently unpredictable because it depends solely on the will and whims of one man. (To the best of my knowledge, there has never been a female dictator.) Adolf Hitler drove the German General Staff to anger and frustration at his irrational direction of military affairs. Because by definition dictators answer to nobody, a structure of accountability is almost completely absent in such systems.

Traditionally, dictators seized and maintained power through the use or threat of the use of force with an attitude of "the public be damned." They did not have to care what the public thought. This format may be called simple dictatorship, a dictatorship that is seized and maintained through a monopoly of the use of force without any pretense of ideological justification. However, in the modern era of a mobilized public, dictatorships tend to be legitimized by the claim that the dictator somehow embodies the spirit and the values of the masses or the folk, almost as Rousseau's leader justified his/her rule as the embodiment of the general will. In such a system, generally known as a populist dictatorship, there is no formal measurement as to the extent to which the dictator actually speaks for the masses; yet, modern dictators unquestionably articulate widely held values, speak to widely held concerns, and enjoy widespread popular support. Hitler, it should be recalled, received a clear plurality in the last free election of the Weimar Republic and President Hindenburg had little choice but to name him chancellor. Daniel Goldhagen, in a widely discussed and heavily documented study, showed that the Nazi's anti-Semitism reflected a widely and strongly held "eliminationist" anti-Semitism among the German people at the time, a feeling that the Jews were a "pestilence" that needed to be somehow removed from German society.[10] Moreover, he shows that thousands of ordinary Germans willingly and eagerly participated in the gathering, transporting, and ultimate slaughtering of the Jews. Hence, the worst attributes of the Third Reich were not something that a small band of Nazis secretly implemented unknown to ordinary Germans. Hitler did not bring anti-Semitism to Germany; he rode the wave of the preexisting sentiment to power.

Scholars differ as to whether the concept of totalitarian dictatorship connotes a distinct and useful category of dictatorships. As with the concept of populist dictatorship, totalitarian dictatorship, if it exists, is a distinctly modern phenomenon. In fact, the dictatorships that have been identified as belonging in the totalitarian category all take on the populist character as well, the aforementioned Third Reich constituting a prime example of this.

A totalitarian system is essentially one that obliterates the distinction between the public and private domains. It does not recognize a fundamental or defining principle of a free or liberal society such as constitutes the West, that there are some things that are none of the government's business. These things include what we choose to read or view in our own homes, what styles we choose to wear, how we worship, and the more recent inclusion of how we conduct our sex lives with willing adults in private. The ability to control such things among a vast and diverse citizenry requires an efficient and effective government, in short, a modern political system. Therefore, the famous despots of history, e.g., Roman Emperors and Egyptian Pharaohs, while their role as leaders of their political systems was beyond challenge, had little impact on or control of the lives of many of their ostensible subjects in the far flung corners of their realms. To fulfill an aspiration to control all aspects of the lives of all of its subjects, a political system would have to possess great regulative and extractive capabilities.

A populist and totalitarian dictatorship needs to mobilize its population to support the purposes of the regime. It does this through an eschatological and millennial ideology, an ideology that posits that human history and evolution will come to a halt with the achievement of some millennium, an idealized time of peace, prosperity, and social justice.[11] For the Communist Soviet Union, it was the future classless and stateless society. For the Nazis, it was a return to an apocryphal past in the dark ages, a time of the glory days of the Germanic warriors who emerged from the Black Forests to help bring down Rome, an age romanticized in Wagner's opera, *The Ring Cycle,* what Henry Ashby Turner called "utopian anti-modernism."[12] This ideology appealed to those strata whose socioeconomic roles are threatened by modernization, the clerks and shopkeepers of the lower middle class (the *petit bourgeoisie*) and the peasantry, strata romanticized in Germany's *volkish* ideology.[13]

In addition to the official ideology, totalitarian regimes keep their populations in line using the technique of terror. Terror, as perpetrated by the state, consists of severe punishment, not meted out consistently or rationally but rather unpredictably when one of the ruling elites is displeased for whatever reason or for no reason. In this situation people, unable to know the limits of permissible behavior, bend over backwards to please the elites, to give them no possible reason to be displeased. In this unpredictable meting out of punishment generating severe anxiety among nonvictims, totalitarian terror is much like the terrorism in which Middle East militants engage and with a similar result. Terrorists strike targets that are available and this unpredictable selection of victims causes those who are not attacked to alter their lifestyle in order to minimize risk.

The level of control that totalitarian regimes seek to maintain over individuals is such that it eliminates all traces of individuality in trying to bring about a complete identification with the state. This was the point of Hannah Arendt's analysis of Adolph Eichmann, the man in charge of implementing the Holocaust, the slaughter of the European Jews, with her phrase "the banality of evil."[14] While one might have expected a sadistic monster to be able to set up and administer the extermination camps, she found an individual without any personal feelings, a man totally subsumed by the Nazi system to the point of suspending independent moral judgments, what she called the "inanimate man."[15] The remarkable spectacle of men doomed by Stalin's purge trials justifying and supporting the state that was about to execute them is another example of the totally subsumed totalitarian man.

Critics of the utility of the concept of totalitarianism argue that the two regimes that came closest to establishing totalitarian control, Nazi Germany and the Soviet Union, no longer exist and probably did not have full totalitarian control anyway.[16] Recent and current dictatorships are found among less-developed nations that do not have the capability of establishing that kind of control. Hence, the concept creates an empty category; it does not describe anything that actually exists in the real world.

Nevertheless, there are distinctions to be made between dictatorships that appear to crave power for its own sake or for the possibilities of self-enrichment through corruption among the elites, and regimes that seek control of a state in service of an ideology and a sense of mission and attempt to control aspects of life that we in the West would regard as matters that ought to be considered private. For example, the Khmer Rouge regime in Kampuchea (formerly Cambodia) tried to impose a peasant lifestyle on that society through forced relocation of people from urban settings to rural ones and mass murder of intellectuals or anyone who did not fit the Maoist ideal of a peasant society. The Islamic Republic of Iran attempts to impose a rigidly theocratic regime on the people of that country, to impose a lifestyle in strict accord with the constrictions of the *Shariah* or Islamic law. These regimes clearly aspire to a level of control that sets them apart from ordinary dictatorships. The fact that they fall short of those aspirations does not nullify that distinction. Hence, such regimes may be regarded as aspirational totalitarian systems. Totalitarianism therefore becomes a model or ideal type by which to place the openness of a society in perspective and which actual societies resemble to a greater or lesser extent rather than precisely defining a real world phenomenon.[17]

BUREAUCRATIC AUTHORITARIANISM

We noted at the outset of this chapter that the concept of dictatorship does not exhaust the universe of autocracy. Guillermo O'Donnell has identified a regime type that he found widely prevalent, especially in Latin America, in which the power in a state is in the hands of an institution such as a bureaucracy and/or in which the leaders are constrained by deeply ingrained traditions and norms. In such a setting, the leader is not free to rule on the basis of whims of the moment. These institutions guarantee the dominance of a strata of society, especially "a highly oligopolized and trans-national bourgeoisie."[18]

This type of regime is common in late developing nations that suffer from low product diversification (i.e., "banana republics") and which are therefore uniquely vulnerable to market forces. When the price of bananas goes down, the banana republic suffers. These nations therefore seek to produce some of the goods they have been buying from West, a practice that has been draining their capital. This process of diversifying an economy is known as import substitution industrialization (ISI). This process is hindered by a lack of capital. In an effort to squeeze capital from the masses or working classes, the consumption levels of these classes, who are already living at near subsistence levels, must be coercively reduced. Because of this need to coercively accumulate savings for investment in LDCs in which consumption levels are already quite low, David Apter has argued that "mobilization systems,"[19] capable of coercively mobilizing the scarce resources of such societies, are the most effective political format for the early stages of modernization. Such systems are characterized by a hierarchical authority form and "consumatory" (sacred and ultimate) as opposed to "instrumental" (secular) values. However, at later stages of modernization, the need for free flow of information to sustain a higher state of technology requires a more open "reconciliation" format. Here Apter is suggesting a logically plausible reason for the relative rarity of open democratic systems among the systems at the lower stages of modernity, as well as the wave of democratization as these nations approach later stages of modernity.

Hence, bureaucratic authoritarian regimes are generally quite repressive, often under domination by the military. As will be discussed in the following chapter on modernization, military domination or disproportionate military influence on the affairs of government is a common occurrence in less-developed countries, a phenomenon known as a *praetorian* society.

Other institutions besides the military may constrain the discretion of an autocrat preventing him/her from assuming the role of a dictator. After Stalin and certainly after Nikita Khrushchev, the effective head of the Soviet Union was constrained by the *apparat,* a massively bloated, centralized, and thoroughly nonaccountable bureaucracy. This bureaucracy actually ousted Khrushchev in 1964.

DEMOCRATIZATION: THE FIRST WAVE

Each of the three waves of democratization identified by Professor Huntington occurred in a unique cultural, geographic, and temporal context driven by unique causes. The first wave occurred from the late eighteenth century to World War II in the wake of the great liberalizing revolutions in the Western world: the British (so-called "bloodless") revolution of 1688, the American Revolution of 1776, and the French Revolution of 1789. These cataclysmic events were carried out in the name of major democratic values derived from a corpus of philosophic literature produced to justify them: works of men such as Locke, Montesquieu, Rousseau, Voltaire, Jefferson, Paine, and Madison. The conquests of Napoleon Bonaparte, although he was an autocrat pursuing wars of aggression, were fought in the name of liberty, equality, and fraternity, as he spread the then-novel ideal that the masses had rights.

The first wave of democratization occurred in relatively industrialized nations in what we call the West, a fact that contributed to the proposition that contextual factors associated with the Western industrial societies constituted prerequisites for stable and effective democracy.[20] Other scholars argue that elites may choose to adopt a democratic format irrespective of contextual factors such as culture, to "craft a democracy" as a conscious political act.[21] They point to the establishment of what appear to be healthy democratic systems in countries whose culture is definitely not Western. Japan is noted as a glaring example of this. Yet, even here, despite major differences between Japan's cultural traditions and those that define the West, there are similarities on key attributes such as trust in one's fellow man and in one's government and a degree of tolerance of different points of view. It is hard to imagine a successful democracy without some of these cultural attributes. Thus, while it is tempting to believe that democracy can be crafted anywhere by elite will regardless of the context, a conclusion that gives hope to emerging democracies outside the West and which underlies the American effort to transform Iraq (ongoing at this writing in mid-2006), the debate over the cultural requisites of democracy continues.

In the Western states that experienced the first wave, the democratic institutions developed and evolved over a long period of time. Huntington claims that no democracy existed at the national level in the middle of the eighteenth century but by 1900 a number of them existed.[22] One would not call Parliament a democratic institution in Britain before the reform acts of the nineteenth century enfranchised first the middle class (1832 in which the franchise depended how much rent you paid or property ownership, giving about one male in thirty the franchise) or perhaps the second great reform bill (1867), enfranchising a million or so city workers and artisans. However, the fact that Parliament had been in existence at least since the thirteenth century gave it a legitimacy lacking in many of the institutions created for the express purpose of serving a newly crafted democracy in the twentieth century. In fact, parliaments under various guises (cortes in Spain, diets in Germany, estates general in France) began springing up throughout the West. Of course, as we discussed in Chapter Three, the key institution that identifies a polity as democratic is more or less regular competitive elections. Diamond and others call this minimal criterion "electoral democracy." Huntington further suggests that 50 percent of the adult males should be eligible to vote.[23] The establishment of electoral democracy does not, as discussed above, guarantee that regime will be able to resolve the difficult issues regimes ultimately face, a condition we call consolidation.

FIRST-WAVE REVERSALS

The importance of the legitimacy of these institutions in consolidating democracies may be seen in the fact that all but one of the reversals of first-wave democracies occurred in countries that became democratic in the twentieth century. These newly crafted democracies faced several challenges to the legitimacy of their regimes in the interwar period (1919–1939), a period historian E. H. Carr called "the twenty years crisis."[24] They were besieged by newly mobilized Bolsheviks on the left and fascists on the right as well as pressures of the Great Depression and what John Bissel calls hyperinflation (26-billion percent in the Weimar Republic in 1923) that destroyed that key ingredient for successful democracy, the middle class.[25] Austria, Poland, and Hungary also experienced such hyperinflation and challenges from the far right and far left.

The expansionist Soviet dictatorship subsumed several of the fragile new democracies of central and eastern Europe, rendering them satellites of the USSR, while expanding fascism on the far right subsumed other democratic experiments such as Austria, Czechoslovakia, and Poland. The romantic perspectives on the Bolshevik Revolution spread the ideology of militant class conflict while the economic crises were already impoverishing the industrial working class thereby alienating that group from the besieged democracies of which it was a part. The point is that idiosyncratic factors of the interwar period contributed to the first wave of reversals. The principle that one might derive from the analysis of the first wave of democratization and reversals is that emerging democracies are more likely to weather such crises and establish consolidation if they rely on institutions with a preestablished legitimacy. Britain was not a democracy in the early nineteenth century but it had established institutional processes that made consolidated democracy possible. Parliament's strength was well established by the close of the civil wars and the execution of Charles I in 1648 and, when it was democratized in 1867, it was able to withstand the challenges of the interwar period. Of course, those challenges were much less severe to England than to central Europe. The first wave of democratization and the first wave reversals are shown in Table 5–1.

Table 5–1　First Wave Transitions to Democracy and First Wave Reversals

Nation	Reversals
Argentina	Military coup, 1930
Australia	—
Austria	*Anschluss*, 1934
Belgium	—
Brazil	Military coup, 1930
Canada	—
Chile	—
Columbia	—
Czechoslovakia	Coopted by Nazis, 1930, as result of Munich
Denmark	German occupation, 1940
Estonia	Military coup, 1934
Finland	—
France	Vichy regime imposed by Germany, 1940
Germany	Weimar Republic supplanted by 3rd Reich, 1932
Greece	Occupied by fascist Italy, 1936
Hungary	—
Iceland	—
Italy	Mussolini's fascist coup, 1936
Japan	Military coup, parties banned, 1931
Latvia	Military coup, 1934
Lithuania	Military coup, 1934
Netherlands	—
New Zealand	—
Portugal	Military coup, 1926
Spain	Civil War, Franco regime, 1939
Sweden	—
United Kingdom	—
United States	—
Uruguay	Military coup, 1933

Source: The list of first-wave countries is adopted from Samuel Huntington, *The Third Wave* (Norman: University of Oklahoma Press, 1991), p. 14. The list of reversals is culled from various reference works.

THE SECOND WAVE OF DEMOCRATIZATION

The victory of the Allied Forces in World War II legitimated the corpus of democratic values in whose name the war was ostensibly fought and justified, while it punctured the myths of authoritarian efficiency and martial power for the dictatorial formats of the defeated Axis powers and their close allies: Germany, Japan, Italy, Austria (who had merged itself with Nazi Germany through *Anschluss*), and France (who spent the war years as a pro-Nazi puppet regime named for its capital city, Vichy). The victorious British and, in particular, American forces clearly imposed a democratic format on Japan and those parts of Germany under their control. Italy, reacting to the role of their prewar king in facilitating Mussolini's rise to power, deposed him and established a democratic republic.

Western democracies also were swept up in the groundswell popularity of the concept of democracy and installed electoral democracy in the following new nations: Israel, the Philippines, and the two former British colonies of India and Nigeria. Among these nations, the attributes of what we call liberal democracy—tolerance, a sense of identification with the nation, trust in one's fellow man, deference to authority, in short the *Civic Culture* values—were confined to Israel, a nation founded by Holocaust survivors and Zionist-driven Ashkenazi Jews who brought with them a European cultural heritage.

Among these second-wave countries, the newly installed democracies seemed to thrive best in those countries that shared some of the attributes of the industrialized West, especially that of economic development. Consolidation occurred and the democratic regimes appeared to be functioning in the former Axis powers, formerly occupied European powers, Israel, and a relatively prosperous Costa Rica, all relatively industrialized countries with some experience with a democratic format. This pattern appears to reinforce the well-established literature expounding a putatively causal relationship between economic development and democracy.[26] This relationship makes intuitive sense in that such development creates a middle class and a source of wealth and therefore bargaining power independent of the state. It might be recalled from Chapter Two that the beginnings of power flowing out of court to the landed gentry in Britain in the fourteenth century came as a result of the independent financial base and hence bargaining power of that gentry. Democracy seems to have a better chance of flourishing where there are a number independent actors with resources and bargaining power. A middle class appears to be critical, as Barrington Moore so bluntly stated, "No bourgeoisie, no democracy."[27]

SECOND WAVE REVERSALS

It was precisely in the less-developed countries that a series of authoritarian takeovers, mostly in the form of military coups, ended their fledgling electoral democracies within a decade of their establishment. This pattern was especially pronounced in Latin America where electoral democracies in Argentina, Bolivia, Brazil, Chile, Ecuador, Peru, and Uruguay were displaced by military juntas. These were countries in which the political institutions were new and still not consolidated while the respective military structures of the new states, due to the technological requirements of modern warfare, are frequently the most modern parts of those societies.[28] Imperial powers frequently created strong military institutions in their colonies so that order and security could be maintained with minimal cost to the mother country. Obviously, since imperial powers were not anxious to sacrifice political control, it was not in their interest to build representative institutions in their colonies. The fragility of the fledgling democracies in Latin America through the 1960s was exacerbated by the influential Catholic Church which had consistently supported and indeed often had an almost symbiotic relationship with authority. Up to the 1968 Medellín Conference, the Church was primarily concerned with salvation rather than with an egalitarian conception of social justice.

Democracy proved to be nearly as fragile in Asia. Whether or not Syngman Rhee's presidency of South Korea was actually democratic, his successor was ousted in a military coup in 1961. The already autocratic Philippine presidency of Ferdinand Marcos abandoned its democratic façade when Marcos declared martial law in 1971. Despite the misleading label of "guided democracy" applied to the Achmed Sukarno presidency in Indonesia, opposition was not tolerated. Even this façade was ended by a military coup in 1965.

Sukarno was one of a number of leaders of movements for national liberation from Western colonialism who became autocratic leaders of their respective nations once independence was achieved by identifying themselves and their rule with national independence itself. Kwame Nkrumah of Ghana and the Ghandi family in India are other examples of this. The Congress Movement that led India's struggle for independence became the Congress Party, the unopposed rulers of that country. Indira Ghandi ended even this sham democracy when she declared an emergency and martial law. The transitions to democracy in the second wave and the second-wave reversals are presented in Table 5–2 which dramatically shows the fragility of these attempts at democracy in less-developed countries.

THE THIRD WAVE BEGINS

Given the pervasiveness of second wave reversals as shown in Table 5–2, by the mid 1970s only 39 states, concentrated almost exclusively among the advanced industrial and predominantly Protestant nations of the Western world, were classified as free by a Freedom House survey.[29] In most of the world containing a substantial majority of the world's population, a democratic format seemed to be the exception rather than the rule. The widespread pessimism about the ability of democracy to

Table 5–2   Transitions to Democracy and Second-Wave Reversals, 1945–1975

Nation	Second Wave Reversals
Argentina	Military coup, 1966
Bolivia	Military coup, 1964
Botswana	—
Brazil	Military coup, 1964
Burma	Military coup, 1958
Czechoslovakia	Soviet backed coup, 1948
Ecuador	Military coup, 1971
Fiji	—
Gambia	Military coup, 1994
Guyana	—
India	Suspended constitution declared emergency, 1975
Indonesia	Guided democracy, 1957; Military coup, 1965
Israel	—
Jamaica	—
Lebanon	Palestinian and Syrian occupation
Maylaysia	—
Malta	—
Nigeria	Military coups: 1966, 1975, 1976
Pakistan	Military coup, 1977
Peru	Military coup, 1968
Philippines	Martial law declared, 1972
Sri Lanka	—
Trinidad	—
Tobago	—
Turkey	Military coups: 1960; 1971
Venezuela	Military coup, 1948

Source: The list of second-wave countries is derived from Figure 1.1 in Samuel Huntington, *The Third Wave* (Norman: University of Oklahoma Press, 1991), pp. 14–15. Second-wave reversals are compiled from various sources.

flourish in the soil of less developed countries or in Catholic countries seemed to be confirmed by the record of the first two waves and their reversals.

Yet, beginning with the collapse of a century-old dictatorship in Catholic and somewhat less industrialized Portugal in 1974, the world experienced a wave of democratization spreading that political format to precisely those parts of the world regarded as inhospitable to democratic regimes. Over a period of about two decades largely in the 1970s and 1980s, the number of democratic regimes increased from the aforementioned 39 to 118 encompassing some 61 percent of the world's regimes by the mid 1990s.

Several factors may have played a role in the spread of democracy in the third wave. The liberalizing transformation of the Catholic Church after the Vatican II Council of 1963 presided over by Pope John XXIII constitutes one of the most important of them. The Church, which was primarily concerned with protecting its authority structure and only the salvation of its flock, tended to support a number of oppressively autocratic regimes. The Church had had such a symbiotic relationship with the old regime in France and took such an uncompromising stand against even the moderate phase of the Revolution that anticlericalism became inexorably associated with support for the first four French republics. The Church in Spain took a similar position of opposing the Second Republic and supporting the quasi-fascist rebellion of Franco in the Spanish Civil War, 1936–1939. After the reforms of the Council, the Church in both countries was concerned with social justice, allying itself with opposition to such regimes. Out of the aforementioned conference at Medillín came "liberation theology," a concern for economic equality which brought Church personnel in alliances with some Marxist-tinged movements to overthrow existing autocrats. In other places such as in the Philippines, the Church emphasized democratic and civil libertarian values. In either event, the Church was transformed from an institution supporting autocrats to one contributing to their downfall.

The second major factor in encouraging the Third Wave was the unexpected collapse of the Soviet Union. The reasons for this collapse are complex and beyond the scope of this volume. Part of it stemmed from the inefficiencies of their command economy which subsidized inefficient enterprises and unproductive work forces and became unable to compete in the world markets. Part of it stemmed from the identities problem—the failure to create a Soviet identity and thus failing to quash the identities of the myriad of nations, many of them Muslim, on the Steppes of Central Asia, who would never feel comfortable as subjects of a Russian-dominated empire. In the previous chapter on political parties, one could find an extensive discussion of how identity as a value including subcultural defense has largely displaced the classic centrality of class-based issues on which the Marxist world view depends. This collapse of the Soviet Empire discredited the Leninist model that had been, as discussed at the outset of this chapter, the preferred model for the emerging nations that eventually made up "The Third Wave."

The autocratic regimes of the Latin countries encountered several delegitimizing crises rendering them vulnerable to liberalizing challenges. Brazil's economy suffered severely with the rapidly rising oil prices. The junta governing Argentina was weakened by years of economic stagnation followed by a decisive defeat in the war for the Falkland Islands, a war they provoked. Mobilizing opposition to the junta was further facilitated by the regime's having seized and tortured thousands of suspected dissidents. This mobilization was further facilitated by the visit of Pope John Paul. The Bolivian dictator, Juan Suarez, assuming a continuing oil boom, incurred significant foreign indebtedness leaving the country's economy in a disastrous state. The dictator of Paraguay, General Alfred Stroessner, lost the main basis of legitimacy for his 40-year old rule, his opposition to Communism, with the collapse of the Soviet Union.

In fact, as Edgardo Boeninger argued, many of these Latin American military juntas were weakly legitimized by what they were preventing—to control Bolshevism and terrorism, to curb inflation, to halt corruption, to restore order—rather than by what they were expected to accomplish.[30] They were able to seize power as the only viable alternatives to a failed regimes unable to protect the nations' vital interests; they were never able to command the pride and respect of their nations for their own sake. When they failed to deliver on their promises—as to restore economic prosperity—or when the threat that they were called on to confront was ultimately ended—as the threat of the leftist Tupamaro Revolutionary Movement in Uruguay—the juntas were not able to command much diffuse support for their regimes.

THE COLLAPSE OF THE WARSAW PACT REGIMES

The abortive revolutions in the Warsaw Pact nations in the 1950s and 1960s in Poland, Czechoslovakia, and Hungary clearly showed that these dictatorships were held together by the threat of Soviet military might. Antiregime riots broke out in Poland in 1956 followed by the outbreak of a revolution in Hungary in which some 32,000 people died, a revolution put down by the raw power of Soviet armor. Twelve years later the "Prague Spring," a liberalization of Czech communism under Alexander Dubcek was similarly put down by the infusion of Soviet armor. Despite some elliptical encouragement of the revolutionary forces in Hungary by America's Eisenhower Administration, the Soviets acted in the confident knowledge that in the nuclear age America would not go to war with the Soviets to save any of the Eastern European countries. Michael Roskin argues that Soviet tanks or the threat of their use kept the communist regimes of East Germany, Hungary, and Czechoslovakia in power for decades longer than they otherwise would have been.[31]

Two immediate factors contributed to the rapid unraveling of the Warsaw Pact. First, Soviet leader Mikhail Gorbachev, struggling with a stagnant economy, apparently decided that the Soviet state could no longer afford the cost of imposing Soviet control of Eastern Europe by military force. Once the East European masses realized that the Soviets were no longer going to prop up the Warsaw Pact regimes with military force, the demise of these regimes was probably inevitable.

Secondly, in the effort to build an effective industrial infrastructure in one generation, savings and investment had to be wrung from the heretofore powerless masses. The resulting relatively poor performance of the Soviet economy meant that the living standards of the East European masses were lowered just when awareness of the prosperity of their Western neighbors was being buoyed by the economic boom of the postwar West. All of this caused something like Ted Gurr's "relative deprivation"—a feeling that they were getting less than they deserved—to add to the frustration of the East European masses.[32]

In the face of the aforementioned strains on their systems, several of the regimes in the Soviet orbit including the USSR itself attempted to stave off the pressures for change by liberalizing their regimes. Gorbachev led the way with his policies of *perestroika* and *glasnost* (roughly, reform and openness) in 1985. Other communist leaders similarly tried to offer reforms without sacrificing the essential communist structure of the regime. In the face of near economic collapse, Polish communist leader Wojciech Jaruzelski attempted a power sharing plan with Solidarity trade union leader Lech Walesa, a plan that could not be sustained as Jaruzelski was forced by Soviet leader Gorbachev to name a Walesa aid, Tadeusz Mazoweiki as prime minister replacing his communist predecessor, Mieczyslaw Rakowski. Shortly after Poland abandoned communism, Hungary's communist regime also liberalized to the point of abandoning its communist essence. It began to appear that a liberal communist regime is an oxymoron; once such a regime compromises its hard line toward political opposition, it is nearly impossible to maintain its communist nature.

The liberalized Hungarian government opened its border to Austria and the West allowing East Germans a route to circumvent the Berlin Wall and escape Erich Honecher's hard-line dictatorship. In one month, September 1989, 13,000 East Germans fled their country by that route. When Czechoslovakia allowed East Germans passage across its border to West Germany, another 17,000 fled by that route. After large antiregime demonstrations in Leipzig, Honecker was replaced by a more "liberal" communist president, Ergon Krenz. Once again, the liberalizing strategy spelled the end of the regime as Krenz was forced out of office. Free elections were held in East Germany in March, 1990. The former "Democratic Republic" of East Germany was absorbed in a reunited Federal Republic of Germany in October of that year. The transition from a communist autocracy to a more "liberal" communist regime unable to sustain its communist nature was repeated in Bulgaria. The liberal communist elite changed its label from communist to socialist. The transformation of Czechoslovakia closely followed the events in East Germany. Possibly emboldened by the collapse of the other communist regimes that fall, students, intellectuals, and workers demonstrated against the suppression of civil liberties and the stagnant economy. The regime responded with ineffective and heavy-handed attempts at suppression. The popular playwright, Vaclav Havel, who had been imprisoned earlier in the year, was installed as president of the new Czech Republic after a million-person march demanded the ouster of the communist government.

The collapse of communist regimes in the former Warsaw Pact nations of eastern Europe followed one another in quick succession in an almost domino fashion in the fall of 1989. The success of the first east European transformations beginning with Lech Walesa's Solidarity Union movement in Poland showed the frustrated masses throughout the region that real change was possible. Successful revolutions always make surrounding autocrats less secure. That these regimes fell so quickly and with little resistance from the displaced communist elites was probably in part due to the fact that the Soviet Union, which had formerly taken a leading role in suppressing liberalizing reform in the 1950s, was now, under the reformist Gorbachev, counseling accommodation of these movements for liberalizing change. Gorbachev had made it clear that he would not expend his country's scarce resources to preserve communist eastern Europe.

The exception to this pattern of relatively peaceful transition was Romania which under Nicolae Ceauçescu had operated independently of the Kremlin and was therefore less susceptible to Gorbachev's reformist pleas. Romanian security guards killed several hundred people before Ceauçescu's own military removed him from office. Although he managed to stay in power for about a month longer than the other Warsaw Pact autocracies, the violence Ceauçescu used to try to hang on to power resulted in a violent end to his regime as he and his wife were executed on Christmas day, 1989. Ceaucescu's fall completed the removal of the communist regimes of eastern Europe.

DEMOCRATIZATION IN ASIA

The cultural determinists, those scholars who advance the cultural-requisites-of-democracy argument, regarded Asia as inhospitable ground for the consolidation of democratic regimes.[33] The predominance of Confucianism in much of that continent would seem to constitute a significant impediment to democracy taking root there. Confucianism teaches the value of the group rather than the individual, of authority over individual liberty, and of responsibilities over rights.[34] Purity of thought is valued over compromise and dissent is often regarded a disloyalty. Yet, democracy has been established and appears to be functioning effectively in at least four Asian countries: Japan, the Philippines, Taiwan, and South Korea. Buddhism, another important religion in Asia (the leading religion in Myanmar—formerly Burma) actually has attributes that are more conducive to more democratic values than some of the traditional versions of Christianity. According to Donald Smith, it is nondogmatic, individualistic, and egalitarian.[35] Meanwhile, Myanmar, although repressively governed by the military since 1962, has experienced a vigorous prodemocracy movement throughout this period.

The case of Japan was similar to the case of Germany discussed in Chapter Two; democracy was imposed by the victorious allied powers and the school-aged children were deliberately socialized in democratic values. As in Germany, cultural support for democracy in Japan was not so much a matter of changing the orientation of its adult population as a matter of generational change.[36] Moreover, Confucianism in Japan was less influential than it had been in China and other parts of Asia. Shintoism is strong in Japan but it takes the form of ritual rather than deeply held values that shape the culture, Moreover, religion in Japan had been modified by being blended with that nation's indigenous culture. Meanwhile, as was the case with Germany, a vigorously healthy economy insured passive support for the regime and enabled a strong middle class to develop. Nevertheless, following the war the Liberal Democratic Party maintained a strong grip on power for nearly four decades, hardly a model of vigorous multiparty democracy. The party only lost in 1993 to a seven-party coalition in the face of massive corruption scandals. It returned to power in a minority government in 1996, raising a question about the health and viability of political opposition in that country.

In both South Korea and the Philippines, there was also a strong American influence, in the former case because of America's participation in the Korean War and the subsequent American presence there, in the latter case because the country had been an American colony. In each of these two countries, moreover, Confucianism had been substantially displaced by widespread conversion to Catholicism, a religion that, we have seen, has become much more hospitable to democracy since Vatican II and Medellín.

All four of these countries, while classified with the less-developed world, were relatively more modernized and industrialized than most of the other countries so classified. Like Japan, Taiwan and South Korea experienced substantial economic growth and the growth of the critical middle class, a source of power and wealth independent of the state. The Korean middle class was instrumental in mobilizing almost daily demonstrations against the regime of Chun Doo Hwan that had come into power as a result of a military coup in 1980. Chun's associate, Roh Tae Woo agreed to a presidential election in 1987 in which Roh was elected president in a four way contest.[37] Thus, while Edward Friedman is correct in his assertion that the east Asian experience belies any assertion that Western cultural attributes must be in place before democracy can be established, a closer examination of these four countries reveals that they actually possessed the putative requisites to a substantial degree. They were relatively modernized, they were prosperous, they had a strong middle class, and they had absorbed a substantial degree of Western religious influence.

The experience of India is similar to that of a number of countries emerging from colonial status to independence; they were ruled by the same movement that led the fight for independence. Because the Congress movement was associated with independence, opposition to the Congress Party was regarded as tantamount to disloyalty to the independent republic. The elected leader of the Congress Party, Indira Gandhi had been exercising "emergency" powers which gave her autocratic control of the government. Under the apparently mistaken assumption that she could further legitimize her regime by a sweeping electoral victory, she called for an election in 1977, an election that swept Congress out of power for the first time since independence. Congress regained power but was swept out of power with a defeat in the 1989 general election. Congress temporarily regained the prime ministership as a minority government in 1991 but the era of its hegemonic dominance was over. India now has a vigorous multiparty system led by the *Bharatiya Janata* party (Indian People's Party) who, having obtained a 40 percent plurality in the last general election, formed the government as of 2006 under Prime Minister Atal Vajpayee. Congess, with 33.8 percent of the vote in that election, is in opposition. With a strong growth of civil society and the growth of other democratic values, India, having clearly met the two-turnover test, appears to be a consolidated democracy despite remaining problems stemming from its multiethnic and still stratified society.

THE SPREAD OF DEMOCRACY TO AFRICA

Africa stands as testament to the argument that electoral democracy can be established and even work effectively at least in the short run without the previously discussed "social and cultural requisites" being in place. Despite the fact that some of these attributes are glaringly absent on that continent, by 1995 three-quarters of the African states had multiparty systems and 14 of those states (Benin, Burundi, Cape Verdi, Central African Republic, Congo, Lesotho, Madagascar, Malawi, Mali, Namibia, Niger, Sao Tome, Principe, and Zambia) had actually transferred power on the basis of an election.[38] The social requisite that is most glaringly absent on that continent is a moderately high level of economic development with the consequent strength of that crucial middle class. Of the 151 nations for which data are presented for per capita GNP in the *World Handbook of Social and Political Indicators,* Botswana is the highest-ranking African state in 87th place. While major Western powers have figures in the $10,000 range, the corresponding figure for most African nations is under $500.[39]

As we have discussed at various points in this volume, much of the leading scholarship in the discipline of comparative political analysis argues that there is a causal link between modernization with its concomitant higher level of economic prosperity and democracy. The causes of the degree of modernization are discussed at length in the following chapter. Therefore, many of these same causes that are advanced to explain the impediments to democratization on the African continent will only be briefly noted here.

Although nature has dealt some of the African nations near the rim of the great Sahara Desert an economic challenge—little arable land and few natural resources—other African nations are blessed with one or both of these assets. Nigeria, although its northern tribes extend to the Sahara rim, has both arable land and substantial petroleum reserves. Zimbabwe (formerly, Rhodesia) used to be a major food exporter from its rich farm lands. Botswana and South Africa have diamonds. Sierra Leone and Zaire abound in mineral resources and arable land. Hence, the roots of African underdevelopment must lie elsewhere.

The cultural segmentation and tribalism of Nigeria is only the most extreme African example of a state without a culturally defined sense of nation or community. Economic crises in the 1980s brought about by economic mismanagement by inexperienced elites resulted in a debt crisis that seriously impeded the ability of these countries to invest in economic growth. Africa is also a classic case of Huntington's model of "political decay"—in which the rapid infusion of education, literacy, and basic sanitation that promoted explosive population growth all contributed to the mobilization of demands.[40] This mobilization preceded the development of legitimate institutions to process these demands into policy. This is the negative side of what Chapter Two called "stage theory," the advantages of the sequential resolution of the crises of nation building.

The breakdown of institutionalized racism known as *apartheid* and the consequent establishment of electoral democracy in South Africa was one of the more widely followed examples of transition to democracy on that continent. South Africa had the advantage of a sizable minority population of British stock who brought with them many of the cultural attributes that had fostered democracy in their homeland. However, over half of that country's white population were of a populist, *volkish* (in the German sense of that term), and racist Dutch stock known as Boers or Afrikaners. In two great "Treks," they migrated inward from the coasts and the centers of European civilization and its values. Isolated in the remote interior, they had been enslaving native Africans since the seventeenth century. The clash between these two culturally distinct settler populations resulted in two Boer Wars around the turn of the century.

In the aftermath of the Second World War, the Afrikaners' National Party gained control of the government and imposed the *apartheid* policy, a policy of overt racism that deeply offended the international community in reaction to the genocide of the World War and more recently to the American Civil Rights movement. International pressure in the form of sanctions and widespread condemnation was brought to bear on the regime. Pressures to end the *apartheid* policies of the regime were mobilized within the political system by the institutions of civil society, institutions that maintained their autonomy from the regime. Hence, protests against the racist policies were mobilized by the African National Congress, a moderate group in existence since 1912, the more radical Pan African Congress, and the Anglican Church led by the charismatic Bishop Desmond Tutu. Eventually, some 700 protesting organizations were coordinated by the United Democratic Front. Meanwhile, in the wake of the Sharpsville Massacre in 1960, in which 67 black demonstrators were killed and 187 wounded by police, international pressure continued to build against the regime, which was isolated to the extent that its athletes were barred from Olympic competition, a penalty not even foisted on the likes of North Korea. Under the leadership of Prime Minister F.W. DeClerk, the regime released famous dissident leader Nelson Mandela from prison and negotiated the reform of the regime with him. South Africa was one of the few transitions achieved through negotiations rather than force or violence.

DEMOCRATIZATION IN THE ISLAMIC WORLD

Turkey stands out as the one state with a predominantly Muslim population that has successfully operated under a regime of electoral, multiparty democracy over a significant span of time. (Indonesia held elections in 1999 for the first time in nearly half a century. Democracy is even more rare among Arab countries.) However, Turkey is unique among Muslim countries in having adopted a secular regime independent of Islamic clergy and Islamic law. Until the attempt to impose electoral democracy in Iraq by American forces in 2006, no other Arab regime has adopted a democratic political format.

The conflict between the West in general and militant Islamism that came to a head in the attack on the World Trade Center in 2001 and the American response in its attempt to import democracy to Iraq, a country without democratic experience, renders the question of the viability of democracy in an Islamic context one of major salience.[41] The fact that—the secularized example of Turkey aside—Islamic civilization is the only significant group of nations without a single consolidated democracy raises the question of whether militant Islamism—the radicalized and ideological brand of Islam—presents insuperable impediments to the installation and consolidation of a democratic format.

Whenever militant Islamic forces come to power, they attempt govern in conformity with the *Shariah* (Islamic Law), a body of rules that have been variously interpreted from one Islamic sect to another but which generally stands in conflict with Western ideals of modernity and human rights. It generally forbids the education of women: it commands death by stoning of women for adultery but not of men; it commands the cutting off of limbs for simple theft; and it forbids listening to music. Islamic scholars differ as to whether the concept of *Jihad* commands the imposition of the faith on infidels by force. Whether or not *Jihad* actually means a requirement to spread the faith by military force, a number of prominent Imams and other Muslim leaders have stated their mission to spread their faith by either the conversion or the killing of infidels. This clear intention to stamp out heresy, somewhat reminiscent of the Medieval Christendom, is incompatible with the freedom of thought inherent in the concept of pluralist democracy. The putative imperative to govern in accordance with the *Shariah* suggests to Islamist leaders like Abu Musab al Zarqawi that democracy, governing in accord with the will of the voting public, is anathema. Zarqawi, ostensibly leading the "insurgency" in Iraq, vainly exhorted Iraqis to boycott the elections of 2005 and for his followers to fight the very idea of democracy, which draws into question the assumption of President Bush that when given the choice, the preference for political freedom is universal.

Bernard Lewis, widely regarded as one of the foremost authorities on Islam, has explored the reason why this once flourishing and promising civilization languishes in medieval authoritarianism. He suggests, for one thing, that the mandated second class status for women by denying them access to education and the work force, not only denies that society half of the productive and creative potential of its population, but insures that the crucial task of raising the younger generations will fall to the most ignorant and superstitious parts of the population. Indeed, as Lewis points out, even those moderate Islamic leaders who want to modernize in the sense of adapting to modern technology resist Westernization against which their chief grievance is the nearly equal status of women.[42]

The almost complete failure of the "third wave" of democratization to penetrate the Muslim world raises again the question of cultural and social requisites for the successful implantation of democracy. Its temporary existence in Nigeria and the Sudan were reversed by military coups. Nigeria at this writing has an elected president, former General Olusegun Obasanjo, but given the predilection of the Muslim-dominated military to quash earlier attempts at Nigerian democracy, the future of Nigerian democracy is uncertain. Moreover, Nigeria with a predominantly Christian population in its southern tribal areas is hardly your typical Muslim nation. If the American attempt to install democracy in Iraq is successful, an enterprise that is either promising or hopeless depending on to whom you listen at this writing in mid-2006, that would clearly support the Edward Friedman—Giuseppe De Palma position that democracy may be "crafted" in various settings and contexts by elite decision, thus rejecting the cultural determinists argument.

The third wave of democratization and third-wave reversals are presented in Table 5–3.

CONCLUSIONS: THE REQUISITES OF DEMOCRACY

In surveying the waves of creating and undoing democratic political formats from the mid-nineteenth century to the present, this chapter has been concerned with the very salient question, at this point in America's relationships with the rest of the world, of whether there are contextual requirements for the successful establishment and consolidation of such a constitutional format. Scholars remain divided over the utility of the concept of consolidation but most would agree that there is a point, albeit one that is hard to pinpoint, where the question of the nature of the regime is no longer on the agenda, which is another way of stating Linz and Steppan's "only game in town" criterion discussed at the beginning of this chapter.

Among the so-called requisites of democracy, one finds the claim that a common sense of nationhood or identity is required as measured by Almond and

Table 5–3   Third-Wave Democratizations and Reversals

Nation	Second Wave Reversals
Argentina	—
Bolivia	—
Brazil	—
Bulgaria	—
Chile	—
Czechoslovakia	—
Ecuador	—
El Salvador	—
German Democratic Republic (Reunification)	—
Greece	—
Haiti	—
Honduras	—
India	—
Indonesia	—
Mali	—
Mongolia	—
Namibia	—
Nicaragua	—
Nigeria	Military coup, annulled elections, 1983
Pakistan	—
Panama	—
Peru	—
Philippines	—
Poland	—
Romania	—
Senegal	—
South Korea	—
Spain	—

Verba's "pride in the nation" factor in their profile of a "civic culture."[43] Yet, as we will see in the following chapter on political development and modernization, many of the newly established democracies are less-developed societies that are severely segmented along tribal, ethnic, or religious lines. One may take some comfort in recalling, however, that a number of established Western democracies are or have been similarly segmented along cultural, ethnic, linguistic, and/or religious lines.

This kind of segmentation usually entails low levels of trust between the social and ethnic groupings, not to mention common objects of identity or a sense of community among them. In such a setting, one model is the classic majoritarian model of democracy in which the minority, the losers in the electoral contest, may be unwilling to accept exclusion from the national decision making process.

This problem applies par excellence to the efforts of the United States to install a democratic format in Iraq, a country strongly segmented between three communities that have never cooperated with or trusted one another: the Kurds who were slaughtered by the tens of thousands by the Hussein regime, the minority Sunnis who were supported by the Hussein regime and who participated in the oppression of the other groups, and the Shi'ite majority who had been oppressed by the Sunnis and who, in a majoritarian system, would threaten to exert a measure of revenge. Clearly, a majority system would not work in such a situation.[44]

There are two alternative formats in such a situation. One is the Belgian solution to transfer all the significant powers to elites of the subcultures, in effect to become a confederation, a loose alliance of the three now-sovereign political systems unable to act in concert to solve common problems. As suggested in Chapter Three, weak national governments such as Belgium and Switzerland work to the extent that not a great deal is expected of them. Neither of these two countries are major players in the world system. Whether Iraq, situated in a volatile area of the world, could survive with an ineffective national government is uncertain.

A second alternative is the model first articulated by Professor Lijphart and practiced to varying degrees in the segmented societies of Canada, the Netherlands, and Austria—a format he calls "consociational democracy."[45] In this model, the various cultural segments are guaranteed a role in major decision making structures proportionate to the electoral outcome, structures such as the cabinet or the higher civil service. In this way, no major subcultural segment is ever frozen out of the policy making process for a period of time. Enough cooperation and guarded trust may build up among the interacting elites over time to enable the system to function. Such a format may have applicability in a highly segmented society like Iraq or a society rent by tribalism such as Nigeria.

The question posed at the outset of this chapter, the question about whether there are cultural requisites to the successful establishment and consolidation of democracy, yields a mixed result. On the one hand, democracy has been established and appears to be operating effectively in several venues, most notably in East Asia, that clearly do not have a Western culture. We have seen, e.g., in the cases of Germany and Japan, that democratic values may evolve after the successful establishment and operation of a democratic format.

On the other hand, these countries with apparently successful transitions to democracy have increasingly acquired some of the attributes characteristic of a democratic society: economic prosperity, a middle class, trust in the nation and its leaders, a measure of tolerance of other points of view, and even a growth of Christianity, a change from the historic dominance of Confucianism and Buddhism. We saw how in Korea, the Philippines, and Japan the transition to democracy was accompanied by or even preceded by a period of economic prosperity, a growing middle class, and the declining influence of Buddhism. Hence, the cultural determinists may still be able to argue that if not the entire Western cultural package—and scholars disagree as to what the content of that may be—at least some cultural or social attributes may be highly important for, if not absolutely essential for, the successful operation of a democratic format over time. The debate over the extent to which cultural and social attributes are to some degree essential for democracy remains unresolved.

ENDNOTES

[1]Samuel Huntington, *The Third Wave: Democratization in the Late Twentieth Century* (Norman: University of Oklahoma Press, 1991).

[2]Francis Fukuyama, "The End of History," *The National Interest* Vol. 16 (Summer, 1989), pp. 3–18.

[3]These numbers are taken from Table 1.1 in Huntington, *The Third Wave*, p. 26.

[4]John Kautsky, "An Essay on the Politics of Development," and Maurice Watnik, "The Appeal of Communism to Underdeveloped People," in Kautsky, ed. *Political Change in Underdeveloped Countries: Nationalism vs. Communism* (New York: John Wiley, 1962), pp. 3–122 and 316–334; Lawrence Mayer, *Redefining Comparative Politics: Promise vs. Performance* (Newbury Park, CA: Sage Publications, 1989), pp. 81–62.

[5]Larry Diamond, et. al., eds., *Consolidating Third World Democracies* (Baltimore, MD: Johns Hopkins University Press, 1997), pp. xvi-xvii; Larry Diamond and Marc Plattner, *The Global Resurgence of Democracy,* 2nd ed., (Baltimore, MD: Johns Hopkins University Press, 1996), pp. ix-x.

[6]Juan Linz and Alan Steppan, "Toward Consolidated Democracies," in Diamond, et. al., *Consolidating the Third Wave Democracies, op. cit.,* p. 15.

[7]Huntington, *op. cit.,* pp. 266–267.

[8]Guillermo O'Donnelll, "Illusions About Consolidation," in Diamond et. al., *Consolidating Third Wave Democracies,* pp. 39–53.

[9]Carl Friedrich and Zbigniew Brzezinski, *Totalitarian Dictatorship and Autocracy* (Cambridge, MA: Harvard University Press, 1956), p. 3.

[10]Daniel J. Goldhagen, *Hitler's Willing Executioners: Ordinary Germans and the Holocaust* (New York: Vintage Books, 1997).

[11]Friedrich and Brzezinski, *Totalitarian Dictatorship.* In this classic treatise, the authors list the possession of such an ideology as the first listed attribute defining such a system.

[12]Henry Ashby Turner, "Fascism and Modernization," *World Politics,* Vol. 24, no. 2 (July, 1972), pp. 547–564.

[13]George Mosse, *The Crisis of German Ideology: Intellectual Origins of the Third Reich* (New York: Schocken Books, 1981) for the centrality of *volkism,* the racial defining of German in German political thought.

[14]Hannah Arendt, *Eichmann in Jerusalem: A Report on the Banality of Evil* (New York: Penguin Books, Twentieth Century Classics Edition, 1994).

[15]Arendt, *The Origins of Totalitarianism* (New York: Harcourt Brace and Janovich Harvest Books, 1951 and 1973), p. 441.

[16]See Carl Friedrich, "The Failure of a One Party System: Hitler Germany," in Samuel Huntington and Clement Moore, eds., *Authoritarian Politics in Modern Society* (New York: Basic Books, 1970), p. 239, for the argument that despite the "uncertainties" surrounding the application of the term totalitarianism, few would deny the National Socialist regime was the archetypical example of that concept.

[17]For a discussion of Weber's use of the concept of ideal type as applied to organizations, see Max Weber, *The Theory of Social and Economic Organization,* trans. and ed. by Talcott Parsons (New York: The Free Press, 1964), pp,. 329–334. See also H.H. Gerth and C. Wright Mills, eds., *From Max Weber:Essays in Sociology* (New York: Galaxy Books, 1958), p. 59.

[18]Guillermo O'Donnell, "Tensions in the Bureaucratic Authoritarian State and the Question of Democracy," in David Collier, ed., *New Authoritarianism in Latin America* (Princeton, NJ: Princeton University Press, 1980), p. 287.

[19]David Apter , *The Politics of Modernization* (Chicago: University of Chicago Press, 1965), pp. 22ff.

[20]See, e.g., Seymour Lipset, "Some Social Requisites of Democracy: Economic Development and Political Legitimacy," *American Political Science Review,* Vol. 53, No. 1 (March 1959), pp. 69–105; Gabriel Almond and Sidney Verba, *The Civic Culture* (Boston, Little Brown, 1965).

[21]Giuseppe Di Palma, *To Craft Democracies* (Berkeley: University of California Press, 1990). One of the most forceful rejections of the practice of over-generalizing about the requisites of democracy from the western experience is Edward Friedman, *The Politics of Democratization: Generalizing from the East Asian Experience* (Boulder, CO: Westview Press, 1994).

[22]Huntington, *The Third Wave*, pp. 13–14.

[23]Huntington, *The Third Wave,* p. 16.

[24]Edward H. Carr, *The Twenty Years Crisis, 1919–1939 2nd* ed. (New York: St. Martin's Press, 1964).

[25]See John Bissel, "The Crisis of Modern Democracy: 1919–1939," in David Potter et. al., eds., *Democratization* (Cambridge, UK: The Polity Press, 1997), pp.71–93, for a summary and analysis of first-wave reversals.

[26]One of the earliest and most forceful expositions of this relationship is Seymour Lipset, "Some Social Requisites of Democracy: Economic Development and Political Legitimacy," *American Political Science Review,* Vol. 53, No. 1 (March, 1959), pp. 69–105. See also Juan Linz and Alfred Steppan, "Toward Consolidated Democracies," in Diamond et. al. *Consolidating Third World Democracies*, pp.17–20.

[27]Barrington Moore, *The Social Origins of Dictatorship and Democracy* (Boston: The Beacon Press, 1966), p. 418.

[28]Lucien Pye, "Armies in the Process of Political Modernization," in John Johnson, ed., *The Role of the Military in Underdeveloped Countries* (Princeton, NJ: Princeton University Press, 1962), pp. 69–90.

[29]Cited in Larry Diamond, "In Search of Consolidation," in Diamond et. al. eds., *op. cit.*, p. xlvi.

[30]Edgardo Boeninger, "Latin America's Multiple Challenges" in Diamond et.al., eds., vol. 2, p. 31.

[31]Michael Roskin, *The Rebirth of East Europe* (Englewood Cliffs, NJ: Prentice Hall, 1994), p. 126.

[32]Ted Gurr, "A Causal Model of Civil Strife: A Comparative Analysis Using New Indices," *The American Political Science Review,* Vol. LXII, No. 4 (December, 1968), pp. 1104–1124.

[33]See, e.g., Francis Fukuyama, "The Primacy of Culture," in Diamond and Plattner, eds., *Global Resurgence of Democracy*, p. 325.

[34]Huntington, *The Third Wave*, p. 300.

[35]Donald Smith, *Religion and Political Development* (Boston: Little Brown, 1970), pp. 195–197.

[36]*Ibid.*, pp. 264–265.

[37]Hsin Huang, Michael Hsiao, and Hagan Koo, "The Middle Classes and Democratization," in Diamond et. al., eds., *Consolidating Third World Democracies*, p. 315.

[38]John Wiseman, "The Rise and Fall and Rise (and Fall?) of Democracy in Sub-Saharan Africa," in Potter et. al., eds. *Democratization*, p. 285.

[39]Charles Lewis Taylor and David Jodice, *World Handbook of Social and Political Indicators*, 3rd ed., vol. 1 (New Haven, CT: Yale University Press, 1983), pp. 111–112.

[40]Samuel Huntington, "Political Development and Political Decay," *World Politics*, Vol.17, No. 3 (April, 1965), pp. 386–430.

[41]The thesis that Islamic civilization is in a state of long-term conflict with the West is cogently argued in Samuel Huntington, *The Clash of Civilizations and the Remaking of the World Order* (New York: Simon & Schuster, 1996).

[42]Bernard Lewis, *What Went Wrong: The Clash Between Islam and Modernity in the Middle East* (New York: Harper-Collins Perennial Books, 2002), pp. 69–73 and esp. p. 157.

[43]Garbriel Almond and Sydney Verba, *The Civic Culture* (Boston: Little Brown, 1965).

[44]See the distinction made between majoritarian and consensus models of democracy in Arend Lijphart, *Patterns of Majoritarian and Consensus Governments in Twenty-One Countries* (New Haven, CT: Yale University Press, 1984).

[45]Arend Lijphart, *The Politics of Accommodation: Pluralism and Democracy in the Netherlands* (Berkeley: University of California Press, 1964).

6

Political Change and Modernization

During the more than four decades of the Cold War in which the United States with its NATO allies and the Soviet Union with its Warsaw Pact allies confronted one another in what appeared to be a bipolar world, all of the nation states not aligned with either of these two power blocs were grouped as a category known as "The Third World." Despite their being grouped or categorized together, this large and variegated group of nations had little in common except for two things: they were not part of either the Western democratic bloc of nations nor of the Marxist group of autocratic nations, and they were somewhat less industrialized and modernized than the nations of the two dominant blocs.

The concept "Third World" referred to such a diverse group of societies and states that it was analytically useless; it became even more so upon the breakup of the Soviet Union and the democratization of much of the former communist world described in the preceding chapter. The analytic usefulness of these concepts is further weakened by the wide diversity of social, economic, and political attributes among the countries so classified.

This group of nations had also been widely identified as less developed, less modernized, or non-Western. Others, using the terminology associated with a globalist or world economic system perspective, refer to them as the periphery as opposed to the industrialized core. Each of these terms has lacked specificity rendering it difficult to unambiguously assign all nations to particular categories.[1] Nevertheless, there seems to be wide agreement that these terms refer to the relatively less industrialized nations of Asia, Africa, and Latin America. Less modernized or less developed seem to be the preferred terms for referring to these nations. In this chapter, the term "less-developed countries" or LDCs will be used.

As stated above, the only attribute that the Third World countries shared was that they did not belong to one of the two blocs of the bipolar world. For example, among the nations that comprise what we call South America there is Argentina, a country that meets the widely accepted criterion of being a postindustrial society with 52 percent of its 32.7 million people in the tertiary or service sector of the economy and only 14 percent in agriculture, on the one hand, as contrasted with Bolivia with only 26 percent of its 7.1 million people in the service sector and over half still in agriculture. The diversity of South America alone is shown in Table 6–1.

Thus, by economic and political criteria, relatively more developed nations, albeit in the non-Western or less developed category, such as South Korea or Argentina, have more in common with supposedly Western nations such as Italy, especially the southern half of that country, than they do with such severely underdeveloped countries in subSahara Africa as Chad, Mauritania, or Ethiopia. Indeed, some scholars have suggested that nations such as these, lacking resources to provide even the minimal level of sustenance for their respective populations, should be considered as a separate category below the developing nations of the Third World—a Fourth World.

TABLE 6–1   The Diversity of South America: Size and Modernity

Nation	% in Agriculture	% in Service	Area (Sq. Miles)	Population
Argentina	14	52	1,072,070	32,664,000
Bolivia	51	26	424,163	7,157,000
Brazil	42	38	3,284,426	155,356,000
Chile	21	52	292,257	13,287,000
Columbia	31	46	459,513	33,778,000
Ecuador	47	29	109,483	10,752,000
Guyana	—	—	83,000	750,000
Paraguay	51	30	157,047	4,799,000
Peru	40	40	496,000	22,362,000
Suriname	—	—	55,155	402,000
Uraquay	12	56	72,172	3,121,000
Venezuela	21	32	352,143	20,189,000

Sources: *Comparative World Atlas* (Maplewood, NJ: Hammond Corporation, 1993), pp. 4–5. Charles Taylor and David Jodice, *World Handbook of Social and Political Indicators*, 3rd ed., Vol. 1 (New Haven, CT: Yale University Press, 1983), pp. 208–216.

A concern with these LDCs has not coincidentally been associated with the drive to make political analysis more "scientific" and hence explanatory, a transformation of the field described in Chapter One. The conceptual tools of traditional comparative government, a parochial focus on the constitutionally designated structures of Western democracies, were ill suited for the study of the newly emerging nations that frequently either lacked such structures or had given them different roles and meanings. Hence, scholars concerned with the LDCs turned to social and other contextual factors that had previously been ignored in the traditional study of comparative government. Thus the geographical expansion of comparative analysis was accompanied by a conceptual expansion that was crucial to the construction of explanatory theory, as shown in Chapter Two. However, the goal of rendering explanatory theory as general as possible—applicable to the widest variety of nations or cases—has had its cost in sacrificing precision. Generality and empiricism are frequently conflicting imperatives because the behaviors that serve as indicators of the concepts we use take on different meanings in different settings. It is therefore no accident that students of these LDCs have given greater attention to the formulation and specification of new concepts than have their more traditionally oriented colleagues, with their focus on advanced Western political systems.

CONCEPTUALIZING THE LESS-DEVELOPED COUNTRIES

It was argued in Chapter One that in order to build explanatory and predictive theory in the field, we must specify indicators for our major concepts, criteria for unambiguously assigning cases to one category (i.e., concept) or another. The key concept here is modernity, a concept that has multiple dimensions. For example, Welzel, Inglehart, and Klingemann identify three components of modernity: economic development, cultural change, and the spread of democratic institutions.[2] Although this chapter will explore the relationships among these dimensions, they are conceptually distinct. In fact, a nation might operate under a distinctly nonmodern political format (such as a noninstitutionalized, charismatic form of authority) while possessing a modern industrial plant and advanced technology.

The economic dimension of modernity first concerns industrialization. This entails becoming efficient enough in the cultivation and herding of food sources—the agrarian sector—so that society can move people from that primary sector to the manufacturing of raw materials into finished products. The commonly used indicator here is the percentage of the population in the secondary or manufacturing sector; when 50 percent of the population is in the manufacturing sector, that is an industrial society. Industrialization, of course, entails the concentration of a work force around the manufacturing site, the beginnings of urbanization. Urbanization in turn, produces other social consequences that will be discussed below in the context of "modernization theory."

The economic dimension generally entails classifying societies in four categories: a primitive society in which people acquire food by hunting and gathering, an agrarian society in which people acquire food by deliberate cultivation and herding of animals for meat, an industrial society in which a majority of the population is involved in the manufacture of products from raw materials while only a minority are involved in the acquisition of food, and a postindustrial society in which a majority of the population is in the service sector, mostly in the creation of ideas and the dissemination of information. A postindustrial society necessarily involves an advanced state of technology, which in turn requires functional specialization in decision making roles (as discussed in conjunction with the administrative state in Chapter Three) and is reflected in the structure of society.

Hence, the social dimension of modernization involves role specialization to manage the explosion of knowledge and information that drives the advanced state of technology. As noted in Chapter Two, social modernization also entails secularization defined in terms of the declining influence of closed, comprehensive thought systems that restrict the free flow and interchange of information on which modern science depends. It is in this sense that David Apter argues that in the later stages of modernization mobilization systems, designed to concentrate resources to common purposes through a "consumatory" ideology (one that is closed and defined by final goals), are replaced by "reconciliation systems," designed to promote inquiry through instrumental, essentially pragmatic, values.[3] This poses the question of whether a society can enjoy the advantages of Western technology in such areas as medicine, transportation, or weapons systems while rejecting the social and cultural attributes of the West in which the technology was created. Technology can be purchased—but it must be operated and maintained.

A modern society is one in which the population is mobilized, becomes part of and identified with the wider society: there is an expansion of intellectual horizons beyond the confines of one's village or tribe to a sense of nationhood.[4] This mobilization entails an expansion of the politically relevant strata of the population, those strata of whom government must take account. Among the indicators of social mobilization are literacy rates, average duration of formal education, or media exposure—factors that might be expected to generate a higher level of awareness and a higher volume of demands and expectations. When social modernization generates a greater volume of demands, there is a question as to whether the political system can adapt to this stress.

Political development may therefore be conceptually distinguished from industrialization and social modernization. While Karl Deutsch assumes the stress of a newly mobilized society would automatically cause the political structures to respond to this challenge, Samuel Huntington warns that mobilizing a society before it develops a constitutional format able to process the higher level of demands can cause that regime to collapse or "decay."[5] Huntington suggests that institutionalization, which will enhance the capacity of the state to cope with the stress of the level of demands coming from a mobilized society, should precede such mobilization. He says, "Institutionalization is the process by which organizations and procedures acquire value and stability."[6] Developed institutions should be complex (with functionally specific roles), autonomous, and adaptable.

With his concept of institutionalization, Huntington is moving toward a conceptualization of political development as opposed to social modernization. He is talking about enhanced capabilities from the governing structures. This idea of enhanced system capabilities as the essence of political development was further developed by Gabriel Almond and G. Bingham Powell when they specified five capabilities that should be associated with the modern political system: regulative, extractive, distributive, symbolic, and responsive. The implication is that to the extent that a political system has lower levels of capabilities on one or more of these five dimensions, they would be less modern.[7] Both Huntington and Almond among others focus the concept of political as opposed to social modernity or industrialization on the capability of the systems' institutions to adapt to the stress created by changes in the quantity and intensity of demands.[8]

In so doing, they have conceptually distinguished political development from social modernization or industrialization, thereby opening the possibility of finding a relatively modern society governed by a military junta or simple dictatorship or other combinations of modernity in one sector and lack of modernity in another. Moreover, in defining political development in terms of system capacities, these scholars avoid the parochial ethnocentrism of defining political development in terms of some particular constitutional format or regime. Yet, in assessing whether a society can sustain industrial modernization with its modern technology, one needs the ability to measure the level of modernity in each of these dimensions, a daunting challenge for concepts supposedly universally applicable. Huntington does suggest some potential indicators for the dimensions of institutionalization. For example, he suggests that the concept of adaptability can be indicated by the age of institution, from which can be inferred the system's ability to withstand crises over time. There is an element of tautology here, however. We know a system is adaptable because it has lasted. Yet, it has lasted because it is adaptable. We also lack the means to precisely distinguish system breakdown, the presumed consequence of failure to exercise the foregoing capabilities, and system change. For example, when France in 1959, in the face of crises both domestic and foreign, replaced the Fourth Republic with the Fifth Republic, was this a case of system adaptation and change—or was it a case of system breakdown?

The foregoing reflects that lack of consensus among scholars as to the meaning of concepts such as development and modernization, not to mention the indicators of their presence in the real (sensory) world. Moreover, there is an underlying normative content in the way these concepts are applied. For example, Huntington's focus on institutionalization connotes a concern for the maintenance of order, while those concerned with mobilization are interested in generating change to enhance some controversial notions of social justice.

MODERNIZATION THEORY

The foregoing discussion of the degree of modernity in the economic, societal, and political dimensions concerns states of being. Yet, the literature on development ultimately implies change, a process of going from one state of being to another.

In the decades following World War II, the early writings on political development envisaged a process of moving inexorably from a less-developed to a more-developed state, a process widely known as "modernization theory."

Modernization theory propounds a process of moving from an agrarian society in which the majority of the population is needed to produce the food. As technology advances efficiency in cultivation and herding, peasants are no longer needed in these enterprises, and they are therefore driven into the urban work force. Urbanization provides the concentration of labor and capital to feed the emerging factory system. With the closer patterns of interaction in the emerging cities, resources can be allocated to an expanding public education and literacy, which in turn drive media exposure and social mobilization, which then drive expanding political participation.[9] Participation, an indicator of a mobilized and hence modern society, does not necessarily mean democracy. Recall the phenomenon of populist dictatorships discussed in Chapter Five.

This developmental scenario is presumed by modernization theorists to be linear, moving in the same direction (as from less modern toward more modern), to be universal (all political systems eventually going down the same modernization path, and being the product of the forces of history rather than the choices of individuals. The path of modernization theory is shown in Figure 6–1.

Max Weber, the famous German social scientist of the early twentieth century, similarly conceptualized the modernization process as an inexorable rationalization, a movement away from charismatic and traditional bases of authority to rational and legal bases of authority and the increasing pervasiveness of the

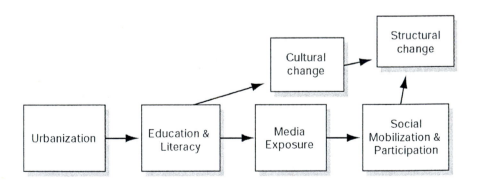

Figure 6–1   Modernization Theory

bureaucratic form of organization, as discussed in Chapter Three.[10] This focus on basis of authority adds another perspective on political modernity. Max Weber argues that Protestantism facilitates the rise of capitalism. With capitalism comes a rising middle class with the resources to invest in infrastructure and economic growth. The importance of the middle class for modernization is seen when looking at the slow economic development of parts of Latin America with its two-tiered social structure, European absentee landlords and a native peonage comprised of people of color.

With his work on the impact of Protestant values on the development of modern capitalism, discussed in Chapter Six, Weber also pioneered a consideration of the cultural dimensions of modernization. Early modernization theorists such as Lerner posited that the modernization process brought about a new psychological orientation. Vicky Randall and Robin Theobald summed up this conceptualization of modern man as follows:

> Modern man is adaptable, independent, efficient, oriented to long-term planning, sees the world as amenable to change and, above all, is confident of the ability to bring change about.[11]

Ronald Inglehart, Hans Klingermann, and Christian Welzel, leaders in exploring the impact of cultural factors on modernization, also find modernity associated with people having a sense of the ability to control their own destiny.[12] Rather than suggesting simple linear causal path, they suggest that the relationships between the dimensions of modernity are actually recursive; the causal arrows go both ways. Thus, while economic development or industrialization causes cultural modernization, cultural modernization drives economic development.

With the sense that man can control his own destiny, Inglehart and associates find a concomitant decline in the impact of religiosity, a phenomenon we noted in Chapter Two, with regard to the European democracies. Religion is dysfunctional for modernity and democratization for several reasons: In claiming to have a monopoly on truth and salvation, it made tolerance of different points of view illogical. Clearly, the suppression of heresy is not conducive to the creation of new ideas. In focusing on other-worldly concerns, it distracted people from the attention and effort to control life on earth as we know it.

It is far from clear, however, that this putative secularization of society—the declining salience of religiosity—is a universal phenomenon. Indeed, the growing power and assertiveness of Islamist fundamentalism in the Muslim world in the first decade of the twenty-first century would suggest the opposite trend, as would the increasing salience of the politics of identity displacing the politics of interest discussed in Chapter Four. Identity, as Ashutosh Varshney argues, is in the realm of ontology rather than rationality.[13] It is about the questions, who am I? and what is my purpose in life? The more modern politics of interest rather is about the question, how do I get what I want? Thus, the assumption by modernization theory of linearity cannot be sustained. Clearly, for example, present day Iran is less socially modern than it was under the Shah.

The rise of Islamic fundamentalism also indicates that modernization as we understand it in the West is not a universal or inevitable phenomenon. Societies dominated by that perspective hate the West and its values. While they may covet some of the products of Western technology, they utterly reject the values that define the West. The assumption of universality and inevitability will be further challenged by the perspective that the capitalist West is deliberately keeping the LDCs permanently underdeveloped, a perspective we will discuss below in the context of alternative explanations of underdevelopment.

The assumption that all LDCs will ultimately change through the same stages and arrive at the same end of this evolutionary process is a now largely discredited idea called "stage theory," associated with the writings of Walt Whitman Rostow and Kenneth Organski. Organski, for example, postulated that societies will evolve through four stages: political unification, industrialization, national welfare, and abundance.[14] The stages in stage theory, such as Rostow's "take off into sustained growth," are usually conceptualized in such a vague manner that it is impossible to independently identify when a society is in that state.[15]

More importantly, stage theory is an application of the general idea that history inevitably moves toward a common millennium driven by impersonal forces irrespective of human will, an idea that Karl Popper called "historicism."[16] Several important thinkers, including Karl Marx, Georg Hegel, Arnold Toynbee, and Francis Fukuyama have offered a historicist perspective on human history albeit they posit different historical paths and different millennia. The historicist perspective, by postulating a predetermined and inexorable path for the unfolding of human history, denigrates an essential principle of modern and liberal society which is that man can choose to impact his own destiny and, in so doing, distracts the followers of the historisist perspective from the pursuit of social and economic progress.

Thus, although the terms "modernization" and "political development" are widely and casually used in comparative political analysis, these terms are complex, and their meanings and implications are frequently overlooked and oversimplified if not misunderstood. Yet, if we are to explain the vast differences in the levels of development and modernization, these terms must acquire precise and widely accepted empirical content. Comparative political analysts are still striving for that goal.

EXPLAINING MODERNIZATION AND UNDERDEVELOPMENT

Two normative themes have been implicit in much of the literature on political development and modernization; one is that the enormous disparities in levels of economic prosperity and material well being among the peoples of the world constitute an affront to some conceptions of social justice, and second, that with the destabilizing impact of rapid social change, the greater is the propensity for social violence which must be controlled by forces of order. These values are at some points conflicting. The imposition of order may discourage the social change that may herald in greater material equality among the peoples of the earth. The normative nature of these concerns may obscure the distinction between explanatory and polemic purposes in the literature on underdevelopment and social change.

These concerns have led to large bodies of scholarship offering various and sometimes conflicting explanations of underdevelopment and social change and various explanations of the destabilizing impact of that change.

The literature putatively offering explanations of the widely differing levels of economic and social modernization may be grouped in two categories: those that find the causes of these differences in the world economic system and especially in the exploitation of the LDCs by the industrialized and capitalist West, from here on called *external explanations*, and those that find the causes of these differences in the attributes of the LDCs, heretofore called *internal explanations*. Each of these explanations will be judged by their internal logic and by their fit with available evidence, especially in comparison with that fit for any alternative and competing theories.

EXTERNAL EXPLANATIONS: THE IMPACT OF COLONIALISM

As stated above, the enormous disparities in material well being between the West and the LDCs have been a central concern to scholars. Monte Palmer gave, as an example of this disparity, the fact that in 1989, the "Big Seven" democracies: the United States, the United Kingdom, the Federal Republic of Germany, France, Italy, Canada, and Japan comprised just 14 percent of the world's population; yet, they consumed 42 percent of its energy and enjoyed 53 percent of its goods and services.[17] To recommend a cure for this affront to egalitarian values, one must diagnose the causes.

It is not difficult to conclude that the relationship between the industrial West and the rest of the world has by and large been an exploitive one, given the pervasiveness of colonial control of much of the Asian, African, and Latin parts of the world by the West. Colonialism, as that term has traditionally been understood, means the political subjugation and control of one country by another such that the former is deprived of sovereign power, the defining attribute of a modern nation state. As such, colonialism is an inherently exploitive relationship. The destiny and well-being of the colonized nation is completely at the will of the imperial power.

The impact of colonialism varied a good deal with the attributes of the land being colonized and the policies of the imperial power. Scholars, for example, drew a distinction between direct and indirect rule. The former, common among the French colonial possessions such as Indochina, has Europeans monopolizing po-

litical and administrative roles down to the lowest official level, effectively ex-
cluding the native population from any experience in self-governance. The latter,
characterized by British rule in India, involved the development of administrative
and police functions leaving a body of institutions and trained officials to carry out
essential political functions once independence was achieved. These same British,
however, utilized a more direct rule in their African possessions such as Kenya,
Uganda, and Ghana.

When the empires of the European powers collapsed in the immediate post-war
years, scholars, who wished to attribute the difficulties of many of the newly independent nations to exploitation by the West, created the concept of *neocolonialism*
to refer to the economic and political influence that stronger political systems of
the West continued to exercise in the countries without maintaining formal political control. *Neo* is a prefix meaning "a new form of," allowing one to apply a term
to a situation to which it logically would not apply. This allows those who wish to
indict the West for putative exploitation with the now pejorative term *colonialism*
although Western colonialism has in fact disappeared.

EXTERNAL EXPLANATION: LENINISM AND DEPENDENCY THEORY

A large literature therefore developed attributing the major cause of the continuing
gap between the West and the rest of the world in material prosperity to be continuing exploitation by the West. Much of this literature was an adaptation of V. I. Lenin's theory of imperialism. The appeal of the Leninist model to the LDCs was
discussed in the previous chapter.

In co-opting the Russian revolution of 1917, Lenin adopts Marxism to justify a
peasant-based movement to which classical Marxism clearly would not apply.
Marx predicted a proletarian or industrial working-class revolution from the internal contradictions of advanced capitalism while Russia had neither a capitalist
economy, an entrepreneurial or bourgeois class, nor significant industrialization.
Lenin, in a major reformulation of Marxism, argued that the leadership (i.e., Lenin) of the exploited strata can impart revolutionary class consciousness without
waiting for it to develop through the evolution of the capitalist system. More significantly, he attributed the failure of Marx's predicted collapse of Western capitalism to Western imperialism.

Marx argued that the workers or proletariat in an unskilled and generally interchangeable work force had no bargaining position. Hence, the bourgeoisie were
able to force the workers to longer hours without additional pay, which was kept
near subsistence levels. With no body of consumers able to purchase this excessive
production and with no outlets for the growing supply of capital, the system would
be faced with recurring economic crises. Enterprises would fail and most of the
bourgeoisie would fall into the ranks of the proletariat.

However, with imperialism, the Western powers were able to siphon off their excessive production (or, in Marxian terms, "surplus value") in the captive markets of their imperial possessions and to exploit their resources creating an artificial prosperity for the West, thus staving off its otherwise inevitable collapse. The task of bringing about the collapse of Western capitalism now becomes a matter of halting their exploitation of the LDCs and then co-opting these nationalist movements for his socialist objectives. Lenin redefines the agenda of Marxism as a two stage revolution: first, end Western imperialism which will cause the collapse of capitalism, then effect a communist take over of the putative nationalist movement.

Lenin has now transformed Marx's class struggle between the bourgeoisie and the proletariat as a struggle between the West and the LDCs in which the West including Marx's erstwhile heroes, the industrial labor force, becomes the exploiter and the LDCs including their rich elites become the oppressed. For example, in Vietnam the United States was fighting a front of noncommunist nationalists and communists, the *Viet Minh*. While the United States saw the struggle as the containment of communism, Vietnamese saw it as a nationalist struggle against foreign domination. Thus, in the short run, the interests of the communists and the nationalists converge, which may partly account for the popularity of the Leninist model in the newly independent nations in the early post-World War II period, as discussed in the preceding chapter. In the longer run, however, Marxism-Leninism entails a surrender of a distinct national identity and its subsumption in an international movement. This longer run divergence of interests between the forces of nationalism and those of international communism may have contributed to the widespread rejection of the latter forces in 1989.

Lenin, borrowing heavily from J. Hobson, argues that the capitalist West must exploit the LDCs in order to prevent their system from collapsing.[18] This argument is the basis of dependency theory, a literature produced initially by scholars specializing in Latin America that claims that underdevelopment in that area was created and perpetuated by Western exploitation of their countries.

Dependency theory, called *dependencia* by the Latin Americanists who first propounded it, adopts Lenin's explanation of the need of Western capitalism to exploit the LDCs. However, dependency theorists go further than the Leninists in that they not only blame capitalism for perpetuating underdevelopment but they claim capitalism caused underdevelopment. Michael Parenti, for example, claims that the image of precolonial Africa as underdeveloped is a myth "created by imperialism's image makers."[19] Thus, Parenti claims that in the early 1400s, Niger, Mali, and the Guinea produced fine fabrics and leathers; Katanga, Zambia, and Sierra Leone produced copper and iron; and Benin produced brass. These essentially cottage or extractive industries are hardly indicators of an industrial society, however. They do not embody the level of technology and productive efficiency associated with a modern industrial society.

The putative exploitation of LDCs includes extracting raw materials from them at low prices and selling finished products back to these captive markets at substantially higher prices, while keeping the technology that makes that production possible esoteric through patent laws. Dependency theorists imply something unsavory in this profit motive and unwillingness to share technology whose creation, often the product of funded research, was not cost free. The structure and skills of the extractive industries, such as building mines and transportation to the seaports, that serve the needs of the capitalist West are funded and encouraged. Investment in native industrial diversification is not. It would not be surprising if Western investors did use their capital, with all the risks entailed in investment, to further their own interests. Dependency theorists, however, charge that capitalist prosperity was created out of this exploitive relationship, that development and underdevelopment emanate from the same historical process. As Julius Nyerere, former president of Tanzania put it, "You are rich because we are poor; we are poor because you are rich." Out of this assumption, dependency theorists derive a moral imperative for the redistribution of material well-being between the LDCs and the West.

It is unrealistic to expect the Western elites to adopt an altruistic attitude out of guilt and to effect a massive redistribution of economic resources. The West has been maintaining its domination and ability to exploit the LDCs through what the dependency theorists call *the infrastructure of dependency.* Their superior military power is utilized to install native elites whose position and interests depend on their serving the needs of the West, not of their own people. Western supported puppet dictators, such as Fulgencio Batista of Cuba (overthrown by Fidel Castro in 1959), Anastasio Samoza of Nicaragua (ousted by the Sandinistas in 1979), and Rafael Trujillo of the Dominican Republic (assassinated in 1961), oppressed their own people while protecting Western investment in their countries in return for Western military and economic support. These men epitomized native elites who formed part of the infrastructure of dependency. As noted above, patent laws serve to prevent economic independence and hence are part of the infrastructure of dependency, as are the development of enterprises and skills to get native resources to Western industry.

As dependency theorist Susan Bodenheimer argues, capitalism can and will use its power and resources to maintain this infrastructure and the exploitive relationship with the LDCs. The solution to her, therefore, is the replacement of capitalism with a more humane and egalitarian socialism.[20] Bodenheimer along with Andre Gunder Frank represents the left-oriented strand of dependency theorists who find the degree of economic inequality between the West and the LDCs to constitute one of the world's most egregious moral failings and the capitalist economy of the West to be the major culprit.[21]

DEPENDENCY THEORY CRITIQUED

Useful explanatory theories are consistent with relevant data. That is, the phenomena that are logically predicted from the theory do in fact occur in the appropriate circumstances. Since the fit between theory and data in the social sciences is a matter of degree, due to the ever present exogenous factors that affect outcomes, the best theories account for more of the relevant data than alternative explanations.

Since dependency theory posits that exploitation of LDCs by the capitalist West constitutes the strongest explanation of the cause and perpetuation of underdevelopment, those countries that were never colonies nor maintained close economic contact with the West should be the most developed or modernized countries outside the West, while countries that were heavily penetrated by Western influence should be wallowing in throes of the deepest underdevelopment. In fact, the opposite seems to be the case. The two African countries that were never colonized and virtually ignored by the West, Ethiopia and Liberia, are hardly paragons of prosperous modernity. Meanwhile, other countries that were heavily penetrated by Western social and economic influence, such as India and Hong Kong, are among the most prosperous and modernized of the LDCs. The transfer of technology partially explains this.

Conversely, dependency theory posits that the prosperity of the West is built on the exploitation of the LDCs. Therefore, the nations that colonized the most with a more exploitive relationship with their imperial possessions should be the most prosperous and modernized while those nations that lacked substantial colonial holdings and did relatively less trade with the LDCs through their developmental periods should lag behind the colonial powers in modernity and economic prosperity. Yet, as P. T. Bauer points out, some of the most prosperous Western nations such as Canada, Australia, Japan, the Scandinavian democracies, and the United States were not known as colonial powers and, until recent decades, had relatively few commercial contacts with the LDCs.[22] Meanwhile, two of the most aggressively exploitive among the colonial powers, Spain and Portugal, remained among the less prosperous and modernized among Western nations. The data do not seem to support the central principle of dependency theory, that Western influence constitutes the major impediment to economic prosperity and independence of the LDCs while Western prosperity is a product of imperial exploitation of LDCs.

Dependency theorists further argue that Western capital investment in LDCs is done in such a way as to shape the structure of their economies. Especially with reference to the U.S. domination of Latin America with such investment programs as The Alliance for Progress, they argue that such Western capital concentrates the resources of the LDCs on extractive industries that serve the needs of the West. Yet, the total capital investment by the United States in Latin America is hardly sufficient to shape the structure of the Latin economies.

Dependency theorists who hold that this putatively exploitive relationship between the LDCs and the West constitutes *the* principal explanation of underdevelopment have to confront the availability of alternative explanations that account for the variations in question at least as well as the dependency explanation. Of course, these alternative explanations, which largely focus on attributes or behavior patterns in the LDCs themselves, are less satisfying for two reasons. First, they place the blame for their condition on the LDCs themselves, casting an aspersion on their attributes. As Bernard Lewis observed with respect to the once proud and prosperous Muslim civilization now languishing in second-class status, it is easier to ask, "Who did this to us" rather than ask, "How did we do this to ourselves?"[23] Second, attributes of the LDCs themselves are generally rooted in deep-seated cultural patterns that are resistant to change. It is far easier to undo colonialism or even economic exploitation than to change culture; hence, the external explanation is far more optimistic and hopeful than the internal ones.

POPULATION GROWTH AND DEMOGRAPHICS

One major impediment to socioeconomic development is the very high birth rate in many of the LDCs that in most cases results in very rapid, almost exponential population growth. The high birth rate is a function of several factors. One is the importation of hygiene and medical science that allows a high percentage of infants to survive. In many places, couples would give birth to a large number of infants but only a few of them would survive the ravages of high infant mortality. Now they still give birth to as many children but most of them do survive. A second factor is cultural patterns. For example, in many Latin American countries, *machismo*, an aggressive assertion of masculinity, is ingrained in the culture. This masculinity is demonstrated in part by siring a large number of children, as well as by the systematic subjugation of women bordering on misogyny. Machismo is not uniformly strong throughout Latin America: it is especially strong in Brazil and Mexico but less so in Chile and even less so in Argentina. The birth rate in Latin America is not simply a function of their Catholicism with its rules about human sexuality; Italy, for example, has a below replacement birth rate. Other LDC cultures also value large families. The fact that Latin America has the highest population growth in the world is a function not only of their birth rate (some African countries have a higher birth rate) but of the lowering infant mortality rate. Thus Mexico's population growth rate of 3 to 4 percent a year would cause its population to double every 18 to 24 years.[24] India's population is projected to increase by 56 percent between 1998 and the middle of the twenty-first century while Brazil's population is projected to grow in the same period by 48 percent.[25] This population growth is important because if a couple has one or two children, the mother might still be in the work force; hence, half of that family would be productive adding to that country's GDP. However, if a family has eight children, the mother could not work so that 90 percent of that family would be pure consumers, absorbing scarce resources that might have been directed to investment.

Population growth thus may constitute an important impediment to economic development—but it is not a sufficient cause. India and Peru, for example, have high population growth but have higher levels of economic modernization among the LDCs.

CULTURAL FACTORS: RELIGION

Cultural factors may also impede economic and social modernization. This was certainly true in the West for much of its history. Max Weber and R.H. Tawney have propounded a thesis about how Protestantism fostered capitalism and economic modernization while the Catholic Church acted to impede such modernization.[26] The Catholic Church in its medieval guise took an other worldly orientation in glorifying asceticism and in its attitude that the quality of life was regarded as less important than salvation. The Church, with its fixation on the suppression of heresy, discouraged freedom of thought on which the modern world with modern technology depends. Science and the growth of knowledge do not flourish in the context of inquisitions. Finally, the Church banned the use of money to make money (called "usury") which is, after all, the key function in a capitalist system. That is one reason why Jews, who were banned from doing most other things, became prominent among the banking families of modernizing Europe. Protestantism by contrast, especially in the Lutheran and Calvinist sects that appeared in Europe with the Reformation, held that competitive success in worldly pursuits was an indication you were among those predestined for salvation. Hence, in contrast with Catholicism, worldly success and acquisition was given moral and religious sanction. Moreover, the presence of competing truths weakened the hold of religion in general among the European populace, paving the way for the Enlightenment and the dawn of the modern age.

Similar to the West's experience with medieval Catholicism, there are aspects to religions dominant in the less-developed world that appear to be dysfunctional for modernization. Moreover, the impact of these religions is great because the salience of religion itself is much stronger in the less-developed world than in the now largely secularized West. Confucianism, discussed in the previous chapter, fostered a strong reverence for tradition and the past. Buddhism taught that the key to salvation is in the renunciation of the sensory world and of desire, hardly an attitude conducive to the struggle for progressive social change. Islam believes in *Kismet* or fate. Yet, the belief that everything is preordained would not encourage one to improve one's own lot let alone that of the world about oneself. Some scholars have suggested that the perception that the events of the world have causes that can be humanly controlled is the first step for inquiry into those causes and eventually actually gaining some control over human events. Even more strongly than with the *machismo* elements in the Latin culture, Islam believes in the subordination of women. Some segments within Islam forbid even the right of women to an education, a practice that not only robs Islamic society of half of its creative and productive potential but, as Lewis points out, condemns the children of that society to be raised by the most ignorant parts of the population.[27] The more fundamental parts of Islamic society have percolated to the leadership of that society and insist on strict adherence to the *Shariah* or Islamic law. Not only does this bar the adoption of the Western idea of popular sovereignty but it fosters a kind of dogmatism that is incompatible with modernity. The less-developed parts of the world never went through an Enlightenment; they are still in the grip of closed thought systems resembling the grip of the medieval church in the Western "dark ages."

TRIBALISM AND A SENSE OF NATIONHOOD

The task of building a modern, effective nation state requires that a sense of nation (a culturally defined shared identity with a people) should be more or less coterminous with the state. We have seen in our examination of Western systems that a number of segmented societies exist in which isolated and alienated subcultures actively refuse assimilation and do not accord the state the legitimacy needed to govern effectively over a range of contentious issues. The subcultures in Canada, Belgium, and Spain prevent the citizens of those countries from sharing a sense of common identity. The politics of subcultural defense in the West was discussed at greater length in Chapter Two.

Among the LDCs, tribalism constitutes the major impediment to the development of a strong sense of nationhood. European imperial powers drew the boundaries of their colonial possessions on the basis of politics and power realities among themselves and with little regard for the tribal and ethnic lines in the areas under imperial control. These tribal identities had long antedated the artificial national identities drawn up among imperial powers and many place tribes with a long history of conflict between them within the borders of a single state. We saw how these Western countries have had difficulties functioning as coherent nation states (as Belgium evolved into a confederation and Canada barely survived two secession votes in recent decades), although these countries have had over a century to build the legitimacy of their nation state.

Nigeria is perhaps the apotheosis of a country without a national identity among its people. Estimates vary but most scholars claim that there are close to 300 mutually unintelligible languages spoken among its people, divisions buttressed by geographically defined cultural and religious diversities. The extreme segmentation of the country is underscored by the fact that none of the competing political parties draw significant support from more than one tribal area. The northern part of the country near the Sahara rim is dominated by Muslims of the Hausa and Falani tribes. Lacking a private sector to absorb their able people, they dominate the military and the government and, like other Muslims, viewed the state as an instrument to spread the faith. The southern part of the country includes the seacoast where Western colonizers arrived and congregated. Consequently, the southern and southwestern tribes such as the Ibos, the Yorubas, or the Edos acquired western values including individualism, tolerance, education, secularism and/or Christianity, whereas the Muslim north was relatively insulated from such Western values. The educated Nigerians are predominantly southerners who therefore dominate the civil service jobs even in the north, generating much resentment from the northerners. A Middle Belt with such tribes as the Tiv and the Nupe exemplified native African culture and religion. This region is the source of Nigeria's vast deposits of crude oil.

These divisions have made it nearly impossible to form effective governments legitimate to the various segments of the country. The country has been torn by instability since it acquired independence in 1960. Since then, the country has experienced six coups d'etat and a bloody civil war in which the Ibos tried to secede from the country and set up its own state to be called Biafra. The country has been governed by six military juntas and two military dictatorships with only ten years of civilian rule between 1960 and 1999.

PRAETORIANISM

The election of a former northern general, Olusegun Obasanju as president of Nigeria in 1999 was a result of severe international pressure to return to civilian rule. The previous apparently democratic election of Mashood Abiola, a Yoruba, in 1993, upset the northern Hausa—Falani establishment and was voided by then military dictator Ibrahim Babangida. Under international pressure, Babangida resigned in favor of a transitional council, but Sani Abacha seized power and ran a particularly corrupt and brutal regime until he died of a heart attack. Abiola also died suddenly while in prison. Obasanju was reelected in 2003 and remains in office as of this writing in 2006. Hence, the regime has not yet transferred power by an election, and the military remains a potent force in the country whose notorious political corruption, called "dash," continues unabated. The consolidation of this democracy is very uncertain at this writing.

This disproportionate role for the military in civil and political life is not atypical for LDCs. The military may exercise this influence either by figuratively pulling the strings of a nominal civilian leader or by directly seizing power as they have done so often in Nigeria. When a small group of officers jointly run a state, this is known as a *junta*. This situation of disproportionate military influence, known as a *praetorian society,* is common in LDCs because the military is frequently one of the earliest and best-organized institutions while competing civilian institutions have not yet attained strong legitimacy.[28] Thus, praetorianism is more common where civilian institutions are either weakly legitimated or are performing poorly.

Argentina is one of a number of Latin American systems with a history of praetorianism. Since 1930, the country has been ruled by military juntas six different times, interspersed with a series of populist leaders, playing havoc with the national economy in order to cater to their mass base of support.[29] The first such populist leader was Hipólito Yrigoyen, who came to power supported by a disaffected and alienated middle class. The disastrous management of the economy in his second term was exacerbated by the Great Depression. His term was ended by a coup. Juan Perón, a former colonel, came to power in 1946 with a charismatic wife, Evita, and the support of a peasant and worker base known as the *descamisados* (shirtless ones).[30] Playing to this base was an economic disaster and he was deposed by another coup. During his 18 years out of power, he turned to the support of the fascist regimes of the Axis during World War II, showing that populism is not neatly placed on a left to right dimension. Perón died two years into his second reign and was succeeded by his second wife. Evita, his first wife, succumbed to cancer in 1952. His second wife, Isabela, made shambles of the economy and was deposed by another coup. The latest junta to govern Argentina carried on a policy of repression in which thousands of people simply disappeared, having been arbitrarily imprisoned and tortured. The junta tried to divert attention from a failed economy by seizing the British controlled Falkland Islands off the Argentine coast, resulting in the humiliation of the Argentine military by the British. The failed regime had little choice but to return the country to civilian rule and in 1983 Raul Alfonsin was elected president.

Because the military must view itself in competition with the military in other states with regard to the technology demanded by military hardware, the military frequently possesses a higher level of technological skills than the country in which it is situated, and structurally the military is the epitome of a modern organization. Hence, the military in LDCs become sources of both technical and administrative resources giving it disproportionate influence in these societies where such resources are still scarce. Finally, the military is oriented toward fighting wars; hence, the leaders of praetorian societies may be more inclined toward military adventurism. Saddam Hussein of Iraq, a leader who came to power with military support and who usually dressed in military attire, led his country into a fruitless seven-year war with Iran and then invaded Kuwait. Clearly, the enormous expenditure of resources in these adventures did not advance the cause of economic modernization.

DEBT CRISES AND CORRUPTION

It may be discerned from the foregoing that recurring financial crises plague LDCs, crises *not* the result of exploitation by the West. One common form of these crises is heavy indebtedness to foreign creditors. This indebtedness and its attendant interest drains off capital from investment purposes, preventing economic growth. One of the key tasks for modernizing the economies of LDCs is the accumulation of capital for investing in an industrial infrastructure (e.g., building factories, etc.). Saving is difficult in a near subsistence agrarian economy. Mexico and Nigeria are oil-rich countries nevertheless plagued by that kind of foreign debt. They borrowed heavily against projected oil revenues in the 1970s and were stuck with the debt when the price of oil did not continue to rise as expected. The consequences of this bad judgment were exacerbated by the all-too-common practice in LDCs of spending their money on symbolic luxury rather than investing it in ways to promote economic growth. Nigeria and Brazil, for example, built showy new capital cities, Abuja and Brasilia respectively. Saddam Hussein's Baathist regime in Iraq spent millions erecting a dozen ostentatious presidential palaces, rewarding the families of Palestinian suicide bombers, and bankrolling terrorist training and operations.[31]

Corruption—the self enrichment of officials at public expense—is all too common in LDCs when rulers find themselves in power for the first time without a sense of responsibility to their public. Zimbabwe (formerly Rhodesia), previously a food exporting country, had its agriculture and hence much of its national revenue ruined when strongman ruler, Robert Mugabwe, took the land from the white farmers who knew how to work it and gave it to cronies who did not know how to farm and ruined the land. The massive corruption in Nigeria, called *dash*, was mentioned above.

It is clear that a number of factors perpetuated underdevelopment, some of them being more important in some places and others in other places. There is some truth to each of these "explanations" of underdevelopment. Any single factor explanation of something as complex as the level of modernization of a country's economy is at best going to be a partial truth. While the level of exploitation by a Western power over an LDC, which varied from one relationship to another, had some impact on the degree of modernization, the contextual factors discussed above also clearly played an important role.

INSTABILITY AND VIOLENCE IN RAPIDLY CHANGING SOCIETIES

Despite a widespread perception that violence and political instability is born out of the despair and hopelessness of great economic inequality and abject poverty, a large body of research indicates that such violence and instability is associated with rapid political and economic change, including modernization. The institutions of the more traditional societies—feudalism, tribalism, traditional religions—are breaking down in periods of rapid change, leaving many without a sense of purpose, a sense of meaning in their existence. Psychologist Erich Fromm argues that this breakdown generates a need for the now-alone individuals to subsume themselves in some larger movement, what he calls "the escape from freedom." "In contrast to the feudal system of the Middle Ages under which everybody had a fixed place in an ordered and transparent system," he argues, "capitalist economy put the individual entirely on his own feet."[32] Seeking to explain the then highly salient phenomenon of Naziism and its appeal, Fromm theorizes that as modernization breaks down traditional institutions and thereby eliminates socioeconomic roles, whole strata of people are marginalized and alienated from modernizing society.

The earliest supporters of the Third Reich, a system that absorbed and gave dignity to such marginalized people, were peasants, shopkeepers, clerks, the unskilled unemployed—people whose place was threatened by modernization. Henry Ashby Turner could therefore refer to fascism as "a revolt against modernity."[33] While other revolutionary social movements looked to a millennium in the indefinite future, and while the true socialists fought for the industrial labor force, the Nazi elite glorified a mythic model drawn from the early Middle Ages and before, to cults of blood and soil, and to reinstate the role of the peasantry and *petit bourgeoisie*. The Nazis seemed to represent the cause of the losers of modern society.

Thus, there are strata who are marginalized as their socioeconomic role is eliminated by modernization. Such people, not receiving a personal stake in the well-being of their societies, will tend to resent the modern world and its attributes and become alienated from the society in which they live. Faced with unemployment and a loss of sense of identity and worth, these strata are far worse off in the early stages of modernization than they were in premodern agrarian society.

The essential idea behind the theory that early modernization exacerbates violence and instability is that modernization brings about social mobilization, the psychological induction of the masses into the broader society and political system. As such, it generates demands and expectations faster than the relatively inefficient political institutions of early modern societies can satisfy them. This idea is sometimes called "the gap hypothesis," since the gap between demands and ability to satisfy them is maximized when the economy slows after a period of rapid economic growth, while demands keep rising. This is when frustration is maximized and hence the disposition to engage in political protest or violence is greatest. The gap occurs because the rise in economic growth is ultimately limited by the scarcity of resources or other economic factors, therefore it levels off while the revolution in rising expectations has no such limits. James Davies who first propounded this idea calls it the "J-Curve" hypothesis from the shape of the want satisfaction curve as shown in Figure 6–2.

The essence of Davies' hypothesis is that the ratio between the formation of wants or demands, on the one hand, and the rising level of the satisfaction of these wants, on the other, determines the level of frustration among a population. That the level of frustration determines the level of political violence makes intuitive sense. However, Davies presented no data to subject his ideas to an empirical test.

The task of adapting data to test the frustration, aggression, and violence hypothesis initially fell to a psychologist—political science couple, Rosalind and Ivo Feierabend who constructed complex indirect indicators of the inherently imprecise concepts of frustration and of the disposition to engage in violence using aggregate data (widely available data on attributes of whole societies). For example, they conceptualize violence as a ratio between want formation and want satisfaction. The former is indicated by urbanization and literacy rates; the latter by caloric intake per capita, GNP, and physicians and telephones per unit of population. By using easily accessible aggregate data, they were able to apply their test to 84 poli-

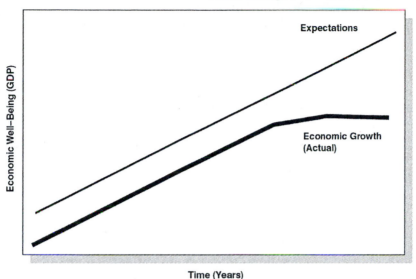

Figure 6–2 Gap hypothesis

ties.[34] The complexity of the model is enhanced by adding the factor of coerciveness of political systems. Strong correlations were found among the variables over the wide sample of polities included in the studies. However the impact of coerciveness appears to be curvilinear. Lower to moderate levels of coercion anger the population without being effective; hence, they increase the levels of violence. However, high levels of coercion are effective in curbing internal violence.

The use of such indirect indicators or inferential measures raise the question of validity—that is, the extent to which they actually measure the concept. These measures involve an inference from the observed data to a conclusion about the extent to which a psychological attribute is present. Such inferences are always imperfectly valid. The inference of psychological factors from aggregate data raises concerns about the "ecological fallacy," an assumption that relations between aggregates or whole systems are necessarily the same as the relationship between individuals within those systems. Thus, although nations with a higher aggregate index of frustration tend to have a higher level of violence, it does not follow that the individuals who most contribute to that index are the ones most likely to engage in violence. However, what is not necessarily true may still be probably true.

This research into the psychological foundations of violence is complemented by the work of Ted Gurr, whose principal explanatory concept, called here "relative deprivation," is defined as the relationship between the values "to which they believe they are justifiably entitled and those values they think they are able to get and keep."[35] This concept has the advantage over the Feierabends' "systemic frustration" by going beyond what people want and focusing on that to which they think they are entitled. This brings in the idea of justice denied without which, Crane Brinton tells us, no revolution can occur.[36]

Despite the sophisticated conceptualization and measurement of relative deprivation, Gurr finds that it explains very little of the variation in political violence among LDCs. Rather, he finds much of that variation is explained by two factors: structural facilitation (which refers to the presence of institutions capable of mobilizing discontent into action such as an antisystem party) and legitimacy.

Rapid industrialization may be inherently destabilizing for a number of reasons summarized by Mancur Olson.[37] To begin with, economic growth requires capital for investment. Capital comes from savings, resources diverted from consumption. However, in LDCs, the masses are frequently at or near the subsistence level of well being and require all of their resources for consumption. Any savings will have to come from a coerced reduction in their level of well-being. To build the infrastructure of industrial society (factories, roads, etc.), the masses will have to eat less or forgo other essentials of their daily lives. While the masses are therefore worse off than they were as peasants in a relatively stable agrarian society, a few entrepreneurs introduce new technologies, becoming very wealthy and possibly creating resentment among the impoverished working class. These new technologies at the same time render much of the work force structurally unemployable, meaning they lack the skills and training to operate at this higher state of technology. In summary, in early modernization, there are far more losers than winners and, because wages tend to be more sticky than prices, the gap between rich and poor will increase.

The differences between the elite strata and the masses that can generate frustration and resentment are not just economic. It is of course possible in times of rapid social and economic change for an ambitious and talented or creative person from the lower strata to acquire wealth and experience upward mobility. However, normally economic prosperity rises faster than social status. Hence, these *nouveaux riches* (new money) may now be as wealthy as the old landed gentry but they cannot intermingle socially with them, and the children of *nouveaux riches* are not considered suitable suitors for the children of the gentry. Modernization and their new wealth has weakened the bonds of these *nouveaux riches* to their old caste or class but they are not accepted among the gentry; hence, they are *déclassé*.

This points to the basic impact of rapid modernization alluded to at the outset of this section, the breakdown of the institutions and belief systems of the traditional world—institutions and belief systems that did much to assuage the fears, sufferings, and uncertainties of temporal life. The Church in Europe's Middle Ages performed a valuable function of giving a short and difficult life meaning and purpose, as does the Islamic faith in the contemporary Middle East. The weakening hold of religiosity in the West, a fact documented and discussed in Chapter Two, whatever good that has done for tolerance and freedom of thought, has left individuals adrift, without a sense of purpose and the sense of security that religious certainties can provide. Moreover, those critical strata whose economic roles have been rendered atavistic by modernization—the peasantry or owners of small family farms; the shopkeepers, clerks, and artisans of the lower middle class; and unskilled workers—are especially hurt, losing both their spiritual and their economic anchors.

Huntington advocates institutionalization prior to the mobilization of demands as a strategy for maintaining order in rapidly changing societies—societies he recognizes that are more prone to violence and instability for the reasons discussed above.[38] More complex, autonomous, and legitimate institutions may inhibit the tendency toward violence in three ways: they add to the political system's capabilities to satisfy the demands created by rapid modernization; they add to the legitimacy of the regime format; and they may enhance the regime's capacity to maintain order by coercion. While coercion—the use of force to deter or suppress violence—will theoretically keep order, scholars have found that the relationship between the use of coercion and political violence is curvilinear as noted above. When coercion is weak or ineffectively applied, it is more likely to generate increased resentment and anger than it is to restrain violence or protest activity. Violence and protest is more likely when the level of coercive potential is such that the protesters have a fair chance of winning. Hence, the relationship between coercion and violence at lower intensities of coercion is a positive one. However, as the intensity of coercion is increased, coercion becomes increasingly effective in curbing violence and protest activity. At higher levels of coercion, the relationship between coercion and violence becomes negative. In a police state, there is very little protest activity or domestic violence. The curvilinear relationship between coercion and domestic violence is shown in Figure 6–3.

Of course, the foregoing is focused on the socioeconomic and psychological causes of protest activity and violence that are exacerbated by the process of modernization and rapid socioeconomic change in general. This theoretical literature would be incomplete if it did not more precisely conceptualize and measure the dependent variable(s) of violence and instability. There are not only levels but types of political violence. Incidents of protest, instability, violence vary with respect to their extent or pervasiveness, their duration, and their intensity.[39] The extent of violence refers to such factors as the number of participants, the geographical range of the incidence (did it encompass the whole country or was it confined to a single province?), or the proportion of the total population involved. Duration refers to how long it lasts. The intensity refers to such factors as the number of casualties and fatalities and the total value of property damaged or destroyed. These dimensions are not necessarily linked. An incident may be of high intensity but of short duration or vice versa. Hence, it is well to apply each dimension in assessing any given incidence.

The ultimate form of political violence or contentious politics is social revolution, an event that involves not only regime change but the establishment of a new social, economic, and political order mobilizing a substantial portion of the popu-

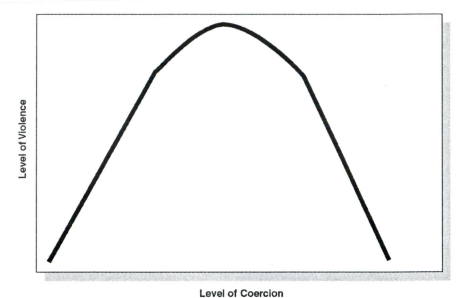

Level of Coercion

Figure 6–3   Violence and Coercion

lation of that society. Huntington calls it "an explosion of popular participation in national affairs."[40] Social revolutions have been treated as a distinct category of political violence and studied from a distinct perspective. Rather than examining specific and indirectly-measurable psychological concepts in the works of the Feierabends and Gurr, scholars have treated social revolutions from a macro perspective, examining broad socioeconomic and structural trends. In his seminal work in the first half of the twentieth century, Crane Brinton identified broad trends such as the desertion of the intellectuals, the impoverishment of the elites, and a lag of social acceptance behind economic success for at least one class.[41] Theda Skocpol made a major impact on the study of revolution and violence with her work on the social revolutions in France, Russia, and China which focused on the role of institutions and macro conditions in the sociopolitical order.[42] Skocpol's implication is that such social revolutions are *sui generic*, requiring the analysis of the interaction of numerous variables as opposed to the single-factor explanation of studies like those of the Feierabends. This approach of a more integrated perspective in the study of contentious behavior has been advocated in the work of McAdam, Tarrow, and Tilly.[43] An integrated approach generates one of the recurring problems in comparative analysis: too many variables for too few cases. Obviously, one cannot use statistical analysis on a study like that of Skocpol with three cases.

Despite this, Skocpol finds patterns in the three social revolutions under consideration. In each case, the system was governed by what she calls "agrarian bureaucracies," a recurring format in LDCs in which a developing bureaucracy shares control with a landed gentry. Since most policy reforms threatened that gentry, agrarian bureaucracies had difficulties adapting to the imperatives of a modernizing world. Secondly, the systems were faced with the ubiquitous alienation from the modern world and perpetual discontent of the peasantry. Thirdly, each of these systems faced a reduced capability in their administrative and military institutions as a result of combined pressures from more modernized countries.

In contrast to the effort to formulate general principles of such broad phenomena as social revolutions, MacAdam, Tarrow, and Tilly focus on the numerous interacting factors in smaller events such as Kenya's Mau Mau Revolt while, with their broader concept of contentious politics, they break down the artificial boundaries between such concepts as war, revolution, social movements.[44] These studies all support the basic point that modernizing societies are especially vulnerable to violence, protest activity, and political instability—and from Brinton to Skocpol, they find patterns in the factors behind these events: the weaknesses of the traditional elites, the pervasiveness of the peasantry and other "crisis" strata, and reduced system capabilities. These attributes are found among so-called Western countries as well. France, for example, has had substantial peasantry and weak central governments for much of the modern era until the midtwentieth century (and a dozen unscheduled and illegal regime changes in the two centuries following their great social revolution of 1789). However, these attributes associated with political instability and violence are clearly more prevalent among the LDCs. Thus, while economic and social modernization may in the long run generate progress toward some conception of social justice, in the short run it produces widespread frustration and the instability and violence associated with it. Such instability and violence may be an inexorable side effect on the road to modernity.

CONCLUSIONS: THE DIFFERENT PATHS TO MODERNITY

Confronted with a bewildering array of new and different political systems entering the world stage in the post-World War II era, political scientists sought to make sense of them by imposing a familiar set of concepts on the analysis of these systems—concepts drawn from the Western democracies with which political scientists were familiar. In a landmark effort to rise above ethnocentrism while charting new paths to the understanding of these emerging LDCs, Gabriel Almond replaced the traditional focus on the structures of regimes such as parliaments and cabinets with eight functional categories that could, it was hoped, apply to all systems: rule making, rule application, rule adjudication, interest articulation, interest aggregation, political socialization, political recruitment, and political communication.[45] However, Almond admitted that the functional categories he came up with, the efficient performance of which was to constitute their conception of "developed," were drawn from the Western democracies that he considered the apotheosis of modernity.[46] His first three functions, for example, closely correspond to the legislative, executive, and judicial functions of Western countries.

The logic of functional analysis was critiqued in an earlier chapter. What is even more vulnerable to criticism in Almond's conceptual scheme is the implicit obeisance to modernization theory with the unstated assumption that there are universal paths to modernization. This assumption, we have seen, is found in much of the early literature on the LDCs and the rapid changes occurring in many of them. It underlies the attempt to dichotomize the nations of the world into Western and non-Western categories, with the assumption that when the "non-Western" LDCs change, they will move toward the Western model.[47] Even assuming that the countries in a given category share some significant attributes, the overlap of such attributes between the categories renders a rigid distinction between Western and non-Western countries theoretically useless.[48] For example, Pye lists a charismatic basis for legitimizing authority as an attribute of non-Western systems as opposed to rational-legal bases such as demonstrated competence or credentials; yet, charisma has clearly been the power basis of numerous Western leaders (such as De Gaulle, Churchill, or FDR). As noted at the outset of this chapter, placing the nations of the world in two broad categories ignores too many significant differences for the categories to be analytically useful.

It is apparent from the examination of the variety of patterns among LDCs and present-day industrialized countries in their past that sociopolitical change is neither universal nor inevitable let alone suggesting that some particular pattern or direction of change is either universal or inevitable. From the pop philosophy of Frances Fukuyama, concluding that the achievement of Western liberal democracy would bring about "the end of history," to the impressive and creative theorizing of Gabriel Almond, scholars have been looking at LDCs from the perspective of a Western model whose terms or concepts take on very different meanings in non-Western contextual settings. Edward Friedman argues that even terms like "democracy" must be adjusted to the realities of the experience and culture of Japan.[49] Concepts co-opted by LDCs from the West take on very different meanings in their new settings. Political party, for example, refers in the West to an institution that nominates candidates for office and articulates policy choices while serving as a link between that state and the public; in many LDC settings parties function to mobilize power to implement policies virtually coterminous with the state itself.

The Western model is clearly not descriptive of the path of many LDCs. Some societies or cultures virtually reject what we consider modernity. The current Islamist leadership in the Muslim world works to resist modernization of that particular culture. Other societies modernize along one or more dimension without moving toward the entire Western model. The conclusion most clearly suggested by this examination of the LDCs is that social, economic, and political change is *context specific*. Modernization and political development will take as many different paths as there are contexts in which they occur.

ENDNOTES

[1]Christian Welzel, Ronald Inglehart and Hans Deiter Klingermann, "Economic Development, Cultural Change and Democratic Institutions: Causal Linkages Between Three Aspects of Modernity," Paper presented to the Annual Meeting of the American Political Science Association, Atlanta, Georgia, September 2–5, 1999, p. 3.

[2] *Ibid.*

[3]David Apter, *The Politics of Modernization* (Chicago: University of Chicago Press, 1965).

[4]For a classic example of defining modernization in terms of mobilization, see Karl Deutsch, "Social Mobilization and Political Development," *American Political Science Review*, Vol.LV, No. 3 (Sept. 1951), pp. 493–514; Daniel Lerner, *The Passing of Traditional Society* (Gencoe, IL: The Free Press, 1958) also sees this broadening of intellectual horizons as a key element of modernization.

[5]Samuel Huntington, "Political Development and Political Decay," *World Politics*, Vol. XVII (March, 1965), pp. 386–430. See also Huntington, *Political Order in Changing Societies* (New Haven, CT: Yale University Press, 1968), chap. 2.

[6]Huntington, "Political Development and Political Decay," p. 394.

[7]Gabriel Almond, "A Developmental Approach to the Study of Political Systems, *World Politics*, Vol. 17, No. 2, pp. 195ff. Gabriel Almond and G.Bingham Powell, *Comparative Politics: A Developmental Approach* (Boston: Little Brown, 1966), chap. 8.

[8]Cf. S.N. Eisensradt who defines political development as "A potential capacity to sustain continuously changing new types of political demands and organizations ..." S.N. Eisenstadt, "Bureaucracy and Political Development" in Joseph LaPalombara, ed., *Bureaucracy and Political Development* (Princeton, NJ: Princeton University Press, 1963), pp. 98–99.

[9]This model was propounded by several scholars. See, e.g., Daniel Lerner, *The Passing of Traditional Society* (Glencoe, IL: The Free Press of Glencoe, 1958), chap. 1. Cf. also Phillips Cutwright, "National Political Development: Measurement and Analysis," *American Sociological Review*, Vol. 28, No. 2 (1963), pp. 253–264.

[10]Max Weber, *The Theory of Social and Economic Organization,* Talcott Parsons, ed. (New York: The Free Press, 1947) and Hans Gerth and C. Wright Mills, eds., *From Max Weber: Essays in Sociology* (New York: Oxford University Press Galaxy Books, 1958), Parts VIII and IX.

[11]Vicky Randall and Robin Theobald, *Political Change and Underdevelopment: A Critical Introduction to Third World Politics* (Durham,NC: Duke University Press, 1985), p. 18.

[12]Christian Welzel, Ronald Inglehart, and Hans Dieter Klingemann, "Economic Development, Cultural Change and Democratic Institutions: Causal Linkages Between Three Aspects of Modernity," cf. also Inglehart and Welzel, *Modernization, Cultural Change and Democracy* (Cambridge, UK: Cambridge University Press, 2005), p. 12 and *passim.*

[13]Ashutosh Vasahney, "Nationalism, Ethnic Conflict and Rationality," *Perspectives on Politics*, Vol. 1, No. 1 (March, 2003), pp. 85–100.

[14]Kenneth Organski, *The Stages of Political Development* (New York: Alfred A. Knopf, 1965).

[15]Walt Whitman Rostow, *The Stages of Economic Growth* (London: Cambridge University Press, 1960).

[16]See the devastating critique of historicism in Karl Popper, *The Open Society and its Enemies*, 2 vols. (New York: Harper Torchbooks, 1966).

[17]Cited in Monte Palmer, *Dilemmas of Political Development*, 4th ed. (Itasca, IL: Peacock Publishers, 1989), pp. 2–3.

[18]J. A. Hobson, *Imperialism: A Theory* (London: George Allen and Unwin, 1905). Hobson degenerated into classic anti-Semitism in blaming international finance capital ostensibly dominated by Jews for colonial exploitation and the wars of Europe. In selling the idea of the Jew as the quintessential apotheosis of capitalist exploiter, Hobson set the foundation for the currently popular view that Zionism is an instrument for the exploitation of Third World peoples.

[19]Michael Parenti, *The Sword and the Dollar: Imperialism and the Arms Race* (New York: St. Martin's Press, 1989).

[20]Susan Bodenheimer, "Dependency and Imperialism: The Roots of Underdevelopment," in K. T. Fann and Donald Hodges, eds., *Readings in U.S. Imperialism* (Boston: Porter Sargeant, 1971)

[21]See, e.g., Andre Gunder Frank, *Capitalism and Underdevelopment in Latin America* (London: Penguin Books, 1970)

[22]P. T. Bauer, *Dissent on Development* (Cambridge, MA: Harvard University Press, 1976).

[23]Bernard Lewis, *What Went Wrong? The Clash Between Islam and Modernity in the Middle East* (New York: Harper-Collins Perennial books, 2002), p. 152.

[24]Howard Wiarda and Harvey Kline, "The Latin American Tradition and Process of Development," in Wiarda and Kline, eds., *Latin American Politics and Development*, 3rd ed., (Boulder, CO: Westview Press, 1990), p. 103.

[25]Calculated from data in United Nations Population Fund, *6 Billion: A Time for Choices, The State of the World's Population 1999.*

[26]Max Weber, *The Protestant Ethic and the Spirit of Capitalism*, Talcott Parsons, trans. (1904; reprint New York: Charles Scribner, 1930); R. H. Tawney, *Religion and the Rise of Capitalism* (New York: Harcourt Brace, 1937).

[27]Lewis, *What Went Wrong?* He makes the point through a quote, p. 70.

[28]See Edwrd Shils, "The Military in the Political Development of New States," and Lucian Pye, "Armies in the Process of Political Modernization ," in John Johnson, ed., *The Role of the Military in Underdeveloped Countries* (Princeton, NJ: Princeton University Press, 1962).

[29]See Michael Coniff, ed., *Latin American Populism in Comparative Perspective* (Albuquerque: University of New Mexico Press, 1982).

[30]Marissa Novarro, "Evita's Charismatic Leadership," in *Latin American Populism.*

[31]Robert Hayes, "Case Closed: The U.S. Government's Secret Memo Between Saddam Hussein and Osama Bin Laden," *The Weekly Standard,* Vol. 9, No. 11 (November 24, 2003). In this and in a subsequent book, Hayes details an ongoing pattern of meetings between high level Iraqi intelligence officers and Al Qaeda operatives. Support for the three terrorist training bases at Samarra, Ramadi, and Salman Park in Iraq is detailed in Robert Hayes, "Saddam's Terror Training Camps," *The Weekly Standard*, Vol. 11, No. 17 (January 16, 2006).

[32]Erich Fromm, *Escape From Freedom* (New York: Avon Books, 1941), p. 128.

[33]Henry Ashby Turner, "Fascism and Modernization," *World Politics*, Vol. 24, No. 4 (June, 1972), pp. 547–564.

[34]Ivo Feierabend and Rosalind Feierabend, "Systemic Conditions of Political Violence: An Application of the Frustration–Aggression Theory," in Ivo Feierabend, Rosalind Feierabend, and Ted Gurr, eds., *Anger Violence and Politics,* (Englewood Cliffs, NJ: Prentice Hall, 1972), pp. 136–183

[35]Ted R. Gurr, "A Causal Model of Civil Strife: A Comparative Analysis Using New Indices," *American Political Science Review* Vol. LXII, No. 4 (December, 1968), pp. 1104–1124 at 1104. See also Gurr, *Why Men Rebel* (Princeton, NJ: Princeton University Press, 1970), pp. 24–30 for a full exposition of the concept.

[36]Crane Brinton, *The Anatomy of Revolution* (Englewood Cliffs, NJ: Prentice Hall, 1952). Originally published in 1938, Brinton examines the four "great" revolutions: the British Revolution of 1688, the American Revolution of 1776, the French Revolution of 1789, and the Russian Revolution of 1917. Despite the uniqueness of each of them, Brinton delineates patterns among them.

[37]Mancur Olsen, "Rapid Growth as a Destabilizing Force, *Journal of Economic History* Vol. 3, No. 4 (December, 1963), pp. 529–552 .

[38]Samuel Huntington, *Political Order in Changing Societies.*

[39]Gurr, "A Causal Model of Civil Strife."

[40]Huntington, *Poltical Order in Changing Societies,* p. 266.

[41]Brinton, *The Anatomy of Revolution.*

[42]Theda Skocpol, "France, Russia, and China: a Structural Analysis of Social Revolutions," *Comparative Studies in Society and History,* Vol. 18, no. 2 (April, 1976) pp. 175–203. Cf. also Skocpol, *Social Revolutions in the Modern World* (Cambridge, UK: Cambridge University Press, 1994).

[43]Doug McAdam, Sidney Tarrow, and Charles Tilly, *Dynamics of Contention* (Cambridge, UK: Cambridge University Press, 2001).

[44]McAdam, Tarrow and Tilly, *Dynamics of Contention*, p. 92 ff. and 308.

[45]Gabriel Almond, " A Functional Approach to the Analysis of Political Systems," in G. Almond and James Coleman, eds., *The Politics of the Developing Areas* (Princeton. NJ: Princeton University Press, 1960), pp. 1–63. This introduction was a classic must-read to aspiring scholars of comparative politics in the 1960s.

[46]*Ibid*, p. 16.

[47]Lucien Pye, "The Non Western Political Process," *The Journal of Politics*, Vol. 20, No. 3 (August, 1958), pp. 468–486. Cf. another attempt to dichotomize the world into developed and less developed countries, George M. Kahan, Guy Paulker and Lucien Pye, "The Comparative Politics of Non-Western Countries," *The American Political Science Review*, Vol. 49, No. 4 (December, 1955), pp. 1022–1041.

[48]Alfred A. Diamant, "Is There a Non-Western Political Process? Comments on Lucien Pye's 'The Non-Western Political Process," *Journal of Politics*, Vol. 21, No. 1 (February, 1959), pp. 123–127.

[49]Edward Friedman, *The Politics of Democratization: Generalizing from the East Asian Experience* (Boulder, CO: Westview Press, 1994).

7

Conclusions
An Evolving Field in a
Changing World

Change remains the concept that characterizes the evolving field that is the subject of this volume and the world that it seeks to explain. The transformation of comparative politics from a descriptive enterprise to an explanatory one has been a settled fact for decades. Yet, comparative politics remains a field with unresolved issues regarding its own self-definition.

While the goal of scientifically adequate explanation is now generally accepted by leading scholars in the field, the essential nature of a scientific explanation remains a question that divides these scholars. Chapter One shows how the early decades of the modern explanatory enterprise of comparative political analysis were characterized by a search for a grand unifying theoretic framework within which to integrate political research into a coherent whole. In their zeal to be more scientific, political scientists indiscriminately adopted concepts and ideas from fields they enviously regarded as more scientific, especially from the "harder" biological and physical sciences.

Among the works that mesmerized these political scientists seeking to comprehend the criteria of "real" science was Thomas Kuhn's influential *The Structure of Scientific Revolutions.*[1] Two major themes or ideas that were uncritically adopted by political scientists emerge from this interpretation of the essence of modern science. First, each field of scientific research in a given period or era is dominated by a grand unifying theory or "paradigm," giving theoretic coherence to all the work in that field. The idea that all political research should be within a common paradigm led to the search for a general enough framework to encompass all political research. David Easton's several tomes promoting systems analysis was just such an effort.[2] The problem is that as the concepts in the schemes were pitched at an ever higher level of generality, they lost their empirical content. Since the indicators that give concepts their empirical content come from and derive their meaning from a particular context, generality and empiricism are inversely related. It is impossible to specify any precise event or phenomena predicted by the central proposition of Easton's system model, that is, when the inputs to the system get in sufficient disequilibrium to its outputs, the boundaries of the system will break down.

Second, theoretic change is a process of one perspective gaining acceptance over competing or previous ones, that is, not driven by any objective determination of the explanatory superiority of one paradigm over others; hence, science is not a cumulative enterprise. Kuhn argues that since concepts acquire meaning from the theory, and the data acquire meaning from the concepts, such data cannot be an independent test of that theory. One cannot objectively claim that one theory is superior to others, and competition between theories is not settled by research and experiment. For example, the concept of elastic demand is only meaningful within the confines of macroeconomic theory.

Paradigms (Kuhn's generic term for various kinds of theoretic structures) are conventionally accepted, and the work of "normal science" is to gather data to support the accepted paradigm. According to Kuhn, scientific revolutions occur out of an epiphany, where leading scholars suddenly see fit to replace the existing paradigm, as when relativity in physics replaced Newtonian mechanics.

Actually, Kuhn gives us a distorted view of science on all counts. First, science is *not* dominated by a single paradigm. When relativity theory came into physics, Newtonian mechanics was not displaced. Both of these paradigms have a place in modern physics depending on the research question being addressed. Second, paradigms are not replaced in a sudden event. Rather paradigms are adjusted by an incremental and continuous adaptation of them to a constantly unfolding body of data. The biologists' theory of evolution has changed since Darwin's day by adapting it to new finds in the fossil record. Hence, science is cumulative and theories can be objectively tested. Theories do determine the meaning of concepts, but once that meaning is settled and the criteria for being included in a concept are specified, the decision as to whether a datum refers to that concept or category is objective. To return to our example of macroeconomic theory, once the meaning of the concept of elasticity of demand and the indicators for measuring it are specified, one can intersubjectively say to what extent the demand for a given product or service is in fact sensitive to fluctuations in price.

Kuhn's work, which so mesmerized political science for so long, is counterintuitive. Clearly, current theories are superior to earlier ones. It is patently obvious that we know more in every field of scientific endeavor (although the humanities are still debating the eternal questions that have occupied their attention since ancient times). Scientists know more but so do political scientists. In the many pieces of scholarly research discussed in this volume, political scientists have created middle-range theories that increase our abilities to predict empirical or sensory events of interest to them. To take one glaring example, the Five Nation Study reported by Almond and Verba destroyed what had then been conventional wisdom, the rational-activist model of the cultural requisites of democracy, the idea that democracy requires a politically active and informed citizenry.[3] (Conventional wisdom, on which traditional political science had so heavily relied, is that which is widely assumed to be true but which no one had bothered to test.) Great levels of apathy and low levels of political participation became the new conventional wisdom until partially punctured by the seminal work of Russell Dalton.[4]

WHERE DO WE GO FROM HERE: FUTURE DIRECTIONS FOR POLITICAL INQUIRY

It is therefore not necessarily a liability that we have numerous competing paradigms or principled explanations of the phenomena we study such as stability, democratization, violence, behavior, or modernization. The debate, for example, between the primacy of cultural-explanation advocates, such as Inglehart and his associates, and the elite decision advocates, such as De Palma and Friedman, need not be definitively resolved. The phenomena we study are of such complexity that no single explanation is going to account for all or even most of the variation. Competing theories inquire into the impact of different possible causes of the outcomes we seek to explain. Each of these studies may therefore add to the amount of the variation that is explained. The psychological explanations of violence and revolution in the works of the Feierabands and Gurr, for example, account for a significant amount of the variation in that phenomenon but still a distinct minority of it.[5] A fewer-case but multivariate analysis, such as undertaken by Skocpol, does not cancel out the value of the psychological approach but it may enable scholars to reduce the amount of the unexplained variation.[6]

The aforementioned psychological explanations of violence typified one of the more encouraging trends in modern political research, the creative specification of indirect or inferential measures of some of the inherently soft concepts that dominate any field focused on human behavior. Thus, for example, David McClelland hypothesized that the rates of economic growth and modernization was, to a large extent, a function of an achievement orientation embedded in the psyche of that society. To test his hypothesis in the world of experience, he had to measure the very mushy psychological concept or an "achieving personality." This he did at the individual level with a "thematic apperception test" (TAT), an exercise in composing a brief explanation of a very ambiguous picture which is then coded for "achievement imagery" by trained coders.[7] To characterize an entire culture for achievement imagery, McClelland applied the same coding scheme to that society's children's literature, on the assumption that literature will best reflect the values one wants to preserve in the culture. McClelland did find that the achievement scores in that literature did in fact correlate significantly with ensuing rates of economic growth.

Clearly, there is a degree of inference in moving from the achievement-imagery score to the conclusion about the presence of the psychological concept, as there is in moving from a score on an IQ test to a conclusion about one's innate intelligence. There are, however, means of checking the validity of such inferential measures, the question of whether these measures actually measure the concept they purport to measure.

It is important, however, that theorists assume the responsibility for suggesting tools for measuring the concepts they create. Far too often, leading scholars in comparative politics (especially that influential group of scholars that dominated the Comparative Politics Committee of the Social Science Research Council in the 1960s and 1970s), expended vast resources in funds and time creating elaborate, intuitively plausible, but empirically empty theories. Perhaps driven by their perception of Kuhn's scientific revolution, these scholars competed to make the theoretic breakthrough as the proverbial light bulb bursts into light symbolically announcing the epiphenomenal insight. This book earlier considered congruence theory, the contribution of the late Harry Eckstein, an intuitively plausible but empirically empty attempt to explain an equally vague outcome, the effectiveness of modern governments. Since no testable hypotheses emerged from the several pieces of work embracing this idea, we really cannot say we now know more about the stability or effectiveness of modern governments than we did before Eckstein spun his theories. The empirical emptiness of such grand theories is frequently justified as part of a first step in building actual explanatory theory by a disclaimer in the very title of their works, such as "Toward of Theory of ..." or "Prolegomena to a Theory of..." In this way, as Lee Sigelman sarcastically points out, criticism of the empirical emptiness of the work is deflected with the claim that this is only an exploratory first step.[8] Apparently, the unstated assumption is that there ought to be an academic division of labor, and researchers who are less theoretically gifted can assume the less glamorous task of wallowing about in the data attempting to apply these grand theoretic insights to the sensory world.

There is, however, very little professional reward for fleshing out and testing new applications of existing theory. Major journals are relatively less inclined to publish such applications of existing theories compared to claims of theoretic innovation. The path to the kind of scholarly recognition that leads to appointments and tenure at major research universities is in the *creation* of the theoretic breakthrough. Fortunately, in recent decades, the cutting edge of scholarship in comparative political analysis has been moving away from the creation of empirically empty theories and models. Some of the most influential research in the field does devote serious attention to the measurement of the concepts used. Ronald

Inglehart's work on cultural change discussed at length earlier in this volume goes to great pains to carefully measure his key concepts, such as postmaterialism and postmodernism. Russell Dalton's work on political behavior is similarly well grounded in data. The task of imparting empirical content to the construction of explanatory theory is greatly facilitated by the development of data banks, such as the Inter University Consortium for Political Research, rendering vast stores of aggregate and survey data available to be mined by scholars at universities throughout the Western world.

These developments are crucial because it is through the application, testing, and adaptation or revision of explanatory principles that scientific knowledge is cumulatively built. Knowledge is not gained by creating a nontestable theory or by confirming an explanation. Rather it is built by accounting for the differences between those contexts in which the theory does hold up against the data and those contexts in which it does not. It would therefore be conducive to the theory building goal of the field if journals and other scholarly outlets for research placed a greater value on "wallowing about" in the data as opposed to publishing new theories. Rather than aim for competing grand theories, an enterprise of cumulatively building explanatory theory requires the constant testing and adjusting of the theories we already have, to fit the constantly unfolding body of data.

AN EXPANDING FIELD OF STUDY

This volume has recorded the ongoing debate among scholars as to the most promising sources of explanatory factors. Modern political scientists, those who led the effort to refocus the field to explanatory purposes, also led to the discovery of the impact of contextual factors. In particular, we saw how scholars such as Ronald Inglehart and his associates produced a vast literature on the impact of culture and cultural change on political conflict.[9]

Other scholars argued that we were placing too much emphasis on the contextual causes of the political outcomes we sought to explain. Rather, it was argued that such outcomes were the product of choices made by political and social leaders, and the culture itself was one of the products of those choices. Thus, the emergence of effective democratic governments in Asian settings described in Chapter Five was offered as confirmation that elite choice rather than cultural determinism was responsible for that emergence.

This is a false argument. Obviously, cultural factors being in place are no guarantee that any particular political format will emerge in a given setting, if that setting is not controlled by elites sympathetic to that format. Yet, elite choices are to some extent constrained by the setting in which they find themselves. Chapter Five clearly shows that there are cultural and demographic patterns that are associated with the establishment and consolidation of democracy. These factors may even be a necessary condition for the emergence of that format; yet, without active leaders determined to push a democratic format coupled with the weakness of those trying to resist that format, these demographic and cultural factors cannot be sufficient to guarantee a democratic outcome. Complex outcomes such as the emergence of a particular political format or even of a stable and effective political system are more likely represented by what Abraham Kaplan calls "concatenated theory," which I have earlier referred to as factor theory, as illustrated by Figure 7–1.[10]

Of course, a complete and realistic expression of the model in the figure below would have arrows pointing both ways, showing a reciprocal relationship not only between the central focus of stable democracy but between each of the other factors and all the other factors in the model. Since the logical relationships among all the factors have not been specified, this form of theorizing does not lead to the logical deduction of expected outcomes as in the classic hypothetico-deductive theories in classic philosophy of science.[11] The closest we can come in political science to the ability to logically deduce expected outcomes is in the rational-choice modeling and game theory discussed in Chapter One. This rigorously formalized system can best produce expected outcomes in the real world, however, when the numbers used in the model can be assigned empirical content-precise rules of correspondence with phenomena in the sensory world.

Obviously some aspects of the field of comparative political analysis lend themselves to the kind of precise measurement needed for advanced quantitative analysis. For example, party conflict, coalition formation, and voting behavior can frequently be rigorously quantified as can some of the conflict situations addressed in rational choice models. There may be some danger in the temptation to

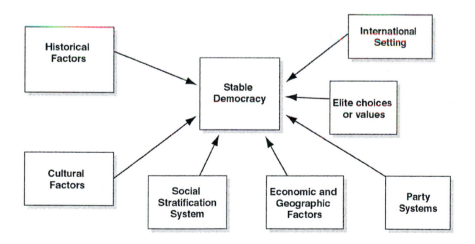

Figure 7–1   A Hypothetical Factor Theory of Stable Democracy

choose questions for inquiry that lend themselves to the use of rigorous techniques at the cost of addressing important questions from the real world of politics. Some critics of the strong emphasis on formal theory argue that we, as political scientists, have a responsibility to shed what light we can on these important questions, some of which do not lend themselves to methodologically rigorous analysis.[12]

A DYNAMIC WORLD

This volume has seen a field in the process of still defining itself while seeking explanations of a world that is itself undergoing processes of fundamental change. While Seymour Lipset and Stein Rokkan could argue in the late 1960s that the political and social cleavages of Western political systems were "frozen,"[13] we have seen these cleavages undergoing fundamental change in the ensuing decades from class- and religious-based cleavages to cleavages based on lifestyle and identity.[14] As the issues generated from class cleavages have been weakened in importance with the spread of postwar prosperity and the issues generated from religion have declined in salience with the secularization of Western society, new cleavages based on identity have grown in significance. These changes in the cleavage structures have transformed the basis of political conflict, which has forced the political party systems to redefine themselves. There is wide agreement that western party systems are undergoing a process of change; yet, the nature of that change is a matter of interpretation on which some of these scholars disagree. For example, as cleavage structures change, political dimensions and the range of issues change as well. A growing chorus of scholars perceives the emergence in the Western world of a class of parties on the radical or far right.[15] The present author sees the category of emerging parties as difficult to classify on the left to right spectrum. The radical right parties seem to be a subset of a broader category of parties stressing identity at either the national or subsystem level, some of which appear as populist right while others seem to be more to the left.[16]

The point is that, in the world of change studied by scholars of comparative political analysis, the nature of that change is still a matter of interpretation. While there is widespread agreement that the West is experiencing cultural change, we have witnessed the leading scholars in the field, with access to the same data, debating the essential nature of postindustrial society, the product of that change.[17] The amassing of data and innovative creativity in measurement are not going to advance us very far toward the goal of explanatory theory until we can reach some consensus on what it is we are trying to measure. We have seen concepts like the radical right, consolidation of democracy, postmaterialism, modernization, or institutionalization either used in different senses by different scholars or used without a precise definition. Thus, as Lee Sigelman points out, one of the most frequently cited propositions in the field, that when institutionalization does not precede social mobilization violence is more likely, cannot be falsified by any conceivable set of observations.[18]

The message of this volume is that the goal of comparative political analysis is and should be cumulatively building a body of explanatory theory in the scientific sense of the term. Progress toward that goal will only come with a reciprocal effort at building consensus on the meaning of the major concepts we wish to explain and their putative causes and creative ways of measuring them. Rigorous mathematical techniques in and of themselves serve to impress the mathematically unsophisticated but do not contribute to this goal unless they measure clearly defined phenomena we either wish to explain or that have a possible causal impact on such objects of explanation. Thus, while the goal of the discipline is now clear to most scholars in the field, much remains to be accomplished: in both the tasks of theoretically conceptualizing the world of politics that is changing at a bewildering rate and in creatively measuring that changing world of politics.

ENDNOTES

[1]Thomas Kuhn, *The Structure of Scientific Revolutions* (Chicago: University of Chicago Press, 1962).

[2]David Easton, *The Political System* (New York: Alfred Knopf, 1953); Easton, *A Framework for Political Analysis* (Englewood Cliffs, NJ: Prentice Hall, 1965); Easton, *A Systems Analysis of Political Life* (New York: John Wiley, 1965).

[3]Gabriel Almond and Sidney Verba, *The Civic Culture* (Boston: Little Brown, 1965).

[4]Russel Dalton, *Citizen Politics* 3rd ed. (New York: Chatham House, 2002).

[5]Ivo and Rosalind Feierabend, "Systemic Conditions of Political Violence: An Application of the Frustration-Aggression Theory," in Ivo Feierabend, Rosalind Feierabend and Ted Gurr, eds., *Anger, Violence and Politics* (Englewood Cliffs, NJ: Prentice Hall, 1972), pp. 136–183; Ted Gurr, "A Causal Model of Civil Strife: A Comparative Analysis Using New Indices, *American Political Science Review*, Vol.LXII, No. 4 (December, 1968), pp. 1104–1124.

[6]Theda Skocpol, *Social Revolutions in the Modern World* (Cambridge, UK: Cambridge University Press, 2001).

[7]David McClelland, *The Achieving Society* (New York: The Free Press, 1961)

[8]Lee Sigelman, "How to Succeed in Political Science by Being Very Trying: A Methodological Sampler," *PS* Vol. 10, No. 3 (Summer, 1971), p. 302.

[9]For example, Ronald Inglhart, *Culture Shift in Advanced Industrial Democracies* (Princeton, NJ: Princeton University Press, 1960); "The Renaissance of Political Culture," *The American Political Science Review*, Vol. 82, No. 2 (December, 1988), pp. 1203–1230.

[10]Abraham Kaplan, *The Conduct of Inquiry* (San Francisco: Chandler Publishing Company, 1964), pp. 298 ff.; Lawrence Mayer, *Comparative Political Inquiry: A Methodological Survey* (Homewood, IL: The Dorsey Press, 1972), pp. 62–63.

[11]For an oft-cited example of this classic philosophy of natural science, see Ernest Nagel, *The Structure of Science* (New York: Harcourt, Brace, and World, 1961), p. 140.

[12]Donald Green and Ian Shapiro, eds. *Pathologies of Rational Choice Theories: A Critique of Applications in Political Science* (New Haven, CT: Yale University Press, 1994). See also Jonathan Cohen, "Irrational Exuberance," *The New Republic*, Vol. 221, No. 17 (October, 1999), pp. 25–32.

[13]Seymour Lipset and Stein Rokkan, "Cleavage Structures, Party Systems, and Voter Alignments: An Introduction," in Lipset and Rokkan, eds., *Party Systems and Voter Alignments* (New York: The Free Press, 1967), pp. 1– 65.

[14]See, e.g., Ronald Inglehart, *The Silent Revolution: Changing Values and Political Styles Among Western Publics* (Princeton, NJ: Princeton University Press, 1977).   .

[15]Herbert Kitschelt, *The Radical Right in Western Europe* (Ann Arbor: University of Michigan Press, 1995). Martin Schain, Aristide Zolberg, and Patrick Hosay, eds., *Shadows Over Europe: The Development and Impact of the Extreme Right in Western Europe* (New York: Palgrave, 2002).

[16]Lawrence Mayer, Erol Kaymak and Jeff Justice, "Populism and the Triumph of the Politics of Identity: The Transformation of the Canadian Party System," *Nationalism and Ethnic Politics*, Vol., 6, No. 1 (Spring 2000), pp. 72–102.

[17]See the debate between Scott Flanagan and Ronald Inglehart, "Value Change in Industrial Societies," *American Political Science Review*, Vol. 81, No. 4 (December, 1987), pp. 1289–1319.

[18]Lee Sigelman, "Understanding Political Instability: An Evaluation of the Social Mobilization Approach," paper presented to the Annual Meeting of the Midwest Political Science Association in Chicago, April, 1978, discussing Samuel Huntington, *Political Order in Changing Societies* (New Haven, CT: Yale University Press, 1968) which, Sigelman reports, was cited over 250 times between 1975 and 1977, while the average scholarly work is cited 2.5 times in its lifetime.

Index